FRANK McGUINNESS
AND HIS THEATRE OF PARADOX

.

ULSTER EDITIONS AND MONOGRAPHS
General Editors
Robert Welch
Joseph McMinn

ULSTER EDITIONS AND MONOGRAPHS
ISSN 0954–3392

FRANK McGUINNESS AND HIS THEATRE OF PARADOX

Hiroko Mikami

Ulster Editions and Monographs: 12

First published in Great Britain in 2002 by Colin Smythe Limited
Gerrards Cross, Buckinghamshire SL9 8XA
www.colinsmythe.co.uk

British Library Cataloguing-in-Publication Data
A catalogue record for this book is available
from the British Library

ISBN 0-86140-448-3

Distributed in North America by Oxford University Press
198 Madison Avenue, New York, NY 10016

Produced in Great Britain
Typeset by Art Photoset Ltd., Beaconsfield, Buckinghamshire
Printed and bound by T.J. International Ltd., Padstow, Cornwall

TO MY PARENTS
Terushige and Sachiko Mikami

CONTENTS

ILLUSTRATIONS

The following paintings are all by (Michelangelo Merisi da) Caravaggio.

(between pages 66–67)

10. *The Musicians*
    New York, Metropolitan Museum of Art, 1595/96.

11. *The Incredulity of St.Thomas*
    Potsdam, Schloss Sanssouci, 1601/03.

12. *Boy with a Basket of Fruit*
    Rome, Galleria Borghese, 1593/94.

ABBREVIATIONS

The following abbreviations are used parenthetically in the text to identify either the play or the collection of plays in which a given play appears. Page references to the plays, which are incorporated into the text, relate to the particular editions indicated below. Unpublished production scripts mentioned in the text are held in the Tilling Archive at University of Ulster and referred to as UP.

Published plays:

CB	*Carthaginians and Baglady* (London: Faber and Faber, 1988)
D	*Dolly West's Kitchen* (London: Faber and Faber, 1999)
F82	*The Factory Girls* (Dublin: Monarch Line, 1982)
F88	*The Factory Girls* (Dublin: Wolfhound Press, 1988)
I	*Innocence* (London: Faber and Faber, 1987)
M	*Mutabilitie* (London: Faber and Faber, 1997)
ML	*Mary and Lizzie* (London: Faber and Faber, 1989)
O	*Observe the Sons of Ulster Marching Towards the Somme* (London: Faber and Faber, 1986)
P1	*Plays 1* (London: Faber and Faber, 1996). Contains *The Factory Girls; Observe the Sons of Ulster Marching Towards the Somme; Innocence; Carthaginians;* and *Baglady*
S	*Someone Who'll Watch Over Me* (London: Faber and Faber, 1992)

Unpublished plays:

Bread	*The Bread Man*, UP90–1.
Bird	*The Bird Sanctuary*, UP94–1.

ACKNOWLEDGEMENTS

I would like to thank my friends at the University of Ulster at Coleraine where most of this book was written as a PhD thesis submitted to the university: Professor Robert Welch, my supervisor, for his encouragement, suggestions, and patience; Mr Philip Tilling for his trust in allowing me to acces to his invaluable archive; Dr Anne McCartney, Dr Frank Sewell and Mrs Wendy Taulbutt from the Centre for Irish Literature and Bibliography for their friendship and support; Mr Martin McLoone and Professor John Hill from Media Studies for supplying me with various films from their archive; Professor Terence O'Keeffe and Dr Michael Green for having made me consider the possibility of doing the research in Coleraine; the Library staff of the University of Ulster for their assistance.

I would like to extend my thanks to Waseda Univeristy for granting me a sabbatical from 1997 to 1998, and Japan Society for the Promotion of Science for awarding me Grant-in-Aid for Scientific Research (Grant-in-Aid for Publication of Scientific Research Results in 2001).

I also wish to recognise the assistance and encouragement of the following: Professor Declan Kiberd, Dr Andrew Hadfield, Dr Angela Bourke, Professor Christopher Murray, Dr Andrew Tomlinson, Mr Paul Hadfield, Dr Noel McGuigan, Mrs Kay Bourke, Professor Junko Matoba, Professor Anthony Newell, Dr Tim Seul, all of whom read chapters in draft and made invaluable suggestions; Professor Colin Smythe for his support and patience; the Archive of Abbey Theatre, Dublin and its archivist, Mairaéd Delaney; the Druid Theatre, Galway; the Field Day Theatre Company in Derry/Londonderry; the Royal National Theatre, London, all of whom supplied me with unpublished play-scripts of McGuinness.

My thanks also go to my friends and colleagues: in Ireland both the south and the north of the border, Jennifer Johnston and David Gilliland, Michael and Edna Longley, Professor Rosalind Pritchard, Mr Denis Smith, Hiroe Kaji, Chie Oda and Michael

Dunne, Chisato Yoshimi, Toshi Akai; at home, Professors Hiroshi Suzuki, Shigeo Shimizu, and Masaru Sekine from Waseda University.

My greatest debt of gratitude is to Frank McGuinness, the playwright himself, who encouraged me through his works and in person all the time. He also kindly allowed me to quote his plays and writings.

Finally, I would like to thank my parents to whom this book is dedicated.

INTRODUCTION

Frank McGuinness and Ireland in the 1980s and After

I: Ireland Today

The image of Ireland as female, as some womanly noumenon rooted in antiquity, is as various as it is recurrent. Mythographers note that this goddess of sovereignty is imagined into three phases: 'the virgin Ana, flowering fertility-goddess; the mother Badb, "Boiling," the cauldron perpetually producing life; and the crone Macha, "Great Queen of Phantoms," or Mother Death'.[1] From the literary embodiments of Cathleen Ni Houlihan and Dark Rosaleen to the Hibernia of the Victorian cartoons, the representations of Ireland as a female beauty are common. At the same time, the Shan van Voght and the *puella senilis*, 'the woman who is as old as the hills', representing the country in the form of an old hag, are also incessant.

But the second phase, in which Ireland is associated with a bubbling cauldron, seems (unlike the beautiful/ugly figures) to have slipped from cultural remembrance.[2] Yet it is possibly the most relevant image of Ireland today. With her new economic prosperity and cultural vigour, the country is most appropriately likened to a boiling cauldron, which, in the myth at least, is 'the producer of life, wisdom, inspiration, and enlightenment'.[3] Small additions to this cauldron, this flux of modernity, have a catalytic effect on the overall character of the country. Ireland is a small island at the edge of the Atlantic with a little over five million people – three and a half in the Republic and one and a half in the North. Its size means that the cauldron can reach boiling point quickly. Small changes of temperature or ingredients can rapidly alter the whole. An example of this is the widespread modernising of attitudes effected by Mary Robinson, the first female president of the Republic, during her term of office between 1990 and 1997.

1

In her inaugural speech, Robinson expanded the notion of the nation: there are over seventy million Irish descendants living all over the world, ready to receive news and information from the 'home land'. This is the background for the worldwide Irish or Celtic boom being witnessed these days.

On 2 December 1999, the Republic of Ireland removed its territorial claim to Northern Ireland in Articles 2 and 3 of the Constitution; and in the North, a power-sharing Executive held its inaugural meetings at Stormont when direct rule from Westminster came to an end after 25 years.[4] Reg Empey, a Unionist who was appointed as the first Minister for Enterprise, Trade and Investment, talked of 'chasing the Celtic Tiger'. 'Celtic Tiger', a term drawn from the so-called Tiger economies of Asia, is a metaphor for the Republic of Ireland's economic miracle in the Nineties. During that decade, the average living standard of the South caught up with that of the North and will probably surpass the whole United Kingdom's within a few years. Indeed, some argue that it has already done so. This Celtic Tiger is beginning to dismantle the superiority complex Ulster Unionists have always had towards the South. The South is no longer poor, which undermines one of the Ulster Unionists' more pragmatic reasons for keeping Ulster British, leaving aside questions of religion and ideology. Empey's comment shows how attitudes in the North are now beginning to thaw – indeed, the North suspects that it is being left behind.

The Celtic Tiger, on the other hand, has given new confidence to the people of the Republic. They do not need to define their own country, with a tone of self-mockery, as 'an impoverished island'. It was 1988 when Brendan Kennelly wrote in an introduction to *Landmarks of Irish Drama* that:

Ireland is a small, poorish island in the Atlantic, close to Britain, with which country it has had a long and troubled relationship (is that the proper word?) for almost a thousand years. One would hardly think that a rather impoverished insularity would help to breed a world-renowned drama, but it has, because drama thrives on that trouble and conflict which are as much a tragic part of Irish life today as they have ever been. During the past fifteen years, several fine plays have been written about the 'Northern troubles'. Irish drama presents an ongoing re-creation of Irish history.[5]

A sketch of *today's* Ireland, and its theatre, would not look like this. Then, however, it was an accurate summary of the country in the Seventies and Eighties. Ireland was considered irremediably poor. It had had a long, unhappy, and still determining relation with Britain. It was wounded by 'the Troubles' of the North. Yet these elements were nonetheless regarded as vital, if uncomfortable, stimuli, which could generate a high standard of Irish drama; to write a play meant attempting to re-write Irish history. All the negative elements of that time, 'political instability, five general elections within ten years, none of them decisive,'[6] the pro-life constitutional amendment of 1983 and the failure to delete the anti-divorce article from the Constitution, a hunger strike by the IRA in the Maze Prison–all these were, with hindsight, signs of an Ireland which would change, whose changes would be hailed, mirrored, questioned and quickened by, among other things, that re-writing of Irish history.

II: A Child Born Near the Border

Frank McGuinness was born in 1953 in Buncrana on the Inishowen peninsula, Ireland's most northerly area, in County Donegal.[7] Buncrana is only 14 miles from the border between the Republic of Ireland and Northern Ireland. For the people of the Inishowen peninsula, Derry/Londonderry[8] is a natural capital, to which they still commute for work or shopping, crossing the border on a daily basis. Donegal is one of the nine counties of Ulster, the northernmost of Ireland's four traditional provinces. Between the north-western point of Donegal Bay and the south-eastern point of Dundalk Bay, lies a belt of hills, lakes, and forests, which forms a natural border to this territory. When partition was brought into force in 1920, however, this natural border was not adopted. Donegal was excluded, along with Monaghan and Cavan, from Northern Ireland, in order to secure a safe majority for Ulster Unionists. Since then, the name Ulster has often been commonly (if wrongly) applied to Northern Ireland's six counties.

McGuinness is often categorised as a Northern writer, with 'a split between a southern training and a northern temperament'[9] marking his character. In an interview with Carolyne Pollard in 1987, McGuinness said:

I think that sectarianism of any kind is stupid and I feel then, to go around describing myself as a Northern or Southern writer is stupid. I'm both, actually. I was born in the North, which is politically classified as the South, so I've got that lovely confusion – I like confusion a lot.[10]

McGuinness's birth near the Donegal border undoubtedly influenced his development as a dramatist. His writing is always poised between the polarities of Ireland, between north and south, Protestantism and Catholicism, Nationalism and Unionism, England and Ireland. And he addresses wider issues of human polarity, particularly in the area of gender, masculinity and femininity. It is therefore no accident that one of his early plays, written for TEAM Theatre Company in 1983, is about four young boys from Derry/Londonderry, two Catholics and two Protestants, who decide to bury their religious differences – and that it is titled *Borderlands*.

III: The Field Day and the Eighties

It was in 1980, when he was twenty-seven, and unemployed, that McGuinness started his career as a dramatist. He saw Brian Friel's *Faith Healer* at the Abbey Theatre in Dublin, and immediately applied for a writer's bursary to the Arts Council, which advised him to join a Playwrights' Workshop it was organising in Galway. There he wrote the first draft of *The Factory Girls* under the supervision of the director, Patrick Mason, who would subsequently direct the play in 1982 at Dublin's Peacock Theatre.

It was by chance, perhaps, that McGuinness attended the Playwrights' Workshop at that particular time; but it was a happy chance. Ireland was beginning to change. And it was a good time for theatre: regional companies based outside Dublin flourished during the 1980s in Ireland, and successes included Field Day in Derry/Londonderry, Druid in Galway, Red Kettle in Waterford, Charabanc and Tinderbox in Belfast, and others. The Field Day Theatre Company, set up by Brian Friel and Stephen Rea in 1980, was the most prominent of all. It produced[11] a new play or a new adaptation every year in Derry/Londonderry and toured both north and south of the border. It provided a valuable opportunity for people living in smaller towns, who normally have little chance to go to the theatre, to see plays of high quality, such as Friel's *Translations* (1980), Thomas Kilroy's *Double Cross* (1986), and Stewart Parker's *Pentecost* (1987).

The first production of Friel's *Translations* was an enormous (though unexpected) success. In 1981, Field Day invited Seamus Deane, Seamus Heaney, Tom Paulin, and David Hammond, in addition to the two founders, Friel and Rea, on to the board as directors. Field day was laying down a solid administrative and creative structure on the back of *Translations'* success. All six directors were Northerners, three Catholics and three Protestants;[12] this mix was an attempt to react positively to the desperate situation in the North which had been born out of sectarian division. In addition to its theatrical activities, Field Day has launched a number of cultural enterprises, which have had an enormous impact on Irish society at large. It has published pamphlets and a three-volume anthology of Irish writing,[13] each of which involved many contributors and editors, both national and international.[14] Seamus Deane wrote in the Field Day pamphlet, *Heroic Styles: the Tradition of an Idea* that: 'Everything, including our politics and our literature, has to be rewritten, ie. re-read. This will enable new writing, new politics, unblemished by Irishness but securely Irish.'[15] This often-cited passage conveys the enthusiasm and firm sense of mission of the decade.

Field Day wanted to create a symbolic Fifth Province, which would stand for 'a new pluralist Ireland'. Though credit for spreading this idea to the public belongs to Field Day – the idea of the imaginary Fifth Province, in addition to Ulster, Leinster, Munster, and Connacht – it was first advanced by Richard Kearney in the Editorial to the first issue of *The Crane Bag* in 1977. Kearney said:

> The obvious importance of the political attempts to unite the four political and geographical provinces would seem to indicate another kind of solution, another kind of unity, one which would incorporate the 'fifth' province. This province, this place, this centre, is not a political position. In fact, if it is a position at all, it would be marked by the absence of any particular political and geographical delineation, something more like a dis-position.

This notion that all Irish traditions could meet on a point of equality in the Fifth Province was so influential that Mary Robinson included it in her inauguration speech as the President in 1990: 'If I am a symbol of anything I would like to be a symbol of this reconciling and healing Fifth Province.'[16]

Thomas Kilroy's *Double Cross*, produced in 1986, was the most successful Field Day play after *Translations*. It is a play about two Irish men during the Second World War: William Joyce and Brendan Bracken. Joyce, known as 'Lord Haw Haw' through Hitler's radio propaganda, was hanged for treason against Britain after the war; Bracken, Churchill's right-hand man, became the Minister of Information. Stephen Rea played both roles and the acting and the play itself won critical acclaim. Kilroy set down his admiration for what Field Day had achieved thus:

Some years ago Field Day asked me to write one of their Pamphlets and I completely failed to do so. It was round about that time that I decided to try and write a play for the company instead, addressing the kind of topics which Field Day has restored to serious debate in Ireland. For me, *Field Day is the most important movement of its kind in Ireland since the beginning of this century.* It has provided a platform for the life of the mind, of whatever persuasion, at a time when mindlessness threatens to engulf us all.[17] (emphasis added)

This enthusiasm about Field Day was shared by many.

The tone, however, dramatically changes in Kilroy's new introduction to the Gallery Press version of the same play, published in 1994: he omitted much of his uncritical praise for the Field Day Movement; and this time he saw nationalism in a different light:

I wanted to write a play about nationalism and in a real sense *Double Cross* derives from the whole debate about national identity which Field Day did so much to promote *in the seventies* and eighties. What interested me was not so much nationalism as a source of self-improvement and the advancement of civil rights but nationalism as a dark burden, a source of trauma and debilitation. It was inevitable, then, I suppose, that I should end up writing about a fascist.[18] (emphasis added)

Field Day was founded in 1980, and thus did not promote the debate about national identity in the seventies. This simple mistake, however, is significant. It implies that the whole enterprise of Field Day, for Kilroy, belongs to the past. Here, he focuses on the question of national identity which 'Field Day did so much to promote'. He has shifted from unconditional praise for Field Day's accomplishments to focus on the dark underside of nationalism, the cousin, as he sees it, of fascism.

The change in Kilroy's tone was in keeping with a general change in attitude to the Field Day movement. Even at the stage when Field Day was being enthusiastically received, critics like Edna Longley (who defines herself as a '"revisionist" literary critic'[19]) criticise Field Day's views on Irish history as being framed by a Catholic Nationalist hegemony which marginalises Protestants in both the North and the South after independence. The plays of Protestant writers, such as Parker's *Pentecost* and Derek Mahon's *High Time*, however, were also produced by Field Day, and the theme for the third series of Field Day pamphlets was 'The Protestant Idea for Liberty' – (Terence Brown's *The Whole Protestant Community: the making of a historical myth* was included in the series). The objectives of the movement, therefore, were not so one-sided as to neglect or exclude Protestant writing. And we should also remember Seamus Deane's unequivocal declaration that Field Day had set out to challenge established explanations of Irish culture, history, and politics.

According to Anthony Roche, those Protestant writers who became Field Day authors, were 'in reaction against that perceived character of Ulster Unionism', which, through a cynical eye, appears 'dour, humourless and generally without culture'.[20] Nonetheless, Roche concurs with Longley, to some extent, when he notes that the Field Day movement in the 1980s was deeply influenced by a Catholic tradition: 'Catholic Nationalism has exclusively appropriated the concept of "Irishness",' he says, and there is more than a grain of truth in this. It is truly remarkable that such heated debates on national identity and the related problems of language and tradition in Ireland stemmed from one theatrical movement; and it would be fair to say that, on balance, the Field Day movement in the 1980s was a cultural enterprise which acted as a catalyst for social and political change.[21]

IV: The History of Mentalities

When writing this book, I kept in mind the title of a chapter in a book by Robert Darnton, 'The History of Mentalities'. In a discussion of the French Revolution, he defines this 'history' as 'the examination of the common man's outlook and perception of events rather than the analysis of the events themselves.'[22] 'It is', he continues, 'a sort of intellectual history of nonintellectuals, an attempt to reconstruct the cosmology of the common man or, more modestly, to understand the attitudes, assumptions, and implicit ideologies of specific social groups.'[23] McGuinness, too, belongs in a context of an Irish history of mentalities. Most of his plays are about the past, both remote and recent: Elizabethan Ireland; seventeenth century Italy;[24] the time of Karl Marx and Friedrich Engels; the periods of the two world wars; the time of Bloody Sunday in 'Derry'. Each play is, in its own way, an 'examination of the common man's outlook and perception of events', to use Darnton's phrase; and they are all mirrors held up to contemporary Ireland.

Fintan O'Toole writes that history plays are written in times of shift from one order of society to another: 'At such times', he says, 'history provided a way of disentangling the contradictions of the present by placing them at a distance. Historical drama is . . . a way of dealing with discontinuity.'[25] Ireland, which had simply missed the Industrial Revolution, apart from the limited area of the north-east of the island, underwent a drastic change from an agricultural and peasant economy to one of high-technology and advanced information systems. In 1960, agriculture accounted for 37% of the workforce: today it accounts for 10%.[26] Ireland has overtaken the United States to become the world's leading exporter, per capita, of software products. For the first time in history Ireland has been experiencing what it is like to be a winner, to enjoy a level of affluence that matches or exceeds that of many 'first world' nations. In this context, national identity and tradition in Ireland and its relation with England should be once again re-examined – in a certain sense, Field Day's achievements in the Eighties have already become outmoded.

However, Ireland, at its core, remains what it used to be. What E. Estyn Evans, a geologist of Scottish origin, who lived and taught in Belfast for forty years, wrote in 1977, still retains relevance about Ireland and its people:

[W]hatever changes may occur – and cultural change is inevitable – its own culture-pattern is so deeply bedded that many of its values and qualities are likely to persist in an environment of strong emotional appeal where traces and memories of the past are ever present, and where the other world seems but a step away. The characteristics of Irishness, it seems to me, are a respect for the past, and indifference to the present time, a sense of the unseen world, intellectual curiosity, the gift of poetic imagination, a cynical sense of humour, a brooding melancholy, a subtle conception of what constitutes truth, an ingenious casuistry and a deviousness which are perhaps related to historical experience, and above all, an inexhaustible interest in words, in people and in spiritual matters.[27]

This 'culture-pattern' is the home of McGuinness's drama. It is lucky for such a writer, who 'instinctively thinks of theatre as a collective or ensemble process',[28] to have worked in a milieu where theatre is regarded as something communal, as something which can connect with, even activate, movements in society. In Ireland, debate about a certain play can spill over into a National paper, such as *The Irish Times*, and reverberate for weeks in everyday 'street-level' discourse. A small addition to the cauldron can make all the difference.

*   *   *

In Chapter One, we look at McGuinness's *Observe the Sons of Ulster*

Marching Towards the Somme (1985) and *Carthaginians* (1988), which represent 'the theological schizophrenia of [his] tradition as an Irishman'[29] from both sides. The folk memory of the Irish, he says, is 'a lethal cultural weapon,'[30] and it is possible to employ this memory 'in that utterly destructive way or use it to some imaginatively constructive end'.[31] These two plays are often thought of as a diptych: *Sons of Ulster* deals with the effect of the Battle of the Somme on Ulster Protestants; *Carthaginians*, on the other hand, deals with Catholic people in the aftermath of Bloody Sunday in Derry/Londonderry. When McGuinness writes about these Irish obsessions and traumas in his plays, there is no hard and fast resolution or reconciliation. His work is always 'a criticism of that obsession as well as celebration of it.'[32] *The Bread Man* (1990) is also examined in this context: its background, how the Northern Troubles affected a particular individual, is also briefly discussed in this chapter.

Chapter Two examines *Innocence* (1986), which was written after the great success of *Sons of Ulster*. McGuinness deliberately changed his way of writing here,[33] and chose Caravaggio, as his protagonist. *Innocence* focuses on the internal complexities of the artistic mind in the context of a Catholic imagination. His way of exploring this mind, with regard both to verbal style and to juxtapositions on stage (for instance, putting whores, rent boys and a Cardinal in the same scene), frustrated the expectations people had about the writer of *Sons of Ulster*.[34] I argue that *Innocence* is a religious play despite its apparently defiant blasphemy.

Three plays in Chapter Three, *Mary and Lizzie* (1989), *Someone Who'll Watch Over Me* (1992), and *Mutabilitie* (1997), could, in one sense, be thought of as dialogues on the unhappy relationship between Ireland and England, and thus as examples of post-colonial discourse, though this term's theoretical overtones threaten to flatten out McGuinness's vital, quicksilver imaginings. *Mary and Lizzie* is another play about historical figures, Mary and Lizzie Burns, who lived with Frederick Engels in Manchester (to whom they 'showed [Engels] the condition of the working class').[35] McGuinness tries to catch 'the voice of the voiceless'[36] and uses surrealistic techniques to evoke a forgotten part of Irish history. In *Someone Who'll Watch Over Me*, a broadly realistic work (and one of McGuinness's most well-received plays to date), Irish/English relations are explored through the interactions of three hostages in Beirut. *Mutabilitie*, set in sixteenth century Ireland, is an imaginary encounter between three poets, Edmund

(Spenser), Willam (Shakespeare), and the File, an Irish female bard – each giving voice to a different perspective on Ireland's unhappy relationship with England.

Chapter Four examines *The Factory Girls* (1982), *Baglady* (1985), and a television play, *The Hen House* (1990), all of which are powerful representations of Irish women. The plays can be read as, among other things, commentaries on social changes affecting women's issues in late-Seventies and Eighties Ireland. Events which most Irish people remember, such as the Ann Lovett case, the Kerry Babies case, the X case, and the several referenda over constitutional bans, are backgrounds for McGuinness's plays in a way which enables them to be re-remembered, that is, remembered from an angle which makes those events forces for progress rather than obstacles in Ireland's political archaeology.

Two plays in Chapter Five are examples of McGuinness's Irish 'comedy of bad manners', to borrow McGuinness's own term. *The Bird Sanctuary* (1994) is clearly to be categorised as such, since McGuinness acknowledged that it was inspired by Oscar Wilde's *The Importance of Being Earnest*. The tone of *Dolly West's Kitchen* (1999) differs from typical works of this genre; but I would like to regard it as a comedy in the same way that Chekhov regarded his own plays as comedies, though one might plump for the subcategory Irish (tragi-)comedy of bad manners when describing it.

* * *

McGuinness regards himself as 'a writer involved with politics' and acknowledges that his task is 'to cause a different type of bother.'[37] For such a writer, who always feels the effect of the past on the present, it would be impossible not to be 'political', in the broadest sense of the word. The wide range of his writings make for a wide variety of vantages on Ireland, on its past and present, on its contemporary political and cultural divides, on issues of gender and sexuality, and on relations with England.

The real attraction and dynamism of McGuinness's theatre is, however, that it opens up the hinterlands beyond both myth and logic. In his plays, people mourn and celebrate, separate and unite. They are living in the contrast between life and death, darkness and light, despair and joy, the sacred and the profane, the temporary and the eternal. Theatre may not change anything. However, in the process of mourning and celebrating, of separating and uniting, people in his plays (and we who watch them) become aware that the experience of theatre can be a celebration and a curse, a charge between positive and negative, out of which, sometimes a channel for expression suddenly opens. This magic in McGuinness's theatre occurs because of his ear, his affinity for contradiction and opposites; because, as he said at a very early stage of his career as a writer, 'theatre is essentially a medium for paradox.'[38]

1

'Folk Memory as Lethal Cultural Weapon': Protestant Ireland vs. Catholic Ireland

Observe the Sons of Ulster Marching Towards the Somme[1]

In 1994, *Observe the Sons of Ulster Marching Towards the Somme*(1985) was revived at the Abbey Theatre following announcements of a ceasefire from both the IRA and Loyalist paramilitaries.[2] Patrick Mason, then the artistic director of the Abbey Theatre, was determined to put it on the stage, since the Abbey as the National Theatre, he believed, should reflect the 'enormous importance' of the ceasefire and the 'momentum of the whole peace process'.[3] David Ervine, a Unionist politician, and some twenty members of loyalist groupings from the Shankill Road, in addition to the politicians from the Republic, which included Dick Spring, were all invited to the opening night, on 19 October. The audience on the night was aware, said Kevin Myers of *The Irish Times*, that 'some sort of history is being made involving the two primary peoples on this island'.[4] This reconfirmed what the audience for its first performance in 1985 felt; the play turned out to have anticipated a new era of reconciliation and understanding in Irish society.

I

This is a play about eight Ulstermen who have volunteered for military service in the First World War. In an interview with John Waters in 1987, McGuinness confessed that he was twenty-seven when he first heard about the Ulstermen who died at the Battle of the Somme in 1916, which occurred only two months after the Easter Rising in Dublin.[5] For a Catholic like McGuinness, the Somme was always excluded from folk memory: 'I was brought up to see the Easter Rising as a triumphant event, and the triumphalism was so strongly Catholic – but then look at the Battle of the Somme: it was a defeat and a terrible betrayal.'[6] 'A southern training' had drummed this kind of mythology about the Easter Rising into generations of Irish school children and ignored the tragedy of the Somme. Easter 1916 had been regarded as 'a blood sacrifice', a term derived from Pearse's famous oration of November 1913, in which he said: 'bloodshed is a cleansing and sanctifying thing'.[7] For a devout Catholic and a true citizen of the Irish Republic, it was one's duty to regard nationalism and blood sacrifice as sacred, and to hate England as the oppressor. The Easter Rising was a symbolic monument for the foundation of the Republic: it held immense significance for twentieth-century Catholic Ireland in ways that may have little relation to the reality of what happened. The ceremony for the fiftieth anniversary in 1966 was a national event. McGuinness, born in 1953, probably belongs to the last generation of children who got this kind of education at school and saw and remembered the ceremony in 1966.

There has been, however, a noticeable change in attitude towards this historical event since the outbreak of the Troubles in the North, since Easter 1916 is thought to be used as a justification for its campaign of violence by the Provisional IRA. People in the Republic have watched one of their own symbols being turned to different ends and consequently looked for new symbols of who they are, and where they are going. *Revising the Rising*, published by Field Day in 1991, the year of the seventy-fifth anniversary of the Rising, is a collection of essays about this event. Máirín Ní Dhonnchadha, one of its editors, wrote in the preface:

Anniversaries are often problematic, and few in recent times have been as loaded with ambiguities and contradictions as the seventy-fifth anniversary of 1916. The interpretation of this key event in modern Irish history has prompted fractures and disputes among historians, politicians, and citizens.[8]

A shift in attitude to Irish history is now under way; naive enthusiasm for the older, somewhat unthinking, allegiances to nationalism is being called into question. Contemporary history textbooks now aim for an evenhandedness, teaching children about, for instance, both Easter 1916 and the Battle of the Somme. Nonetheless, the Easter 1916 is deeply ingrained in folk memory and still looms large.[9] It will probably take a long time to demythologise the Easter Rising, because of the massive momentum it has acquired over the last eighty odd years. And, at the same time, it is difficult for people from a Catholic background to understand the traumatic shadow cast over Ulster Protestants by the Somme.

Michael Longley, a Protestant poet from Belfast, returns us to the particularity of that trauma:

The tragedy of the Somme affects all of Ulster. Every little village and town has its own war memorial, and many of the recorded names fell in that particular battle. My father's own experiences, which he recounted vividly on only a couple of occasions, have allowed me to participate in the community's glum pride. My mother's mentally retarded brother disappeared in the trenches – and from family conversation. His vanishing act haunted my childhood much more than the vast catastrophe ever did.[10]

The Battle of the Somme is not just one of many historical battles for Ulster Protestants: it is a trauma which has been passed on for generations. It was necessary for McGuinness, a playwright from a strongly Catholic family, to live 'among Protestant people' in order to break through this gap between their culture and his own.[11] He was influenced and inspired by *How Many Miles to Babylon* (1974), Jennifer Johnston's pioneering novel, which commemorated young Irish soldiers from the Southern part of the country, who volunteered to serve in the British Army during World War I.[12] Declan Kiberd wrote that 'the 150,000 Irish who fought in World War I, for 'the right of small nations', as most of them saw it, had been effectively extirpated from the official record.'[13] In the Republic, it wasn't just the Somme that disappeared from 'official' remembrance, it was the whole history of Irish volunteers in World War I.

McGuinness made a point of visiting war memorials in Ulster, including those, for instance, in Coleraine and Enniskillen.[14] Johnston's novel and the war memorials were the starting points of his creative enquiry, which eventually brought him to the Somme itself. After investigations about the battle for his play, McGuinness reached a certain understanding:

I think that in the Northern Protestant mind there is a sense of an apocalypse. I don't know if that can be summarised as a death wish, but it is an awareness that the earth will end in some way and I felt that the Battle of the Somme confirmed for many Northern Protestants their darkest and most deep fears. That is why it is still such a truth, such a reality for them.[15]

McGuinness engages with, attempts to understand, this trauma in

Ulster society in *Observe the Sons of Ulster Marching Towards the Somme*. Part One of the play gives dramatic, palpable shape to this trauma, which is crystallised in Elder Pyper, a survivor of the Somme. Its title, 'Remembrance', immediately evokes 'Remembrance Sunday', 'an act of solemn tribute to those who were killed in both world wars and other conflicts which is held at war memorials in towns and villages across the United Kingdom each November.'[16] In Northern Ireland, many Catholics regard even this remembrance of the dead as a Protestant ritual, a view which ignores the immense loss of Irish soldiers in Continental battlefields. In the play, McGuinness tries to remember those Ulstermen killed in the Somme as 'friends, sons and lovers'.[17] At the Remembrance Sunday ceremony, in addition to parades, speeches, and floral tributes, lines from 'For the Fallen', by the British poet Laurence Binyon, are often recited:

> They shall grow not old, as we that are left grow old:
> Age shall not weary them, nor the years condemn.
> At the going down of the sun and in the morning
> We will remember them.
>
> As the stars that shall be bright when we are dust,
> Moving in marches upon the heavenly plain,
> As the stars that are starry in the time of our darkness,
> To the end, to the end, they remain.[18]

'Remembrance', Part One of the play, is a bitter revision of Binyon's poem. Elder Pyper, a fiery old Ulsterman, who survived the Battle of the Somme, sits alone in the dark at the play's start. McGuinness selects the word, 'Elder', rather than 'Older', not only as the counterpart to 'Young' Pyper, but as a reference to a title held by senior members of the Presbyterian congregation. *The Oxford English Dictionary* explains the ecclesiastical use of the word from its Greek origin:

[It is] the title given to a certain order or class of office-bearers in the early Christian Church. The Greek word was adopted in ecclesiastical Latin as *presbyter*, and its historical representative in English is priest. In certain Protestant churches, chiefly those called Presbyterian, the English word *elder* (with *presbyter* as an occasional synonym) is used as the designation of a class of officers intended to correspond in function to the 'elders' of the apostolic church. In the Presbyterian churches the term *elders* includes the clergy (for distinction called '*teaching* elders'), but in ordinary language it is restricted to the *lay* or *ruling elders*, who are chosen in each parish or congregation to act with the minister in the management of church affairs.

'Elder', then, denotes Pyper's role as a leader or a pillar of an Ulster Protestant community. He is expected to 'observe' its rites. Again, *the Oxford English Dictionary* puts flesh pertinent to our theme on this word, 'observe': it is to 'pay practical attention or regard to a law, command, custom, practice, covenant, set time, or anything prescribed or fixed', and 'duly to celebrate a religious rite or ceremony'.

Remembering is, therefore, something people expect from Elder Pyper. He can be counted on to lead the rememberers in their hallowing of the past, but he refuses: 'I remember nothing today. Absolutely nothing'(*P1*, 97). He is tormented:

I do not understand your insistence on my remembrance. I'm being too mild. I am angry at your demand that I continue to probe. Were you not there in all your dark glory? Have you no conception of the horror? Did it not touch you at all? A passion for horror disgusts me. I have seen horror. There is nothing to tell you. Those willing to talk to you of that day, to remember for your sake, to forgive you, they invent as freely as they wish. I am not one of them. I will not talk, I will not listen to you. Invention gives that slaughter shape. That scale of horror has no shape, as you in your darkness have no shape. Your actions that day were not, they are not acceptable. You have no right to excuse that suffering, parading it for the benefit of others. (*P1*, 97)

The audience is plumbed straight into Elder Pyper's darkened psyche. McGuinness knows that 'those who survived the Somme were maimed for life.'[19] Elder Pyper's angry conversation with God (for it is God to whom he talks here) reflects McGuinness's understanding of Protestant culture, in which 'no matter how much of the weight of history [they] inherit, ultimately [they] stand alone before [their] Maker.'[20] The memory of the Somme is a disabling trauma for the whole of Ulster society, but here it is dealt with as a personal horror from which Pyper cannot flee, because he cannot flee from his own mind. 'Darkness, for eternity, is not survival'(*P1*, 98), he groans.

In this living death, he remembers his fellow soldiers who died at the Battle of the Somme.

Is Moore still searching for John Millen? Will he never believe Millen cannot be found? If he were found, would he not return here? Moore must stop searching. It is time to rest . . . Where is Anderson? Still attending McIlwaine? I saw that, you know. Cut into two. Anderson falling on him as if his body could hold McIlwaine's body together. *(P1,* 99)

This is the one and only occasion where the real horror and misery of the battle are directly mentioned in the play, conveyed in the terrible image of a soldier vanishing in the field of battle, mirroring Longley's episode, and of a soldier whose body is cut in two. This image, all the more powerful because it is not overexposed, haunts the audience for the rest of the play. And its sanguinary aspect is entwined with, and thus intensified by, the myth of Cuchullian's fight with the sea. Elder Pyper declares Cuchullian to be the hero of Ulster, rather than that of the Republic:[21] 'we took up arms and fought against an ocean. An Ocean of blood. His blood is our inheritance'*(P1,* 98). Here, Cuchullian's blood symbolises Ulster's deep trauma.

A recurrent device in contemporary drama is the invitation to the audience to step inside the protagonist's skull, a device which has its analogue in the modernist novel's 'stream of consciousness.' It is interesting, in light of modernism's stress on interiority, that *The Inside of His Skull* was the title Arthur Miller originally considered for *Death of a Salesman.*[22] Hugh Kenner regards the stage of Beckett's *Endgame*[23] as the inside of an immense cranium, with its high peepholes.[24] In both cases, a skull or its symbolic equivalent represents an individual agony, which is nonetheless a reflection of the age.[25] The whole structure of *Sons of Ulster* is comparable to these; the audience witnesses, partakes in, the dramatic action of the play, which is set within the walls of Elder Pyper's mind. We feel trapped within the confines of his bruised inner world.

II

In order to understand the mentality of Ulster Protestants as portrayed in the play, we have to go back to the time of the Home Rule debate in the early 1910s in Ireland. McGuinness writes a review for Philip Orr's *The Road to the Somme*:

Orr traces the fears and bigotries that were leading Ulster Protestants' deep suspicion of Home Rule, believing it to be synonymous with Rome Rule, a belief largely justified with the creation of the Free State and its subsequent evolution. Out of this makeshift force there emerged through hard training, both at home in Ulster and in England, one of the most formidable troops of men in the British army.[26]

This catches the general atmosphere in the 1910s, when many Ulster Protestants volunteered for the British army, and explains the connection between their cause and the Home Rule debate as it then existed. In the play, Young Pyper, the protagonist, who is described as 'a bit of mocker' (*P1*, 104), or 'the black sheep' (*P1*, 172) of the family, mockingly imitates the speech of the officer rank in the British army. His speech reflects the climate of Unionist society in Ulster at the time of World War I. 'You are here as a volunteer in the army of your king and empire. You are here to train to meet that empire's foe. You are here as a loyal son of Ulster, for the empire's foe is Ulster's foe' (*P1*, 107). The emphasis put on the word 'Ulster' is crucial.

In 1910, the British Prime Minister, Herbert Asquith, agreed to introduce the third Home Rule Bill[27] for Ireland and it was intended that it become law in three years' time. It was in this context that the Ulster Unionists began to organise their strongest resistance to Home Rule. Edward Carson, also remembered as the lawyer who prosecuted Oscar Wilde, was appointed to lead the anti-Home Rule Unionists and devoted himself entirely to the Ulster cause.[28] On 28 September 1912, Carson led a vast number of Ulster people in signing the Ulster Solemn League and Covenant. 218,206 men and 228,991 women, nearly one third of Ulster's population, signed this Covenant stating that:

Being convinced in our consciences that Home Rule would be disastrous to the material well-being of Ulster as well as of the whole of Ireland, subversive of our civil and religious freedom, destructive of our citizenship and perilous to the unity of the Empire, we . . . do hereby pledge ourselves in solemn Covenant throughout this our time of threatened calamity to stand by one another in defending for ourselves and our children our cherished position of equal citizenship in the United Kingdom and in using all means which may be found necessary to defeat the present conspiracy to set up a Home Rule Parliament in Ireland.[29]

In January 1913, the Ulster Unionist Council, the umbrella body for Unionist and Orange organisations, led by Carson and his right-hand man, James Craig, MP for East Down, decided to recruit a private Ulster army: the Ulster Volunteer Force was officially born. The UVF openly trained for fighting in the event of the Home Rule Bill's enactment. At first, training consisted of drill with wooden replica rifles, but by July 1914, after being supplied with German rifles and ammunition, the UVF was well armed and trained. It threatened open war against anyone who tried to impose a Dublin Parliament on Ulster. David Craig, one of the soldiers in McGuinness's play, has been engaged in the work of supplying arms to the battalions of the UVF. Craig says to his fellows, Millen and Moore, members of the North County Derry Battalion: 'I did a few runs to collect and deliver the wares. We've a couple of vehicles. Was near enough to your part. I could have supplied yous with stuff'(*P1*, 122).

With the outbreak of the War in August 1914, Carson offered 35,000 UVF members to the war effort. Field Marshal Lord Kitchener agreed to the inclusion of 'Ulster' in the names of all the units that would be formed in order to keep their separate identity. Orr writes:

Their 'Ulster Division' was to be an expression of Protestant Ulster power, pride and independence. Their aggressiveness and the fearful reputation they were to acquire as bayonet-fighters were the outcome of the pent-up belligerence of those tense months of drilling, marching and gathering in large public groups. Their efficiency and *esprit de corps* were marks of the ethnic solidarity and separateness which they felt was being ignored by the British government's Home Rule legislation. Most of the men had signed the Ulster Covenant. They were a covenanting army, oath-bound and committed as much to the collective survival of Protestant Ulster as to the survival of the Britain they fought for and were part of.[30]

The 36th (Ulster) Division was swiftly formed from a stock of UVF recruits, and on 8 May 1915, it marched out of Belfast, and crossed to France in October. It then advanced towards the German lines on 1 July 1916, the anniversary of the Battle of the Boyne in 1690 by the old calendar,[31] and 'the Orangemen took that for an excellent omen'.[32]

It has been said that many of them wore Orange sashes, a Unionist symbol of loyalty and love for Ulster, as the men do in the final scene of the play, and that many of them shouted 'No Surrender' and 'Remember 1690' as a battle cry. Orr, however, doubts the truth of this:

My book and the play [*Sons of Ulster*] came out in the mid-1980s when, increasingly, loyalist paramilitaries were taking over the Somme as a loyalists' answer to 1916. In fact, the soldiers probably didn't wear Orange sashes at the Somme, and they didn't go over singing 'this is for the Battle of the Boyne'. People joined for absurd reasons – because they liked bicycles and wanted to be in the bicycle division – many, simply because they had no work. What was it after all? A few thousand people died, but more people died of the 'flu after the war. It's the trenches people have dug for themselves now that make them think it's so important.[33]

Conscious of the fact that it has been used in the loyalist paramilitaries' cause, Orr scrutinises the Battle of the Somme with a clear eye, unclouded by myth. In his review of Orr's book, McGuinness says that 'history tends to be concerned with confusion far more than clarities, and the author is to be congratulated for recording with accuracy and sensitivity the confusion felt by the young men who went to fight in the Great War.'[34] This fidelity to confusion stands opposed to mythologising – and in Ireland, mythologising is a deadly business. As E.Estyn Evans writes, 'until myths of various kinds are exposed, there is not much hope for peace'.[35] Orr, the Protestant writer, tries to demythologise the myth of the Somme while retaining compassion for the dead, wounded and traumatised; whereas McGuinness, the imaginative writer from a Catholic background, tries to remember the dead and the wounded within the context of myth in its most general sense. Together, perhaps, this particular lancing of myth, and this particular embodiment of myth in order that we might see, feel, and understand how one type of myth works, can help to close or bridge the sectarian divide. McGuinness's play, Orr says, 'touches on what Somme commemoration and heritage is all about. The march towards the Somme is the march towards willful[sic] self-destruction, and the inability to choose life. It stands for the dark side of Ulster Protestantism, a culture which seems not to be able to choose positively, and seems to choose instead its own destruction.'[36]

The Battle of the Somme recorded the heaviest losses the British army had ever known in a single day: 20,000 men dead and another 40,000 wounded. From the 36th (Ulster) Division, over 2,700 men were wounded and at least 2,000 died in the first two days of the attack. 'The Somme' became a byword for futile and indiscriminate mass slaughter. Just as the Republicans had made a 'blood sacrifice' in the streets of Dublin at Easter some two months before, now Ulster had made its own for King and Empire.

When Young Pyper first appears on stage in Part Two, he has cut himself peeling an apple. The real action of the play starts with the blood running from his thumb.[37] The blood here is bathetically contrasted with Cuchullian's in Part One, a little cut which thus symbolises Ulster's chronic trauma. Pyper's blood here has nothing to do with that 'blood sacrifice', even though his family's

greatest boast is that 'in their house, Sir Edward Carson, saviour
of their tribe, danced in the finest gathering Armagh had ever
seen'. Tribe, family is one thing: Pyper, the individual, is another,
for he says: 'I escaped Carson's dance'[38] (*P1*, 163), meaning that he
turned his back on Ulster Unionism. Unlike his fellow Ulstermen,
who join the army for the cause of Ulster, Pyper's reason for
enlisting, according to himself, is that he had 'nothing better to
do'(*P1*, 111).

Pyper says that he made a vow, while nearly starving as a
decadent artist in Paris: 'I thought I was dying . . . But I made a
vow I wouldn't die. I vowed that if I survived, I would never go
back to France. If I did go back, I asked that I be struck blind. I
made a covenant, and I survived'(*P1*, 110). The word 'covenant' is
used to evoke an association between Carson's covenant, to which
many fanatical Ulstermen had signed their names in blood,[39] and
Pyper's with his own unconscious. We should understand
'covenant' here as a psychological pact, which reminds us of the
antagonisms between private and public spheres. If a covenant is
'a binding promise that is sanctioned by an oath in the relations
between individuals, groups, and nations and has social, legal,
religious, and other aspects,'[40] then this very private covenant of
Pyper's, which has none of these aspects, is something of a
misnomer. He shows no hesitation when sent back to France as a
soldier, which involves a violation of his own covenant. He
survives the Battle of the Somme; the only soldier, out of the eight
in the play, who does. And the long aftermath of the battle strands
him in a bitter, personal darkness.

In the final scene of Part Two, Pyper intentionally slits his left
hand with a penknife, which echoes that earlier cut. The blood
runs down his skin, which is 'remarkably fine for a man' (*Pl*,
109). Except for Craig, all of Pyper's colleagues in the barracks
ignore this eccentric act of self-violation. Craig begins to tear the
shirt which was given to him earlier by Pyper, and bandages the
bleeding hand. He is simply taking upon himself the healing role
of the blacksmith, which is his trade. Yoko Sato points out that
blacksmiths were, according to folk tradition, believed capable of
curing wounds; and maybe McGuinness knows something about
this since his grandfather was actually a blacksmith.[41] Pyper's
behaviour could be explained as a mock ritual of blood
brotherhood, since he says that '[t]he elect shall bond in God's
brotherhood'(*P1*, 135). Blood brotherhood is a 'special alliance or
tie that binds persons together in a fashion analogous to, but
distinct from, kinship ties. The nature of the alliance thus formed

typically enjoins the members to mutual support, loyalty, or affection.'⁴² The Ulster League and Covenant was a variation of this fictive kinship, which served to bind Protestant people into a metaphorical family, united against an Irish Parliament. Some who signed in blood were following an older ritual of blood brotherhood, although they may not have realised it.

Through this reading, the title of Part Two, 'Initiation', makes sense. Pyper is initiated into Ulster Orangeism, an organisation in which he will eventually become a leader, under the name of Elder Pyper. McGuinness doesn't flinch in his depiction of Orangeism's bigotry. Millen and Moore, two soldiers from Coleraine, boast about their brutal punishment of a Catholic boy who had painted a tricolour on an Orange Lodge: they beat him, shaved every hair off his head, cut the backside out of his trousers, and painted tricolours on his buttocks. Anderson and McIlwaine, another pair from Belfast, begin hunting Catholics as soon as they enter the barracks, saying 'I spy a Taig. I spy a Taig'(*P1*, 132). They smell out Crawford, whose mother is a Catholic. Pyper pretends to perform a conjuring trick, making Anderson touch his hand and then counter-attacks him when Anderson is off his guard. Pyper thus shows how fighting 'dirty' (*P1*, 118) is necessary for survival, and that to fight fairly, according to some rule-book of decency, is to follow an illusion into possible extinction.

Pyper resists being incorporated into the order of the army, which, in important respects, reflects that of Ulster Orangeism. In an interview, McGuinness said that he knew what the last line of *Sons of Ulster* was going to be before he started writing: 'I knew it would be "I love my Ulster" and I knew I had to get a character that would find that as hard to say as I would find it.'⁴³ Pyper is such a character. He does not easily fit into Ulster Orangeism, but he still chooses to give his allegiance, in a very distorted way, to Ulster society, a society which does not make him welcome.

III

Naming is, for McGuinness as for other Irish writers, such as Friel and Beckett, a crucial act for characterisation. McGuinness once said: 'I cannae [sic] write unless I've got the names of the characters.'⁴⁴ His choice of names in the play underlines certain aspects of Ulster society at the time in which the play is set. The name 'Pyper' evokes the famous folktale of the rat-catcher, the

'Pied Piper of Hamelin', who lures the children of the town away.[45] A number of theories exist concerning the origins and meanings of this legend. One links the story with an exodus of young men in connection with the German colonisation of the east. The Pied Piper has also been likened to Nicholas of Cologne, who in 1212 led thousands of German children on the ill-fated Children's Crusade.[46] Common to both these theories is the strong folk memory of an exodus of young men or children, which casts an indelible shadow over its community for centuries. As Craig sarcastically says, reminding us of the ambiguity of the pied-piper figure, Pyper is 'a leader' (*P1*, 192). He leads lines of soldiers into questionable territory, into the dark zones beyond reassuring ideologies. This pied-piper allusion is bolstered by the long title of the play itself, *Observe the Sons of Ulster Marching towards the Somme*.

David Craig's name, the man to whom Pyper feels closest, is also important. 'Craig' reminds us of the historical figure James Craig, Carson's right hand man who later became the first Prime Minister for Northern Ireland after partition. David Craig insists on being called by his surname, emphasising its historical resonances for the audience. However, Pyper always addresses him by his Christian name, David, which has Biblical connotations. Most of the characters in the play call each other by their surname, in cheerful, mocking tones, reflecting army tradition. Therefore, if a first name is used, it will have special overtones – as Anderson says to McIlwaine: 'I know you're up to some badness when you use my Christian name'(*P1*, 147).

In a sense, of course, Pyper knowingly undercuts an ideology which, through a system of naming, empowers the 'tribe' at the expense of the individual. A person's first name is one of the most obvious marks of one's separate identity. In Christian society, a baptismal name represents the bearer's true self, whereas family names usually help establish one's group identification and social code. In the play, the tension between group identification and true self is seen through the ways in which names are used. Pyper is the protagonist who strives for his true self in the context of the homosocial bonding of the army's 36th (Ulster) Division, which requires each soldier to be a son of Ulster by submerging his individuality.

IV

During the five months which separate Parts Two and Three, all eight characters have been shattered by the experience and horror of the war. However, there is no battle scene on stage and we see the effects on each of the volunteers only through their conversations. In Part Three they are on a brief leave at home in pairs: Pyper and Craig on Boa Island, Roulston and Crawford in a church, Moore and Millen at Carrick-a-Rede Rope Bridge, and Anderson and McIlwaine in Finaghy Field, a gathering place for the Orange parade on 12 July. These scattered locations, in addition to the earlier reference to the range of birth places of the characters, (Belfast, Derry, Coleraine, Enniskillen, and Sion Mills), mark out a multi-dimensional map of Ulster, which all at once has geographical, historical and mythological implications. Later, in the final scene, the rivers which run through these areas are added: the Lagan, the Foyle, and the Bann, as well as the Boyne, a symbol of Ulster pride, completing this physical/imaginal map.

Craig takes Pyper to Boa Island on Lower Lough Erne in order to show him the carvings of the double-faced Celtic Janus, deity of duality and entrance, which stand in a Christian graveyard,[47] and strike Pyper as utterly different from the kind of carvings he made in Paris. Pyper feels happy on the island with Craig, for whom the visit to this island means a real homecoming: 'I've brought you home. Home with me . . . I just wanted to wash the muck of the world off myself. I thought it was on every part of me for life. But it's not. I'm clean again. I'm back'(P1, 140). Coming to the island is a private rite of rebirth for Craig. Whenever he washes himself in the waters of the Erne,[48] he is clean and new, purified. The two men sense a release from the socio-historical force of the war into the realm of mythology. They have become closer after the incident in which Craig saves Pyper's life in the battlefield, and a sexual element has entered into their closeness.

In Finaghy Field, Anderson says suspiciously to McIlwaine: 'There's still something rotten there. That time Craig threw himself on him to save him'(P1, 147). Moore, who is at the bridge with Millen, puts the same incident in a different way: 'Courage of a lion. Blacksmith. Risked his life for Pyper's. Together for eternity now. Good man, Craig. Two of them. Good men. Did Pyper come back from the dead that time he fell? I saw it. I saw Craig, what he did. He blew his own breath into Pyper's mouth. It was a kiss'(P1, 159).

In spite of the open gratitude he shows towards Craig, Pyper experiences an inner contradiction between this sense of being saved and a deep death-wish. He uses a biblical metaphor, completely reversing the original, to explain this:

Flesh. Stone. David. Goliath. Why did David save Goliath's life? For
Goliath diminished into nothing through David's faith and sacrifice.
Was David cruel to save Goliath from death? Because Goliath in his
brutality, in his ugliness, wanted death. David would not let him die. He
wanted to rescue Goliath from becoming a god. A dead god. A stone
god. And this stone destroys whoever touches him. (*P1*, 150)

He likens David Craig to David, the king of Israel, and himself to
Goliath, the 10-foot-tall Philistine giant.[49] In the Bible, David's
stone kills Goliath, whereas Pyper-Goliath, the sculptor, creates
images from stones. This kind of distorted biblical allusion in the
play is one of Pyper's favourite devices. In the Borghese Gallery in
Rome, there is a painting entitled *David with the Head of Goliath*[50]
[Plate 2] by Caravaggio, the subject of McGuinness's play,
Innocence (1986). It is commonly accepted among art historians
that this head of Goliath is a self-portrait by the painter. Paul
Hammond, a literary critic, believes that the painting, 'speaks of
the danger of homoerotic involvement, evoking the Freudian
association of decapitation with castration . . . Like many of
Caravaggio's pictures it offers a sado-masochistic pleasure.'[51] This
interpretation of the picture reminds us of the episode in
McGuinness's play about the three-legged whore, whom, Pyper
says, he married then killed by sawing off 'the middle one . . .
shorter than the normal two'. We can see that Pyper's desires
include a sado-masochistic element, hidden in this dirty anti-
Catholic joke. He is the one who castrated the whore, but at the
same time, he says, he himself was the whore, who had been
whoring in Paris: the wish to be both the castrater and the
castrated is obvious. This helps us understand Pyper's
transformed David-Goliath metaphor, which turns on David
Craig's prevention of death. Pyper reaches the contradictory bliss
of being both punished and relieved.[52]

   As a response to Craig's demands, who wants to understand the
mysteries of both the island and Pyper, Pyper begins to explain
the past which has made him what he is now:

I turn people into stone . . . Women and men into gods . . . I turned
my ancestors into Protestant gods, so I could rebel against them. I would
not serve. I turned my face from their thick darkness. But the same gods
have brought me back. Alive through you. They wanted their outcast.
My life has been saved for their lives, their deaths. I thought I'd left the
gods behind. But maybe they sent me away, knowing what would
happen. I went to Paris. I carved. I carved out something rotten,
something evil. (*P1*, 150–1)

Pyper, obsessed with a sense of continuation, or a negative image of regeneration,[53] transmutes his ancestors into gods in order to desecrate them. He 'carved out', as one might carve out, bring to the surface, a cancer, while simultaneously moulding, giving shape to, this rottenness. His version of ancestor-worship, which is irregular in both the Christian and non-Christian contexts, is an expression of his own rebellious spirit, the very thing which helps to make him an artist. Becoming an outcast allows him to 'worship' his Protestant gods, by turning them into stone deities, in itself a kind of personalised Catholic sacramentalism. When Pyper says Protestant gods, he wants us to remember that the adjective rests on the original meaning of the word 'protest'. His personal relation with Craig, and the encounter with his ancestors through the Boa carvings, effigies of the deity of entrance, bring about a sense of new beginning in his life, which, he asserts, involves a recovery of ancient forms.

Pyper then confesses the truth about what happened in Paris: which had much to do with his despair at his artistic creativity, and with his marriage to a Catholic whore, who eventually killed herself. He escaped 'Carson's dance', and the parochial confinements Ulster would have imposed on 'the eldest son of a respectable family' (*P1*, 163), seeking in Paris to gain what he calls 'a whole Northern European Scope'.[54] Pyper wanted to create for himself, not to dance for Carson, yet he is ineluctably drawn back to Ulster by his ancestors.

While you were running with your precious motors to bring in his guns, I escaped, David. I got out to create, not destroy. But the gods wouldn't allow that. I could not create. That's the real horror of what I found in Paris, not the corpse of a dead whore. I couldn't look at my life's work, for when I saw my ancestors, interfering, and I could not be rid of that interference. I could not create. I could only preserve. Preserve my flesh and blood, what I'd seen, what I'd learned. It wasn't enough. I was contaminated. I smashed my sculpture and I rejected any woman who would continue my breed. I destroyed one to make that certain. And I would destroy my own life. (*P1*, 163–4)

Here the confusion and perplexity which Pyper, the ambitious young artist, had to face up to in Paris, are vividly conveyed. In addition to his mental struggle with his interfering ancesters, what he encounterd in France was the new style of visual art, Cubism, which encouraged the complete destruction of traditional means of artistic representations. In fact, cubism affects not just Pyper's life, but the telling of his life, as a stylistic trope outside the narrative. McGuinness has commented that Part Three is modelled, in part, on the 'cubist painting and the artistic revolution that came to a head just during the time of the First World War'. Pyper had to go 'through this enormous creative crisis when the art of representation which he feels himself to embody is completely shattered, overwhelmed by the reality of the cubist invention,'[55] and McGuinness himself draws on this invention as a dramatic means.[56]

Craig responds to Pyper's confession thus:

I wanted war. I wanted a fight. I felt I was born for it, and it alone. I felt that because I wanted to save somebody else in war, but that somebody else was myself. I wanted to change what I am. Instead I saved you, because of what I am. I want you to live, and I know one of us is going to die . . . It was yourself you were talking to. But when you talk to me, you see me. Eyes, hands. Not carving. Just seeing. And I didn't save you that day. I saw you. And from what I saw I knew I'm not like you. I am you. (*P1*, 164)

This is one of the most powerful love scenes acted by two men on stage. It carries echoes of another confession, Catherine's in *Wuthering Heights* – though there it is heterosexual, but, as Pyper says, 'what's the difference?'(*Pl*, 129). Catherine, in stark realisation of heartfelt oneness between herself and Heathcliff, shouts 'I am Heathcliff!' Craig's confession of love is no weaker than Catherine's. And Pyper and Craig's gaze emphatically expresses their passionate sexual desire.

Pyper and Craig's passion parallels other types of relationship or friendship between men. In the previous part, when Pyper meets his old classmate, Roulston, Pyper says, 'Roulston's best friends were always much younger'(*P1*, 119). Roulston was, Pyper implies, taking care of younger boys to protect them at school, perhaps in a patronising manner, in return for their devoted service. The boarding-school experience often fosters this type of relation between boys. As Pyper points out, Roulston's closest friend is Crawford, the youngest of the eight. When they first meet in Part Two, Roulston treats Crawford as 'no more than a lad'(*P1*, 125) and urges him to turn his mind away from Pyper's dirty talk. Even though Crawford's reply to this is neither obedient nor docile, the exchange reflects the authoritarian and bullying ethos which is a common feature of boarding school life.

The most common friendships between men, at several removes from Pyper and David's passion, are also depicted – Millen and

Moore at the Carrick-a-Rede Rope Bridge, for example, and McIlwaine and Anderson at Finaghy Field. Sometimes they feel closer to each other than to their own families: they have chosen, after all, to spend their leave with their friends rather than to stay with their families. McGuinness intentionally juxtaposes these different types of relations between men to underline the point that a sexual relation between men is just a one of the varieties of masculine closeness.

Boa Island, the church, the rope-bridge, Finaghy Field – these four scenes, or better, settings, are now played intermittently.[57] When he was writing *Sons of Ulster*, McGuinness directed Alan Ayckbourn's *Bedroom Farce* (1975), at the New University of Ulster at Coleraine.[58] This is a pioneering work using split-staging devices, and, interestingly, McGuinness acknowledges that the triple structure in *Bedroom Farce* had an influence on his own play.'[59] The influence of Cubist paintings on the structure of this part of the play is also obvious. The scenes are fragmented and presented on stage simultaneously, much as Cubism seeks to show several sides of radically fragmented objects at the same time.

Initially, each of the four scenes is given fairly extensive stage time; then they are lit, by stage light, into pairs: Boa Island with the church; the rope-bridge with Finaghy Field. Two different thematic strands of the play (the tension between creativity and belief, and the tension between onward movement and stasis), thus merge into one. All four scenes are eventually lit together, which is when those strands cohere into a new, alchemical meaning. This makes for complicated description – as opposed to performance, where meaning is powerful and direct.

When the Boa Island and church scenes are run together, two completely different contexts acquire resonance from each other. Pagan and Christian are set side by side. Craig asks Pyper about the carvings on the island and Crawford asks Roulston about what it is like 'being of the elect'. Pyper 'takes Craig's hands and touches the carvings with them', saying: 'It's the only way I can answer you.' Roulston's reply follows immediately: 'It's beyond language'(*O*, 46). When Pyper asks Craig if he has seen the stone, Roulston in the church answers, 'Yes'. And again when Pyper asks Craig if he has heard what he's saying, Roulston answers, 'Yes' (*O*, 47).[60] Pyper and Roulston both reply with the same answer to different questions.

The quotation below is an example of how the two scenes interact, each using powerful imagery in its own religious terms:

Roulston: In the beginning is the word.
Pyper: I turn people into stone.
Roulston: And the word is within me.
Pyper: Women and men into gods.
Roulston: And the word is without me.
Pyper: I turned my ancestors into Protestant gods.
Roulston: For I am the Word and the Word is mine. (*P1*, 150)

When he quotes from the Bible, Roulston, the ex-clergyman, changes the expression slightly, but with crucial effect. St. John's Gospel starts with the dazzling imagery of the Creation of the universe by the Word, which is inseparable from God: 'In the beginning was the Word, and the Word was with God, and the Word was God.' The past tense conveys the immutability of God's work. However, Roulston uses the present tense and intentionally puts himself in the position of God, as if to imply that he is in the midst of the creation of his own universe, which is in complete accordance with Pyper's act of creating the realm of ancestor-gods. It is no accident that Roulston's given name is Christopher, meaning in Greek Christ-bearer. Roulston changes the biblical quotes and thus claims, ironically, a god-like authority. Some such human claim is suggested in McGuinness's deliberate non-use of the capital 'W' in the published version of this exchange.[61] Also implied is the notion that Roulston's world is smaller than the one he once believed in; so this play on capitals indicates a kind of freedom from authority's constraints. Like Pyper, Roulston is another outcast.

A similar interplay of resonance holds for the rope-bridge/Finaghy Field settings:

Millen: Close your eyes.
McIlwaine: Know what I'm thinking about?
Millen: Keep taking your breath.
McIlwaine: That boat.
Moore: I see nothing before me.
Anderson: The *Titanic*?
Millen: The end's in sight. (*P1*, 153)

Millen and Moore are talking about the crossing of the bridge and when Millen says 'the end's in sight', meaning that the end of the rope-bridge is near. But in this context, just after 'the *Titanic*?', we see the terrible end of the trans-Atlantic liner. The *Titanic* was constructed in Belfast during the heated Home Rule debate by a Harland and Wolff workforce, the majority of whom were

Protestant, including McGuinness's Anderson and McIlwaine. Gary Law writes that '[i]n the years that followed her sinking . . . *Titanic* became firmly lodged in the Protestant psyche alongside the Battle of the Somme as the embodiment of an emotional stew that has pride and loss and heroism and futility among its ingredients.'[62]

This climate of Ulster is well reflected in the following exchanges between Anderson and McIlwaine:

Anderson: Every nail they hammered into the *Titanic,* they cursed the Pope. That's what they say.
McIlwaine: There was a lot of nails in the *Titanic.*
Anderson: And he still wasn't cursed enough.
McIlwaine: Every nail we hammered into the *Titanic,* we'll die in the same amount in this cursed war. That's what I say. (*P1,* 154)

McIlwaine connects the unfortunate fate of the ship with the war, in which he is destined to die. So, when Millen says '[t]he end's in sight', it includes every factor: the end of the bridge, the end of the *Titanic,* and the end of the soldiers at the Battle of the Somme.

This kind of juxtaposition makes the audience feel that there is no dividing line between people, that the problems they carry and the fears they experience are all essentially the same: men experience some form of friendship and love; or they are similarly anxious about their energies, as, for instance, Pyper is about his creativity and Roulston is about the strength of his faith. We are watching two tragic ends of Ulster pride: the sacrifice of the proud sons of Ulster to the Somme, and of the *Titanic* to the sea. All is one in this trauma of Ulster – and in the last scene of Part Three, the words of all the eight soldiers converge into one action, 'moving', moving to battlefield:

Pyper: Coming with me?
Crawford: Come on.
McIlwaine: Can you not sleep?
Craig: To the front.
Anderson: I can't sleep, Nat. No sleep.
Roulston: Out we go.
Millen: Move.
Moore: March. (*P1,* 169–170)

V

In Part Four, entitled 'Bonding', these eight men have returned to the front and are sitting in a trench on the night before the battle of the Somme. Their private and personal experience in Part Three is now to be examined in the context of the army again. They are gripped by fear of the battle to come. They realise that what Pyper has said in Part Two, that they are all going to die, is, in fact, almost certainly true. McIlwaine already speaks about his life in the past tense: 'I could never remember words, but I never forgot a tune in my life.' (*P1*, 178) They are waiting for the order to 'go over the top', into battle. And here again a recurrent theme in modern theatre since Beckett, that of 'waiting', is played out. While they wait, they kick a football, sing hymns, tell stories, and play the Battle of Scarva, a re-enactment of the Battle of the Boyne which is held annually at Scarva in County Down on 13 July.[63] (Later, we will see how three hostages in a Beirut cell conduct a similar game in *Someone Who'll Watch Over Me* – writing letters to their families, shooting new movies, driving a car through the air, playing a tennis match, all within the free space of their imagination.)

Craig relates a dream he has had, about home, which reminds the other seven of the rivers which flow through their homeland: The Lagan, the Foyle, the Bann, and the Boyne, (the last, as mentioned before, having huge symbolic importance for Ulster Protestants). In contrast to his fellows who believe that their fate is to die in no-man's-land, Pyper is now fully aware of his identity as a man of Ulster and expresses his commitment to battle in different way. He tries to convince them that the smell of the Somme is the same as those of the rivers at home.

It's bringing us home. We're not in France. We're home. We're on our own territory. We're fighting for home. This river is ours. This land's ours. We've come home. Where is Belfast. Anderson? It's out there. It's waiting for you. Can you hear the shipyard, McIlwaine? You weren't dreaming about Lough Erne, David. You're on it. It surrounds you. Moore, the Bann is flowing outside. The Somme, it's not what we think it is. It's the Lagan, the Foyle, the Bann – (*P1*, 188)

Craig, however, discourages Pyper from continuing this literally misplaced paean to Ulster. This is one of the few occasions when Craig calls Pyper by his Christian name, Kenneth:

It's too late to tell us what we're fighting for. We know where we are. We know what we've to do. And we know what we're doing it for. We knew before we enlisted. We joined up willingly for that reason. Every one of us, except you. You've learned it at long last. But you can't teach us what we already know. You won't save us, you won't save yourself, imagining things. There's nothing imaginary about this, Kenneth. This is the last battle. We're going out to die. (*P1*, 188)

Later, Craig explains to Pyper that he did this 'to stop the heroism'(*P1*, 192). McGuinness always tries to avoid easy rhapsody, and it is clear that there still is dissonance between his characters, even between Pyper and Craig, who have experienced a primaeval Oneness in the previous scene. In this dissonance, Anderson bluntly presents an Orange sash to Pyper, telling him to wear it in the battle in order that he be recognised as one of their own. Pyper snatches it and there follows the exchange of sashes in some spontaneous pre-battle ritual, (bringing to mind Michael and Edward combing each other's hair before latter's departure in *Someone Who'll Watch Over Me*). Now, in contrast to the last scene, all eight men are paired off differently:[64] Craig with Moore, Millen with McIlwaine, Crawford with Anderson, and Pyper with Roulston, the last two pairs being the most unexpected of the four. Pyper then prays:

If you are a just and merciful God, show your mercy this day. Save us. Save our country . . . Let this day at the Somme be as glorious in the memory of Ulster as that day at the Boyne, when you scattered our enemies. Lead us back from this exile. To Derry, to the Foyle. To Belfast and the Lagan. To Armagh. To Tyrone. To the Bann and its bank. To Erne and its islands. Protect them. Protect us. Protect me . . . Lord, look down on us. Spare us. I love –. Observe the sons of Ulster marching towards the Somme. I love their lives. I love my own life. I love my home. I love my Ulster. (*P1*, 196)

This is both homage to Ulster, and a religious covenant, an appeal, as the *Encyclopaedia Britannica* has it, 'to a deity or deities to "see" or "watch over" the behaviour of the one who has sworn'.[65] This is a great transformation for Pyper, who once said: 'Nobody is watching over me except myself'(*P1*, 173). 'Being watched over' is one of McGuinness's perennial concerns, as the title of his hostage play *Someone Who'll Watch Over Me* clearly indicates.

He has asserted in an interview that '[t]he only challenging statement that can be made about the North is to say that if you believe in unity, disunity is the best way to begin the process of unity.'[66] The audience journeys with Pyper through his travails, experiencing the transformation of disunity into unity, and finally, after listening to the line, 'I love my Ulster', to a new form of understanding about an apparently cloistered and bigoted Ulster society.

Observe the Sons of Ulster Marching towards the Somme ends with the word "dance", by the Younger and Elder Pypers.

Younger Pyper: Dance in this deserted temple of the Lord.
Elder Pyper: Dance. (*P1*, 197)

The whole emotional and intellectual enquiry of the play is condensed into this last word, which has several layers of meaning. The play is a *danse macabre*, a dance of death, as Elder Pyper said at the end of Part One, '[d]ance unto death before the Lord'(*P1*, 101). Pyper, as a Pied Piper figure, is leading young Ulster soldiers marching to the catastrophe of the Somme, to death. To this imagery of the *danse macabre*, political elements, expressed as 'Carson's dance', and religious elements, expressed as the 'dance in this deserted temple of the Lord' are added. The whole of Ulster society is dancing.

In the scene on Boa Island, this imagery is transmuted into another dance:

Pyper: David.
Craig: What?
Pyper: Name. Say it. Want to.
Craig: More riddles?
Pyper: No. Talk straight from now on.
Craig: Why?
Pyper: Quicker.
Craig: Dance.
Pyper: The gods are watching.
Craig: The gods.
Pyper: Protestant gods.
Craig: Carson.
Pyper: King.
Craig: Ulster.
Pyper: Ulster.
Craig: Stone.
Pyper: Flesh.
Craig: Carson is asking you to dance in the temple of the Lord.
Pyper: Dance. (*P1*, 164–5)

This is a kind of courtship dance between two men. Craig may say that 'Carson is asking you to dance in the temple of the Lord', but we notice that all the different types of dance in the play are converging into a Yeatsian dance imagery: their dance of love leads them to a unique ecstasy, in which body and soul, creation and creator, and dance and dancer are inseparable. Commenting on the play to Joe Jackson, McGuinness said: 'It was a celebration for those who work hard and fight with all their might for their own corner.'[67] The phrase, 'fight with all their might', evokes the biblical David, who 'danced before the Lord with all his might; and David was girded with a linen ephod' (II Sam 6:14). The dance proclaims and celebrates its identification with the imperishable, with eternity. Such was David's dance before the Ark of the Covenant. Such was also the dance of the eight soldiers who marched towards the Somme.

Carthaginians

I

While *Sons of Ulster* deals with the tragic, traumatising Battle of the Somme, *Carthaginians* (1988)[68] deals with another event which, to many, is equally horrific: Bloody Sunday, as it quickly came to be called. On this day – 30 January 1972 – British troops fired into a crowd of unarmed marchers at a civil rights demonstration in Derry/Londonderry: thirteen were shot dead and another man died in hospital a few days later. The march was banned for security reasons, but this was hardly justification for the slaying of the marchers.[69]

Brian Friel responded to Bloody Sunday with *The Freedom of the City* (1972),[70] a cry of anger about the event itself and the tribunal which followed. In 1988, sixteen years later, Frank McGuinness confronted the challenge of giving the event a theatrical form which could accurately reproduce the echo of it in the Irish psyche. This was an event which, by 1988, had already been consolidated and moulded by collective remembrance. As the programme notes to the Druid Theatre production of *Carthaginians* put it in 1992, Bloody Sunday had left huge numbers of people with 'the memory of wounds' and 'changed a country's history for the rest of the century'.[71]

McGuinness said to Fintan O'Toole that Bloody Sunday was 'one of the worst days of my life'. He described how he felt, when, as a 17 year-old first-year student at UCD, he heard the news in Dublin:

I felt numb. I remembered going in to college on Monday morning and there was a march being organised. The obvious thing for me to have done would be to go back to Buncrana, but in shock you don't do the obvious. I kept walking around and I went over to the restaurant where people were gathering for the march. There were three guys tying a placard around this other guy, and they were laughing because they couldn't get it on properly. I wanted nothing to do with them. I went over to a tutorial and sat there with this unfortunate American. I just remember just sitting there.[72]

Carthaginians was originally written for the Field Day Theatre Company, which was based in Derry/Londonderry. However, the production was withdrawn by the playwright after 'disagreements on casting and direction' in 1987. It was eventually staged at the Abbey Theatre in Dublin.[73]

The play employs allegorical and symbolic tactics. For C. S. Lewis, allegory starts from the immaterial – passions, feelings, or thoughts – and materialises them: symbolism starts from the material and inflects it with immaterial meaning.[74] McGuinness used both. In *Carthaginians,* he started with fathomless anguish and materialised it; yet he started, too, with the irrefutable facts about Bloody Sunday and introduced into them an immaterial dimension.

This framework is especially obvious in the stage setting of the first performance, printed in 1988: the graveyard in Creggan[75] in Derry/Londonderry. 'Three plastic benders', a kind of camping tent, 'of the type used by the women at Greenham Common' (*CB*, 4), suggest that the three women in the play are actually camping in the graveyard. This sit-in method was adopted by the women outside the American air force base at Greenham Common to protest at the deployment of American nuclear missiles on British soil.[76] Elizabeth Butler Cullingford points out that though these benders are never directly mentioned in the script, they 'visually signal women's resistance to violence',[77] representing the flexible vitality of women. Their methods of protesting are totally different from those of the hunger-strikers,[78] who we are meant to understand as contemporaries or counterpoints of the three in the graveyard: these women mean not to sacrifice themselves but to live and survive.

This time-bound setting is, at the same time, timeless. The staging goes considerably beyond standard realism: the row of graves 'should resemble in their shape and symbols those of the grave chambers found at Knowth'(*CB*, 4), similar to the better known neolithic passage-grave at Newgrange. A large pyramid near completion, 'made from disposed objects', is also on stage. These things contribute to an atmosphere which somehow breaks out of the historical particularity of 1972: the pyramid and passage graves, which have been standing on the earth for thousands of years, are powerful symbols representing the historical past and the present, as well as the future and the afterlife. McGuinness seems to have needed these eternal icons of death and burial in order to transcend the potentially limiting context of the play, the contemporary Derry/Londonderry of the troubles.[79] However, the reality of that city and the sting of those events are also explicitly conveyed. McGuinness talked about the city to Liz Penny before he finished the play: 'It is a city with ruins, and the only way you can find out about it is from its ruins and its graveyards.'[80] This echoes his own remark on *Sons of Ulster*, quoted earlier: 'if you believe in unity, disunity is the best way to begin the process of unity'.[81] Paradox is a perennial characteristic, a motif, of McGuinness's theatre; and in his case springs from the intersection of the impulse to transcend, overcome, set right with things as they intractably are.

The opening music, 'When I am Dead and Laid in Earth', from Purcell's *Dido and Aeneas*, used in both versions, is another icon of death and burial. It also imparts mythical, Mediterranean dimensions to the play, which are heightened when Derry/Londonderry is compared to Carthage,[82] and by one of the main characters choosing to call himself Dido. This Dido, however, is a homosexual, not the classical lamenting heroine (the *femme inspiratrice* to such works as Virgil's *Aeneid* or Marlowe's *The Tragedy of Dido, Queen of Carthage*).

In addition to these mythological quotes, the imagery of the death of various forms of life is everywhere in evidence in the setting. Maela spreads clothes over the grave of her daughter, 'as if dressing a young girl'(*P1*, 297).[83] Greta is attending to a wounded bird in the opening scene. She laments the death of the bird in the next scene, saying 'it couldn't fly and it wanted the air. It needed wings. The wings weren't there'(*P1*, 309). Dido has an album of pressed flowers, and says: 'Flowers are more gentle when they're dead. . . . Flowers have more power in them. More magic. You can work spells with dead flowers'(*P1*, 308). A young girl, a bird, flowers are all dead in the graveyard of this 'forbidden city'.[84]

In an interview with Richard Pine, McGuinness points out the tribal elements of the Catholic tradition, contrasting these with the Protestant tradition where people stand alone before their Maker:

The Catholic tradition is very different, you judge yourself not according to your own life but according to the tribal inheritance, according to everything you carry from other people's lives as much as your own, and you are shaped physically and spiritually far more by that simple authority of Rome, which can be an exceptionally destructive force. *Carthaginians* looks at the acceptance of that authority in Ireland, at what happens to a people who move the centre of authority away from their own country to another organisation, a much broader organisation that spreads through Europe, and inevitably that can lead to the shying away from responsibility for one's own life. When you do that you are handing authority to an empire which will destroy you ultimately unless you can confront what's being done to you.[85]

Elder Pyper stood alone before his own trauma: in *Carthaginians* people gather in the graveyard and face their trauma together, communally. *Carthaginians* was first performed at the Peacock Theatre in Dublin in 1988, at a time when the phenomenon of moving statues all over Ireland in 1985 was still fresh in people's memory. The first report of a sighting was in Asdee, County Kerry, in February 1985. A seven-year-old schoolgirl went to the church of Saint Mary and prayed to the two statues of the Blessed Virgin and the Sacred Heart. 'Then she saw the Sacred Heart crook his finger and beckon her over to him. When she looked again, Our Lady's mouth was open.'[86]

Following this, case after case of moving statues were reported: at Ballinspittle in County Cork, at Camolin, Glenbrien and outside Wexford town in County Wexford, and at Carns in County Sligo. During the long rainy summer of 1985, bus tours were organised to carry thousands of pilgrims to these Marian shrines, some of whom later claimed that 'they saw statues move, or visions, or lights in the sky.'[87] It would be quite easy to dismiss the whole phenomenon as mass-hysteria, but to do so simplistically would be to miss something important, because these events can also be read as an index of social changes in 1980s Ireland. One commentator on these incidents wrote:

I know it is an optical illusion, but why in heaven's name do we all start seeing it at the same time? The last reason I would venture would be divine intervention, but whoever thought up the idea for getting more than 40,000 people per week to stand in the rain and say incessant rosaries for peace for the past three months – must at least have had divine inspiration.[88]

For the audience at the Peacock Theatre in 1988, the following exchanges between Dido and Maela must have had a certain currency.

Maela: Was anybody asking for us in the town?
Dido: No, nobody. You're kinda stale news now.
Maela: Us?
Dido: You and your visions. Nobody believes them any more.
Maela: They have no patience. No faith.
Dido: They say they have more sense. They say only the lunatics listen
    to you now. How the hell will the dead rise? (*CB*, 14)

The largely middle-class audience would have vividly recalled
what happened in 1985; the phrase 'the dead to rise' would have
struck a deep chord, reminding them of the miracles, the visions,
the millenarian yearning for salvation and resurrection. But, like
Dido, they were also likely to have considered the phenomena
'kinda stale news'. Compared to Bloody Sunday, these events
could be left behind and forgotten.

McGuinness therefore needed to re-evoke the incidents of 1985
for his audience when he directed the play for the Druid Theatre
in 1992. For example, the exchange between Maela and Dido,
quoted earlier, becomes:

Maela: Was anybody asking for us in the town?
Dido: Nobody. You're kinda stale news now. But the rest of the world's
    beginning to take an interest.
Greta: What do you mean?
Dido flamboyantly produces an Irish Press.
Dido: My media bombardment is starting to pay off. Page seven.
Dido gives Greta the paper.
Greta: (reading) 'Graveyard Girls Greet The Ghosts. Three Derry
    women have solved those holiday blues by turning into ghostbusters.
    They are sitting in Creggan graveyard in Derry waiting for the dead
    to rise. A spokesman for the girls, Mr Dido Martin, said, "They have
    seen a vision. Forget moving statues and Maggiagore[sic], this is the
    big one."' (*P1*, 306)

The phrase 'forget moving statues' slyly remind us of them, and of
the time in which they were seen. In this context of moving
statues, it is worth mentioning another feature of the play: a
parallel between its structure and Holy Week.[89] The play opens on
Wednesday, the day Judas plotted to betray Jesus. McGuinness
has chosen the day of betrayal[90] for his play's beginning, although
there are fewer elements of betrayal in Scene One than in later
scenes, where it grows into one of the key themes as characters
recall traumatic wounds from the past. Scene Four, in which the
characters take part in a play-within-a-play, *The Burning Balaclava*,

takes us through Friday, the day of Christ's passion and death. This structural parody of the liturgy of Holy Week has something in common with the devotional exercise of visiting church, attending services, and doing the Stations of the Cross, imitating the passion of Christ as observed on Fridays and during Holy Week in Catholic devotion. Although *The Burning Balaclava* is acted in mock-heroic style, all the participants gain some emotional release from, and control over, the anxiety which possesses them. On the Saturday night, they sit in a circle and say the names of the thirteen dead of Bloody Sunday.[91] This echoes the Easter Vigil, which properly includes the lighting of candles to symbolise Christ's passing from death into life, and the roll-call is a conjoint act of remembering and of burial. The final scene on Sunday comes, and the play closes in serenity. In this Holy Week framework, the characters of the play are waiting for the dead to rise. The Easter Vigil involves waiting for the light to enter again, for Christ to be reborn, to rise again from the dead. McGuinness simultaneously recalls and parodies this Vigil.

II

Each character in the play suffers psychological disorder in one way or another, and these problems are gradually revealed as the play progresses. Maela cannot really get over the loss of her daughter, who died of cancer on Bloody Sunday. Hark, Paul, Sarah and Seph were all involved with the Civil Rights movement in the 1970s but their idealistic hopes were frustrated. Dido acts as a contemporary wise fool in this confined community of the graveyard. Traditionally, a professional fool or jester in a court was a comic entertainer whose madness, imbecility, or deformity gave him licence to abuse and poke fun at the people he served. The fool represented, or better, re-presented, the weaknesses, vices and grotesqueries of the society in which he found himself. Dido is given this fool's licence because of his homosexuality, which brands him as an outsider of the community. In spite of the fact that the civil rights movement has much in common with the homosexual rights movement,[92] Hark, who was an activist in the former, openly despises Dido when Dido shows affection towards him. Gay political activism over the last thirty years has, to some extent, altered public perceptions of homosexuality: they are now seen less as deviants than as individuals exercising a different sexual preference. Among many people without this preference, however, prejudice against homosexuals still exists. Dido is marginal, even among the social outcasts gathered in the graveyard, because he openly shows this preference, yet it is his very marginality which allows him to function as a wise fool.

It is Dido, the modern jester, who, under a female name, Fionnuala McGonigle,[93] writes and directs the play-within-a-play, *The Burning Balaclava*, a parody of Sean O'Casey's Dublin trilogy or of some recent Troubles plays about Northern Ireland.[94] Mrs. Doherty, who has an obvious resemblance to Juno Boyle in O'Casey's *Juno and the Paycock*, is played by Hark, and her fanatical devotion to the Sacred Heart 'has led to the neglect of her son Padraig', a patriot and idealist, played by Maela. Padraig has a Protestant girlfriend, Mercy Dogherty, whose father is an RUC man. Mercy is played by Paul, while her father is played by Greta. Sarah takes the part of Jimmy Doherty, who is permanently out of work. All gender identities are reversed in *The Burning Balaclava*, apart from Seph's, who takes the role of Father Docherty. Since Seph keeps silent on the stage, because of some secrets from his past he wishes to conceal, he is allotted the part of the priest, who has 'stopped speaking entirely and now communicates only by means of white flags'(*P1*, 333). Dido plays two parts, Doreen O'Doherty and a British soldier.

Thus McGuinness, via comical stereotyping, epitomises life in Ulster. We see the young couple torn apart by the sectarian divide, the devout Catholic mother, the active RUC father, the unemployed youth, the woman who joins the IRA after her beloved (in this case her dog) is killed by a British soldier, and finally the political priest. All of them have variations of the same name: Doherty, O'Doherty, Dogherty, Docherty, and Ó'Dochartaigh. As Hark says, 'everybody in Derry's called Doherty. It's a known fact'(*P1*, 332). Each member of the cast could be anybody, which invokes the Everyman of the medieval morality play, who underlined a commonality of human experience. But Greta also points out the fact that, among those gathered in the graveyard, '[n]obody here's called Doherty(*P1*, 332).' Here again is paradox: everybody is called Doherty, but every single person in the play retains the right to say that their predicament is not universal enough, is too individually complex, to be truthfully depicted in Dido's play.

There is an affinity between McGuinness's work and the medieval morality play in that both are symbolic and allegorical reflections of the predicament of the person in his or her world. People came to 'regard human destiny as "worm's meat" after the Black Death, which ravaged fourteenth century Europe; and from that time on, 'the skeleton figure of death was a potent emblem constantly alluded to in sermons.'[95] It is this skeletal figure, a curious, black anticipation of Auguste Rodin's 'Thinker', that is pondering on the coat of arms of Derry/Londonderry. Despair and apathy, common in Northern Ireland, share with the plague a profound infectiousness. The Black Death skeleton reminded everyone of the unexpectedness of their own end. Derry/Londonderry's coat of arms, found in every corner of the walled city, is a warning to the city and its people of human destiny that they (or we) are mortal. Derry/Londonderry, in whose graveyard *Carthaginians* is set, is a living *memento mori*.

In the last scene of *The Burning Balaclava*, all the characters have water pistols, wear balaclavas, and kill each other. Dido as a soldier is the only one left alive, but all the others who died soon 'rise and shoot Dido' (*P1*, 344). Here again, is a parody of resurrection. As he is dying, Dido says:

They've got me. I join the dying. What's a Brit under the clay? What's a Protestant in the ground? What's a Catholic in the grave? All the same. Dead. All dead. We're all dead. I'm dying. They've got me. It's over. It's over. It's over. (*P1*, 344)

The audience laugh when they hear these grandiose words, but they realise, too, that he is describing human destiny. Dido, 'the queen of Derry', as described in the play, is another living *memento mori*. This meaningless slaughter brings a kind of catharsis for the players. By taking on one of Dido's roles, all the characters find an outlet for their emotions, even though they despise the play itself.

This play-within-a-play could be read as a psychodrama, a group psychotherapeutic practice in which patients with psychological disorders dramatise their personal problems before an audience. J. L. Moreno, who invented the technique of psychodrama in the turbulent period following World War I, and developed it throughout his career, defined it as follows:

One of its objectives is to teach people to resolve their conflicts in a microcosm of the world (the group), free of the conventional restraints by acting out their problems, ambitions, dreams and fears. It emphasises maximum involvement with others; in investigating conflicts in their immediate present form; in addition to dealing with the subject's early memories and perceptions.[96]

Classical psychodrama consists of three stages: warm-up, enactment and sharing. Each of these is essential to the complete psychodramatic process. The structural similarity between the phases of psychodrama and those of *The Burning Balaclava* in

Carthaginians is illuminating. McGuinness once said that 'when one is genetically conditioned for trauma, rehabilitation becomes impossible unless the therapist and the patient become one'.[97]

At the first stage in psychodrama, several warm-up techniques are employed which include 'sharing of names, sharing of experiences, physical activities that involve some degree of touch or non-verbal communication'[98] in order to facilitate interactions within the group. Hark and Sarah, who were lovers in the early 1970s, meet again after a considerable period of separation: Hark is back in Derry/Londonderry from prison and Sarah from Amsterdam. Although both of them want to be close again, their clumsiness prevents them from communicating effectively. But when Sarah slaps him – after he tells her he once believed her (thus implying that he does not now) – they come a little closer to saying how they feel about each other. Hark then picks up a dead bird and says:

Hark: Sarah, the poor bird.
Sarah: What about it?
Hark: It's dead.
Sarah: Did you kill it?
Hark: No.
Sarah: Well, it's not your fault then, is it? (*P1*, 317)

The bird allows them to speak in a roundabout way of themselves, and in this manner they probe for forgiveness and reconciliation, Sarah implying that Hark has no responsibility for her being 'poor'. After this, Hark lies beside Sarah and they sleep together. Their indirect dialogue and their resumption of sexual closeness are a 'warm-up', as it were, before Dido's psychodrama starts. Hark is, therefore, selected as its protagonist, Mrs Doherty, because he is the most sufficiently prepared, from a psychotherapeutic point of view, to express himself, to put himself forward.

The Burning Balaclava, in which we can discern several psychodramatic techniques, moves on to the process of enactment. Reversal of gender identities, for example, is a variation of 'role reversal',[99] the exchanging of roles among the psychodrama's participants. Role reversal enables the participants to experience the world from the viewpoint of the other side and is 'a way of transcending the habitual limitations of egocentricity'.[100]

Dido takes two roles in the play, another variation of a psychodramatic technique, known as 'doubling',[101] which means that one role, in most cases that of the protagonist, is taken by two participants in order to provide 'support in presenting the protagonist's position and feeling'.[102] Dido, a clumsy playwright, performs a scene in which Doreen and a British soldier, both of which roles he plays himself, have a conversation. This is one of the funniest moments in the play, a one-man show, in which Dido wears a helmet and brandishes a gun to play the Soldier one moment, and puts them behind his back to play Doreen the next. The tone of the exchange is absurd, but some truth emerges from this absurdity. When the Soldier confesses his agony at 'being a working class boy sent here to oppress the working class' (P1, 337),[103] for example, the language is convincing.

Psychodrama makes specific use of a method known as 'surplus reality'. This enables participants to experience situations which have never happened in reality, will never happen or can never happen. But they can still generate real emotion. This technique, in other words, extends the boundaries of theatrical reality into the realm of the absurd, in a way which allows the freedom of the absurd to enter into the interaction. Paul Holmes, a psychotherapist and a practitioner of psychodrama, says that 'the ability to experience these scenes is one of the magical strengths of the psychodramatic process. The very act of having experiences in surplus reality is perhaps one of the unique therapeutic potentials of psychodrama.'[104] And in the case of *The Burning Balaclava*, the irony deepens because its absurdity or surplus reality makes people aware that the actuality of Bloody Sunday was even more absurd: truth is more absurd than fiction. But the participants in this play-within-a-play re-experience and work through the traumatic and emotional experience of 1972 and new insight is generated.

Sharing is 'the final stage of the psychodramatic group process, in which all the members are encouraged to share their thoughts and feelings'.[105] When Dido asks Hark if the play is too short, Hark immediately replies: 'It's not short. It's shite'(P1, 344), to which everybody agrees:

Sarah: Dido, you know Hark. He can be a bit rough at times. He just says things straight out. I think this time he's right. It's shite.
Paul: Shite incredible.
Greta: Shite incarnate.
Maela: Dido, . . . you have great courage. I think . . . If I 'd written that shite, I wouldn't show my face for a month. (P1, 344–5)

Everybody except Dido enjoys using and repeating this typical Irish derogatory expression, 'shite', to explain their reaction to *The Burning Balaclava*. Although this word is fairly acceptable in informal conversations in contemporary Irish society, the word still retains a sense of release from taboo, and that is why, here, it functions to bring them together, to a form of sharing – the door to understanding is first prised open by earthy vulgarity, not by the balanced, neutral words of clinicians.

Dido also acts as a director, whose role underlines the theatricality of the play-within-a-play. When Sarah dies too dramatically, for example, he instructs her just to die simply. This kind of interruption by the director reminds the audience of their own position: that they are watching a play. Or when the Soldier played by Dido says to Doreen (also played by Dido) that British soldiers never shoot on sight,[106] the others groan in protest. Dido interjects, as 'himself', to remind them that it's only a play. The audience of 19th century melodrama groaned and hissed at theatrical villains, and relished a shared feeling amongst themselves through these stage conventions. These were recognised techniques of communication between stage and auditorium. Here, all the characters groan, because they become the audience of Dido's one-man show and enjoy watching it. This creates yet another complicated framework: We are watching *Carthaginians* in which *The Burning Balaclava* is played. The characters of *Carthaginians* are watching another theatrical piece, Dido's one-man show within *The Burning Balaclava*, while being at the same time involved in it. This self-conscious theatricality, with its Chinese-box structure, foregrounds and destablises the border between reality and drama to such an extent that we cannot help regarding ourselves as actors in a role, and we are thus led to question the legitimacy of the reality/unreality distinction.

Looking at this play-within-a-play, we realise that we are still in the *Theatrum Mundi* convention, common in Renaissance theatre: 'All the world is a stage [a]nd all the men and women merely players.'[107] We are players on the globe as Shakespearean actors were players on the stage of the Globe Theatre. The Renaissance mind was always conscious of this parallel between microcosm and macrocosm. According to Lionel Abel, the theatricality of the play-within-a-play has always been an index of the *Theatrum Mundi* mindset.[108] If *The Burning Balaclava* is 'therapy' for the characters in *Carthaginians*, *Carthaginians* may be regarded as therapy for people who are 'merely players' in this tormented theatre of the contemporary world – Ulster could be seen as a kind of protracted and collective psychodrama.[109] *The Burning Balaclava* is fun for the people who play it and who watch it. This, however, is just a jolly prelude to the shared pains when their different truths are revealed. To deal with this, McGuinness employs the technique of storytelling – which can, in the right hands, be as good for the psyche as any formalised medicine for the mind.

III

In addition to the ways in which the play-within-a-play structure operates as psychodrama, storytelling has an important role in the furthering of the psychotherapeutic process of the play in its final stages. This is an interesting development, which reflects one of the more crucial concerns, or artistic problems, in contemporary Irish theatre – the priority to be given to either dialogue or monologue in drama. It is fair to say that Irish playwrights are sometimes obsessed with the challenge of using monologue as the basis for an entire play. Brian Friel's *Faith Healer*(1980)[110] and *Molly Sweeney* (1994), Tom Murphy's *Bailegangaire* (1984), McGuinness's *Baglady* (1985), and Conor McPherson's *This Lime Tree Bower* (1995) and *The Weir* (1998), along with, of course, the works of Samuel Beckett, all make fresh and original use of monologue and storytelling. Monologue in contemporary theatre is itself a paradoxical development. Arguably, theatre began with the recognition that dialogue marked a singular, critical difference of human being from animal. Greek theatre sprang out of dithyrambic oration, a style of oration which facilitated proper dialogue when a second actor was introduced. The medieval liturgical play developed out of the broadly monological Matins service held on Easter mornings, specifically, out of that part of the service named '*Quem quaeritis*', which marked the moment when the three Marys on their way to the grave of Jesus were asked whom they were seeking.

In Celtic societies (Ireland, Scotland, and Wales), storytellers have been highly acclaimed and admired for centuries. It is ironic that in Ireland this ability to tell stories might have worked against the formation of a native dramatic tradition. Andrew E. Malone points out that 'the impulse which other Christian countries felt at an early time never affected the Irish people, and those early forms of drama which are such a conspicuous feature in the drama of other countries are without any equivalent in Ireland . . . in Ireland recitation took the place taken by representation in other European countries. The nobles and the aristocracy maintained the bards, and the ordinary folk maintained the shanachies, or storytellers, to provide recreation and instruction'.[111] He regards this as the reason for the absence of any national drama in either the Irish or the English language until the end of the nineteenth century.

> The spoken word was of the greatest importance, and the imagination of the listener supplied all the dramatic action that was needed. The epic poem when recited by the bard in the halls of the nobility, or the story when told by the cottage fireside, brought to all sections of the people that dramatic excitement which their natures desired. In these recitals the fine word was of the utmost importance, and the use of the fine word was governed by a technique that is probably the most finished and elaborate that mediaeval Europe can show.[112]

Of course, socio-economic and political factors played their part, too, in the relatively late birth of drama in Ireland, both in English and Irish. (Gaelic theatre did not come about until the production of *Casadh an tSúgáin*, a one-act play written by Douglas Hyde in 1901.)

The storytelling tradition identified by Malone in *Irish Drama* has, in fact continued into modern Irish theatre, and remains one of its strengths, allowing characters to reveal their thoughts and feelings in a direct and emotional way (and with more psychological urgency, too, than was possible with the older, more reflective style of soliloquy). Indeed, Kristin Morrison has argued for a closer link between storytelling and the psychological compulsion of a character to tell his or her story in modern theatre practice.[113] Discussing the plays of Beckett and Pinter, she argues that:

> The newest convention for expressing psychological inwardness on stage is the technique of storytelling: "narrative" suddenly becomes "drama." . . . Now the telling of a story allows characters that quintessentially "modern," Freudian opportunity to reveal deep and difficult thoughts and feelings while at the same time concealing them as fiction or at least distancing them as narration.[114]

The inner conflict of characters in much contemporary drama, Morrison argues, issues from the contradictory desires to confess and to conceal. In this respect the storytellings in *Carthaginians* can be regarded as rigorously modern in technique, and its characters as descendants of Beckett's own. Frank McGuinness's characters do not tell their stories simply and straightforwardly. The three women, who believe the dead will rise in the graveyard, are disinclined to talk about what they have seen. Greta says: 'The dead will rise here. A miracle. But we can't talk about it, for fear if we talk about it, it won't happen' (*P1*, 298).

Because of this prohibition, they choose to tell dirty jokes, which are variations of storytelling and are repeated several times in the play. But, in the course of the psychotherapeutic process, Sarah can tell the truth about herself after she and Hark are re-united, because the 'warm-up' allows her to do so. When she confesses what happened in Amsterdam, she begins her tale with a very traditional form of storytelling: 'I only know one story. Will I tell it? Once upon a time there were three young fellas, who were pals, best of pals' (*P1*, 327).

Her confession about drug addiction and prostitution in Amsterdam is disguised as an old story in order to create a distance between the story and its teller. Although everybody knows that it is hers, Sarah is able to pretend that the story is somebody else's. This distance gives her the courage to reveal the truth. She continues: 'I was sinking under the weight of powder. I sank and I sank until I felt hands lift me. I thought they were yours, Hark, but they were my own. I saved myself, Johnny. I saw myself dead in Amsterdam. I've come back from the dead. I'm clean' (*P1*, 328). She, then, encourages the others to do the same thing, to come clean about their pasts: 'And if what we saw is true, if the dead are to rise again, then we must tell each other the truth. For us all to rise again' (*P1*, 328).

However, McGuinness does not give the other characters a chance to reply directly to this: Scene Three ends with these words of Sarah's. They are not yet ready to respond to her challenge. But the play-within-a-play, *The Burning Balaclava*, has shown them a way of telling their own truths, a way to rediscover, re-experience and work through the traumatic or troubling events that have made them what they are.

After a long silence, Seph confesses that he betrayed his fellows and ran away. When he came back, he went to those he informed on and asked them to kill him. What they gave him as punishment was to live: literally a life sentence. 'I talked because I lived with what was done here one Sunday. I was here that Sunday. I saw it. I was in Derry on Bloody Sunday' (*P1*, 346). He admits that everything changed after Bloody Sunday. Maela, however, insists that everything is as it was before. When she finishes her story about wandering the streets of Derry after her daughter's death on Bloody Sunday, she keeps saying that she has to go to Mass – at which there is likely to be confession, a ritual which McGuinness seems to be inviting us to understand as religion's re-narrativisation of trauma.

When Greta is asked what kind of miracle she is waiting for, she answers that she wants herself back, that she would like to be what she once was. She does not give any further explanation, and we could easily misunderstand what she says as a metaphor or a cliché about missing the past in general. Which it is not. The story is too painful for her to relate in casual conversation. When Greta talks about her operation for uterine cancer, she can begin only with a 'doctor joke' told in the third person singular: 'This woman had an operation. A woman's problem'(*P1*, 373). The womb imagery and symbolism are intertwined with ideas of fertility and femaleness; Greta's loss of fertility makes her feel futile; she becomes aggressive when Sarah says she would like to have a baby: 'Are you telling the truth, Sarah? About the child? Is it the truth? Wasn't it your big idea to tell the truth?'(*P1*, 366) In the last moment of her confession, she moves from third into first-person voice, making a directly personal cry: 'All gone. All gone. Mammy, Daddy, I'm afraid. Mammy, Daddy, I'm afraid'(*P1*, 373). Through admission of her pain, she is able to take the first step towards recovering herself; she says: 'They will rise tonight, the dead will rise tonight' (*P1*, 374).

All the characters sit in a circle. There is a roll-call to honour the thirteen dead of Bloody Sunday. Then, as morning light breaks through the graveyard, a requiem is chanted to honour and pray for them:

Greta: Forgive the dead.
Maela: Forgive the dying.
Sarah: Forgive the living.
Paul: Forgive yourself.
Hark: Forgive yourself.
Seph: Forgive yourself.
Maela: Bury the dead.
Greta: Raise the dying.
Sarah: Wash the living. (*P1*, 378–9)

Embracing all opposites in the morning light, binding antagonistic forces into a unity, *Carthaginians* yet appears to offer no solution to the problems of Northern Ireland. But if we look with care, we see that a profound resolution underlines its apparent stasis. The perceptions of the characters are irrevocably changed. Dido says: 'What happened? Everything happened, nothing happened, whatever you want to believe, I suppose. What do I believe? I believe it is time to leave Derry. Love it and leave it. Now or never' (*P1*, 379).

Dido, whose etymological meaning is 'a traveller',[115] tales his leave as the others sleep, after sprinkling them with his 'dead flowers'. In doing so he evokes Puck or Ariel, those shape-shifters able to perform magic on the soul. 'You can work spells with dead flowers(*P1*, 308)', he says. The audience knows very well that, on a literal level, the flowers possess no magic, but they might also know that they have been witness to something miraculous: the first glimmerings, perhaps, of the transformation of human souls. This is a moment of magical theatre.

Unlike the tramps of Beckett's *Waiting for Godot*, this traveller, Dido, moves on.[116] His very last word, 'play', echoing 'dance', the last word of *Sons of Ulster*, urges the players of this *Theatrum Mundi*, which includes the actors, *and* the audience, to survive and to live. Derry/Londonderry's coat of arms may bear a symbol of death, but, like one of McGuinness's paradoxes, its motto – Vita, Veritas, Victoria (Life, Truth, Victory) – exhorts us always to strive for life, effort, and hope.

The Bread Man

A brief discussion of an unpublished McGuinness play, *The Bread Man* belongs here with this chapter. It is set in a small town in Donegal near the border in 1970, and was produced at Dublin's Gate Theatre as part of the 1990 Dublin Theatre Festival. It, too, deals with communal trauma caused by the Northern Troubles, though in a less indirect manner than *Carthaginians*: the turmoil of Derry/Londonderry is conveyed through the confusion and agony of a man, 'the Sinner' Coutney, the bread man. He feels guilty about, somehow responsible for, the death of his brother, Philip, in a boat accident. He is not properly able to communicate with his wife and son, and wanders on his own along the beach near his house. The structure of the play is, in its fragmentation and Cubist distortions, similar to Part Three of *Sons of Ulster*.

Northern Ireland's Troubles and the torment of its people haunt the play and the Sinner. If McGuinness's parents are 'the children of partition' (McGuinness's own term), his own generation are 'the children of the Troubles'. When the Northern Troubles broke out in 1968, McGuinness was in his mid-teens, living in Buncrana, fourteen miles from the border. As he responded to the Bloody Sunday in 'Derry' in 1988 in *Carthaginians*, this play written in 1990 is his response to, or survey of, the early stage of the Northern Troubles. Eamonn McCann describes a typical kind of apathy towards the Northern Troubles among Southerners in the early Nineties, the time at which *The Bread Man* was written.

The mass of people in the South are markedly less enthusiastic about the 'Northern struggle' than they were twenty-five years ago . . . And there is a myriad of other, more substantial indications of the widening distance between the concerns of Northerners and the consciousness of the South. From the working-class point of view, the main reason is that Southerners see little connection between what's happening in their own lives and what's happening to nationalists Up There.[117]

This is the climate in which *The Bread Man* was staged in 1990. McGuinness, as a Northerner living in Dublin, must have been conscious of this change in the South. In the late Sixties and early Seventies, to support the Catholic people in 'Derry', for the people from the Republic, was deeply connected with the Republican cause and part of process of achieving a united Ireland. This is why the Sinner of the play carried free bread across the border without a licence: to support the poor Catholics of the city for the sake of a united Ireland. But it seems that bankruptcy and family discord are his only reward.

Even when people of the South seemed to be enthusiastic about the Northern struggle, a kind of indifference was also creeping in. When the Sinner says that 'they are killing each other'(*Bread*, 26), Eddie, a homeless man, replies: 'that's miles away. Fourteen miles away' (*Bread*, 26). This apathy grows; people gradually become less willing to send money to people in 'Derry', even to their own relatives just across the border. Susan, the pregnant wife, complains:

I've had enough of the south of Ireland. I've had enough of dear old Donegal to last me a lifetime. They're fourteen miles from Derry and they're free of Britain's yoke, but to hell with them and their freedom, I'm having my child in the one and only United Kingdom where I'll have a roof over my head, and meat in my belly, and I know where I stand. A Catholic, yes. A Catholic definitely. A Catholic downtrodden. A subject people, for sure. But there, in Derry, I am looked after. Here, I am nothing. (*Bread*, 48)

This expresses the split mentality of many Catholics in the North, who acknowledge both that they are Irish, and that, despite discrimination, there are advantages to being part of the United Kingdom's welfare state.

The play ends without resolution for the Sinner, who suffers the ignominy of being accused by this couple from 'Derry' of having stolen their money. Everything is against him and he is on his knees. However, with an admission that he has nothing, his final affirmative cry, 'I have a son. Son' (*Bread*, 109), reflects a hope, no matter how tiny it would seem to be.

2

Visualising his Verbal Theatre: McGuinness's Interpretation of the Theatricality of Caravaggio's Paintings

Innocence

I

In spite of its realistic outlook, the poetic language of Irish theatre has always evoked visions, and McGuinness belongs to this tradition. Evocation, inspiration of the eye of the mind, is the key. Commenting on the impact of the laughter from backstage[1] in Caitríona Ní Ghallchóir's *Oisín i ndiaidh Na Feínne* [*sic*], a student production at the New University of Ulster, McGuinness said 'sound is more effective [in theatre] than the apparently more appropriate effects of vision.'[2] Although he talks of 'unseen laughter' rather than of language, he reveals his leaning towards the sound effect in theatre, of which language, of course, is part. In the same commentary, he said that 'Theatre is essentially a medium for paradox',[3] implying that theatre, as befits the etymology of the word, is bound up with this powerful, insubstantial 'viewing'.

This paradoxical tension on stage between sound and vision is an impetus for McGuinness's theatre. After his first major success with *Sons of Ulster*, he needed to change his way of writing.[4] 'The way *The Sons* was taken and the seriousness with which it was treated was a shock', McGuinness says. 'You could cod yourself into thinking "I am a sage" . . . *The Sons* is only a play; *Innocence* is only another play. They are not meant to be political programmes. You can change nothing.'[5] But, of course, you can change yourself, your way of representing the world, and we should read McGuinness's declaration of political impotence as a challenge to himself rather than as acceptance. With *Innocence*(1986),[6] McGuinness's approach to politics is much more oblique. He intentionally avoids directly political subjects and for its protagonist chooses Caravaggio,[7] whose paintings he has loved 'since [he] set eyes on them in Florence in 1977'.[8] In order to explore the tension between the language and the visual effect, the play alludes to many of Caravaggio's paintings, which have often been described as theatrical. Alfred Moir explains Caravaggio's paintings in theatrical terms:

He was a master of staging. Most of his paintings of more than one figure resemble the modern theater. We can imagine the genesis of a painting from a shallow stage, shadowy and empty, awakening as stagehands bring in and place a few props and a lighting technician tries out a spot or two or a bank of lights, and coming to life as the actors take their places. He favored very simple sets. Scenery was elaborated only to convey information relevant to the action. His basic unit of scale was the human figure.[9]

If Caravaggio's theatre is constructed from two-dimensional paintings, McGuinness, in contrast, would seem to 'paint' his three-dimensional pictures on stage through language. McGuinness himself uses the word, 'paint', when describing the creation of the play: 'So I began to paint, to play'.[10] He clearly feels an affinity with the painter as a creative artist. *Innocence* deals with the matter of innocence and art. It seems that McGuinness holds the view that to be an artist one must also possess a kind of deep innocence at one's core. The artist somehow stands outside worldliness, and sees with a vision unclouded by guilt or other-directed morality. In this sense, Caravaggio in the play is a direct continuation of Pyper, the sculptor and outcast in *Sons of Ulster*. In *Innocence*, McGuinness deals with the internal complexities of the artistic mind in the context of a Catholic imagination, a mind which should not be treated as though it were simply the antipode of a Protestant one. Heaney's comment on *Sweeney Astray* is pertinent here: 'insofar as Sweeney is also a figure of the artist, displaced, guilty, assuaging himself by utterance, it is possible to read the work as an aspect of the quarrel between free creative imagination and the constraints of religious, political, and domestic obligation.'[11]

II

However, McGuinness's way of explaining this paradox or

tension frustrated the expectations people had about the writer of *Sons of Ulster*. *Innocence* is one of his plays to which literary critics have paid comparatively little attention.[12] Eamonn Jordan's *The Feast of Famine*,[13] a book which deals with most of McGuinness's major plays up to 1994, devotes one chapter to *Innocence*. This is the only extensive discussion of the play, apart from the reviews of its first performance at Dublin's Gate Theatre in 1986. One reason for this critical neglect, in spite of the early publication which followed the first performance, must have been its poor reception by the Dublin audience. The play's iconoclastic features and overt homosexual elements include Caravaggio as a pimp, a Cardinal hiring the rent boys, and a woman masturbating Caravaggio on stage.[14] In 1996, McGuinness looked back on the play:

[I]t *was* 1986 and attitudes have changed an awful lot since then. . . . I don't know if people knew what hit them. There had been plays about homosexuality or with homosexuals in them before in Ireland, but I don't think anyone had ever flashed quite so potently. . . . It's never been done since at home.[15]

In 1986, Lynda Henderson wrote that the production 'has caused quite a flutter . . . among audiences, for reasons which Yeats, Synge and O'Casey would find familiar – the hypocritical sensitivities of an insecure culture.'[16] When the Cardinal turns out to be a client of the two rent boys whom Caravaggio has picked up on the street, Henderson notices that there was '[a]lmost tangible hostility in the audience.' Paul Allen also reported that 'there were ominous takings of notes in the theatre, then orchestrated disruptive walkouts'.[17] McGuinness himself admits that '[i]t is fair to say that it took nerve for any theatre in Dublin in 1985[18] to stage *Innocence* . . . There was a fair degree of uproar, Patrick [Mason][19] and I were branded as a disgrace to the nation and I got a number of anonymous warnings.'[20] McGuinness's iconoclasm seems to have blinded the Dublin audience to the play's real theme: the exploration of the Christian faith of an artist and the matter of innocence at creativity's core.

I would describe *Innocence* as a religious play: a play about Catholicism, in spite, or perhaps because, of its rebellious, apparently blasphemous outlook. What another art historian, Roger Hinks, wrote about the historical Caravaggio and his paintings pertains also to the play:

Caravaggio was, in his own way, a great religious painter, capable of inspiring a Ribera, a Rembrandt: and in his own way, very likely, he was a religious man. But it was precisely because he was religious *in his own way*, and not in the Church's way, that he was under an official cloud: to the orthodox mind error is always more pernicious than unbelief.'[21]

Innocence is, 'in its own way', a religious play. It concerns a man's struggle to realise how he should live and die, the painfully honest processes of self-examination an artist goes through in order to realise his art, and the light and the dark of the soul. In his travails through this dark journey, McGuinness's Caravaggio bears his cross of homosexuality and is stigmatised by it. *Stigma* itself is a paradox in the Christian context: a sign of disgrace is transformed into one of holiness. Caravaggio is a disgrace and at the same time holy. Henderson accurately describes the playwright's thesis as 'the indivisibility of Crazy Jane's fair and foul'.[22] McGuinness's Caravaggio takes his own path towards the imitation of Christ, and perhaps it is no accident, therefore, that Garrett Keogh, who played the title role in the first performance, adopted the look of a conventional Christ-figure.

Innocence is McGuinness's attempt 'to understand Caravaggio and . . . Roman Catholicism'.[23] McGuinness discussed his intentions with Gerry McNamara in a magazine interview in *Out*:

I took very seriously what I think is in Caravaggio's paintings, which is a desire for death, or desire for oblivion. His religion had a lot to do with that – the Catholic Church, with the crucified Christ as its central emblem. That was how he explained himself to himself; that he was born to suffer, to die. And his homosexuality was a burden, another nail in the hand. His painting was the only way to get rid of that burden, his painting took out the nails . . . But his dilemma is a common one . . . Catholicism is just an explanation of that universal struggle; the fact that I must love and I must die. This is something that oppresses everyone.[24]

Religion, among other things, begins in a coming to terms with the universality of human death. 'Religions owe their existence to the unique ability of the human animal to understand that it must die.'[25] Frank Kermode avers that 'Christianity of all the great religions is the most anxious, is the one which laid the most emphasis on the terror of death.'[26] Throughout the Middle Ages, a contempt for this world and an exaltation of the delights of heaven dominated European culture. And there was heaven's dark complement, too, an elaborate theology of hell, which led to an obsession with death as the supreme moment of crisis in the

eternity of human existence. Willard Farnham observes that
'healthy people were writing *memento mori* and picturing the
death's head over their fireplaces, on articles of daily use,
wherever they would be likely to look while they were immersed
in the business of living'.[27] Henry Jacobs notes that 'the *memento
mori* should remind us of death, bring us to the contemplation of
our own sins, detach us from the world and move us beyond
death to thoughts of God and redemption.'[28] These views on the
uses of *memento mori* in the Middle Ages reveal a good deal about
what McGuinness tries to do in *Innocence*. The play has, at one
level, certain affinities with the medieval concept of *memento mori*
and the dark atmosphere of Elizabethan and Jacobean tragedies,
which were written largely under the influence of medieval
tradition. The crucified Christ is a central emblem in the Catholic
Church: Christ died on the cross to redeem people and to set them
free. The ruling authority declared itself the protector of freedom,
but in so doing, it deprived them of freedom as individuals. If
Innocence seems iconoclastic, it is because McGuinness refuses to
be bound by the established authority of the Catholic church. The
play is his attempt to free himself from it.

In order to ground this attempt to understand Catholicism and
to come to terms with Caravaggio, McGuinness used 'the city of
Derry as model for the Rome of [Caravaggio's] day,[29] . . . [Derry]
is now about the same size as Rome was then'.[30] We cannot trace
any clear evidence of Derry/Londonderry as the model for Rome
in the text, but this mention of the city by the playwright reminds
us of another of the play's themes: the desolation of people in
contemporary society. Derry/Londonderry is, as we saw earlier, a
city which has a special meaning for McGuinness, the city nearest
to where he grew up, a kind of hometown for the playwright; it is
also the scene of Bloody Sunday in 1972, which 'ripped Ireland
apart'. It is a locus of national trauma, dealt with in *Carthaginians*,
and serves as Ireland's *memento mori*, a role which the skeleton
figure on its coat of arms eerily reminds us of. In addition to their
similarity in size, twentieth-century Derry/Londonderry, with its
turmoil caused by the civil rights movement and the Troubles, has
much in common with Rome during the trepidations of the
Counter-Reformation, with its daily round of violence and terror.
The shock for many people, including McGuinness, of Bloody
Sunday may well have been paralleled by what people (including
the historical Caravaggio) felt in Rome when they saw Giordano
Bruno burned alive as 'an impenient and pertinacious heretic'[31] in
1600. (Bruno wrote that every great power evolved its own

opposite in order to achieve itself, that from such opposition might spring reunion.) Violence and terror are omnipresent in Caravaggio's paintings throughout his entire career, and probably reflect, to some extent, the actual violence of the world in which he lived. By drawing the two cities closer in his mind, McGuinness is better able to tap into his own imagination and thereby to recreate Caravaggio on the contemporary stage.

Joe Vanek, set designer for the performance at the Gate Theatre, explains his own contribution to this re-creation. He provided a visual accompaniment for the playwright's view of the world:

Caravaggio peopled his [canvas] with the inmates of a teeming, dark and desperate world and elevated them to a divine status. Contemporary Romans adopted the mantle of the sacred and the mythical and earthy realism was born. Frank's play evokes verbal parallels and we searched for a potent visual metaphor of urban desolation and spiritual decay that belongs as much to today as to 1606.[32]

III

The play opens with a powerful visualisation of the *danse macabre*, or Dance of Death, with all the characters on an underlit, sombre stage: Caravaggio is holding a skull, a familiar icon in his paintings, along with other characters, a Cardinal (patron to Caravaggio), Lena (friend to Caravaggio), his brother (a priest), his sister, two rent boys, a whore, and a servant to the Cardinal. The traditional meaning of the *memento mori* is unmistakably clear, although this Dance of Death leads the dancers nowhere: they position themselves in a circle, and Caravaggio, skull in hand, is standing apart from them rather than leading them. It is as if they, in some stagnated condition, are not even allowed to move towards 'death', and Caravaggio, cut off in their centre, suggests that an artist has no authority to guide anyone.

A red cloak, another icon in many of Caravaggio's religious paintings, which Lena caresses, is, according to Christian tradition, 'one of the emblems of Christ's suffering, while he was in the common hall, and is, therefore, one of the symbols of the Passion.'[33] The symbolism encoded in the red cloak here, however, is manifold. This cloak is soon turned into a mad cloak-horse, and 'moves wildly through the characters'(*P1*, 205), breaking into animal sounds. This motif of violence and vital energy is dominant throughout the play. Commenting on *The Taking of Christ* [Plate 6], Caravaggio's painting, discovered in Ireland in

1993, McGuinness writes about the red cloak and violence: 'A red cloak has always a potent meaning in Caravaggio's paintings and here, half-buried in the gloom, the cloak surrounds Jesus and Judas, and the two soldiers, infecting them all with the curse of their violence. This red has congealed to the shade of dried blood.'[34]

Caravaggio's paintings are filled with 'the curse of violence': many severed heads, Goliath's, John the Baptist's, Medusa's, and Holofernes's, are shown in them. Some pictures capture the very moment at which the heads are severed. The red cloak could thus be the blood-soaked cloak, which again is another *memento mori*. As the blood-soaked handkerchief of Horatio in *The Spanish Tragedy*, which broke new ground for Elizabethan revenge tragedies, is a reminder of the revenge which Horatio urges his father Hieronimo to complete, Caravaggio's red cloak reminds us of the terror and violence of many cruel deaths.

But in McGuinness's hands, the symbolism of the red cloak is made broad enough to contain not just blood and death, but tenderness. In the opening scene, Lena caresses the red cloak like a child. This evokes another painting by Caravaggio, *The Penitent Magdalena* [Plate 1]. In his programme notes, McGuinness states that the imaginative origin of the play belongs in this particular painting:

It is dangerous to say where plays come from but with *Innocence* it should be obvious, a painting, an image by Caravaggio . . . I went to Rome, where most of the man's great work is to be seen. Its violence I was prepared for, it's what they say about him, but his tenderness, his gentle power shook me into seeing something else. I watched his painting called the Penitent Magdalena, a woman crying, cradling something invisible. Caravaggio defended the honour of a woman called Lena. The woman he honoured must have been a match for him, and being Caravaggio, it must have been a queer match. So I began to paint, to play.[35]

Mary Magdalena in the painting cradles 'something invisible', whereas Lena on stage strokes the red cloak, like a child. Later she and Caravaggio mockingly play with the idea of having a child. They are indeed 'a queer match', tied to each other in their own peculiar way. We see the proof of this bond when Caravaggio murders a man who has insulted Lena, and she, in turn, gives him what little money she has to aid his flight from Rome. There is historical evidence that Caravaggio fought over a woman called Lena and wounded a man on the side of the head with a blow

from his sword.[36] But whoever this historical Lena was, she was
not (as Hibbard notes in his 1983 study) the model for *The Penitent
Magdalena*. McGuinness, however, disregards this and treats this
woman and the model as one, as Lena, a 'beautiful and angry'
personage, 'girlfriend to the goat, to Caravaggio' (*P1*, 217). The
unexpected tenderness in Caravaggio's painting and in
McGuinness's recurrent theme of childlessness converge in the red
cloak, when it is caressed as a child by Lena – named after Mary
Magdalena, the woman whom Jesus possibly loved most.
Caravaggio as a Christ-figure, then, is matched by Lena as Mary
Magdalena. According to Hibbard, '[t]he repentant Magdalen[37] is
a characteristic theme of the Counter Reformation. . . . Mary
Magdalen was a supreme example of Penance, the sacrament of
greatest importance after Baptism and the Eucharist and one that
was particularly emphasised in this period, when the Church
wanted to welcome back those who had gone astray into
Protestantism.'[38]

Caravaggio's *Rest on the Flight to Egypt* [Plate 4] was painted
during the same period as *The Penitent Magdalena*. If we look at the
two paintings together, it is obvious that 'Mary is painted from the
same model who posed for the *Magdalen*.'[39] The Virgin Mary's
posture is very similar to that of Mary Magdalena, and the Virgin
is of course cradling the infant Jesus: the two paintings are
complementary as if to show that Mary the Whore is only another
form of Mary the Virgin. 'Virgin and Whore', Walker writes,
'constantly exchanged attributes through the Middle Ages; the
Virgin Mary was constantly a special patron of prostitutes.'[40] The
red cloak which Lena cradles in the play is not only an imaginary
baby but also, it could be inferred, the infant Jesus.

In the nightmarish opening scene, two rent boys, who are
fondling each other, and the Whore, who is weeping, are
juxtaposed with the Cardinal, who recites the Offertory from the
Tridentine Mass, representing the authority of the Counter
Reformation. This is a reflection of the world: the young and
beautiful and the old and ugly, the holy and the damned, anarchy
and ultra-orthodoxy are together. This is again the theme of the
danse macabre. McGuinness thus establishes, in his opening, the
themes and images which will run through the play: the suffering
of a Christ-figure who is at the same time an artist, the violence
and tenderness he carries, his childlessness, his partnership with
Lena, which leads nowhere, and the temptation and danger of
sensuous pleasure. The scene ends with complete darkness and
the real action of the play then begins with the light in Lena's

hovel. This extreme contrast of light and dark is the very essence of Caravaggio's paintings, often referred to as 'tenebrism' or 'chiaroscuro'. The influence of his paintings is pervasive throughout the play; however, it is perhaps nowhere more profound than in McGuinness's use of light and darkness in the verbal modelling of the imagery:

I take ordinary flesh and blood and bone and with my two hands transform it into eternal light, eternal dark. (*P1*, 208)

I paint as I see in light and as I imagine in darkness, for in the light I see the flesh and blood and bone but in the dark I imagine the soul of man for the soul and the soul alone is the sighting of God in man and it is I who reveal God and it is God who reveals my painting to the world. (*P1*, 209)

All life is death, all light is darkness, and from the darkness your boys have crawled to bring you the light of love. (*P1*, 238)

Caravaggio is an arrogant artist, assuming a god-like position when he creates. For him, creating any form of art seems to mirror the creation of the world. In a Christian context, however, the artist, at the same time, is tormented and torn apart by this sin of arrogance and pride, which comes first among the seven deadly sins. The light and dark which McGuinness presents in his verbal world are shot through with this strain of guilt. Lena, for example, repeatedly calls Caravaggio 'goat'. In Early Christian tradition, the goat was taken as a symbol of the damned in the Last Judgement: 'When the Son of man shall come in his glory, and all the holy angels with him, then shall he sit upon the throne of his glory. And before him shall be gathered all nations, and he shall separate them one from another, as a shepherd divideth his sheep from the goats.'(Matthew 25:331–32) In the Renaissance, the goat usually symbolised the sinners, the lamb the righteous.

Caravaggio is also defined as a sinner because of his homosexual proclivities. Caravaggio's paintings, many of which are 'apparently homosexual in implication',[41] were visual models for many of the scenes of the play: there are literally dozens in *Innocence* that echo or mimic the paintings. McGuinness's empathy and love for Caravaggio's art amalgamate into drama that is stitched together with visual quotations from the paintings. In the first part, entitled 'Life', most of the quotations are intentionally taken from Caravaggio's secular paintings of the 1590s. The iconoclastic element in the play owes much to

McGuinness's reading of these paintings. *Bacchus* [Plate 3] is one of the paintings to which McGuinness paid particularly close attention. Lucio, one of the rent boys, tells how he posed for Caravaggio as Bacchus or as a tree:

He squeezed grapes all over me. There was even a bunch hanging from my balls. Then he ate them. I have a good stomach but I swear I nearly took sick. He started to call me Bacchus. (*P1*, 225)

Leaves all over my head, right? Rotten old fruit dripping all over me. He had fire burning all about me. My big red cheeks burning like two beetroots. Jesus, I felt a right prick. (*P1*, 225)

Bacchus, the origin of this scene now hangs in the Uffizi in Florence, and about it Giorgio Bonsanti says this:

The important thing to notice here is the absolute newness of the invention, where one does not see a classically idealised Bacchus, but the image of a young man, almost a boy, whose features are hardly refined, and who is dressed – perhaps it would be better to say disguised – as Bacchus, in a manner which today would be considered provocative. Caravaggio deliberately chose a model that could not be associated with the grotesque Bacchus or with the handsome young Bacchus of antiquity. Instead of Bacchus the god, he represents a common person brought in off the street and disguised as Bacchus. It appears as though, after posing for the painter, the model were about to stand up, throw off the drape, drink down the wine, and head off for the tavern.[42]

This seductive Bacchus, crowned with a wreath of grapes, is offering a glass of wine to the viewer. 'He offers', according to Moir, 'not only wine but himself as well: his right hand toys with his sash, which barely holds his drapery together. . . . The sly, dreamy eyes speculate on carnal things and promise gratification of the senses, not of the spirit'.[43] On the table there is a platter of fruits; one apple is worm-eaten and one of the apricots is overripe, implying that the beautiful Bacchus will lose his youth almost as quickly as the fruit rots or decays. In the play, when Caravaggio sees Lucio for the second time, Caravaggio says: 'Soft. Like your face used to be' (*P1*, 230), implying that Lucio's beauty has already gone.

Lucio describes another episode: Caravaggio told him that he had fingers that were carved, that they had the flow of a musician's hands(*P1*, 219). This reminds us of two other Caravaggio paintings: *The Lute Player* [Plate 7] and *The Musicians*

[Plate 10]. These beautiful boys, their mouths half open, again seduce the viewer with their earthly, voluptuous promises. On stage we actually see Caravaggio directing his model into a pose for his canvas. When Caravaggio and the two rent boys, Lucio and Antonio, are in the palace of Cardinal Francesco del Monte, Caravaggio's patron and 'buyer'(*P1*, 231), Antonio offers Caravaggio a bowl of fruit. Caravaggio turns it down but watches Antonio for a while and pulls 'Antonio's shirt from his shoulder to expose the flesh'(*P1*, 228). This scene was inspired by another painting, *Boy with a Basket of Fruit* [Plate 12].[44] In the painting, a beautiful boy, his mouth half open and his shirt hanging from the shoulder, again invites the viewer into the same sensuous world where *The Lute Player* and *The Musicians* live. Here also, the basket of fruit, much of it overripe, again alludes to mortality and decomposition.

Antonio's description of how he was bitten by a black rat recalls Caravaggio's painting, *Boy Bitten by a Lizard* [Plate 9], a connection that is made explicit when he says that he hoped 'it was a lizard. But it was a rat'(*P1*, 235). Antonio associates this with the experience of being thrown into a barrel of rainwater by his father, who was terrified of his son's catching the plague by rat-bite. This allusion to the plague is another *memento mori*, since Caravaggio lived at a time when people still lived under constant threat of the Black Death.[45] Again, many symbolical interpreta-tions of this painting are possible. The lizard could imply death or lust, which corresponds 'neatly with the paired cherries, symbolic of love, and the roses, which, among other meanings, can refer to venereal disease. Both are certainly symbols of venery and would be in keeping with the mock heroic character of the whole painting, as warning of its pitfall.'[46]

These abundant quotations from the paintings create a sensual and seductive imagery on stage, fleshing out a world where Caravaggio struggles with his sense of sin. Urged by the Cardinal to confess, Caravaggio begins his confession by saying that he saw two boys; to which the Cardinal responds by asking him if he has led them astray into sin. This is a dangerous game, poised on a knife-edge, because both the Cardinal and Caravaggio know very well what the gaze thrown at beautiful young boys means. They are accomplices:

I heard them whispering and laughing. I watched them touch each other. Still young, still desired, and I was angry. I was jealous. They were as near to me as you are, but in their youth and desire they were as far away as the stars in the sky. I wanted to raise my fist and grab them from the sky and throw them into the gutter where I found them. I wanted to dirty their white shirts with blood. I wanted to smash their laughing skulls together for eternity. I wanted the crack of their killing to be music in my ears. I wanted them dead. I wanted red blood from their brown flesh to stain their white shirt and shout out this is painting, this is colour, these are beautiful and they are dead. They are not there. The sin, not there. My sin, not there. Just my painting, not my sin. I didn't touch them. I did not kill them. I desired them. Oh my God, I am sorry for having offended Thee for Thou art the chief good and worthy of all love. (*P1*, 244)

This confession, practically a mock confession, closer to moral cat and mouse than it is to a pure shriving, is both strange and dramatically powerful. The artist's urge to destroy the two beautiful young boys, to vent his jealousy, is graphically expressed. After this, we cannot look at the paintings connected with the play, such as *The Lute Player* or *The Musicians*, without hearing 'the cracking sound of their killing', without imagining that horrible noise as a deathly accompaniment to their songs. Caravaggio's wish to combine violence and death with beauty in his paintings is also clear here. He is obsessed with his sense of sin; because of this obsession, this monologue is still relevant as a confession, in spite of its mocking tone. And however sinful Caravaggio may be, his paintings are his attempt to atone for his transgressions: to paint is an act of atonement, at-one-ment, a drive to unify opposites and end painful contradictions. The paintings themselves, however, are transgressions, and McGuinness leaves us with a dramatic sense of the complexity of human motive.

Caravaggio is forgiven, even before he makes his confession. The Cardinal says: 'You remind us of unpleasant truths, Caravaggio. For that you may be hated. Your sins may be condemned. But you will be forgiven, for you are needed. Forgiven everything eventually. Dangerous words. A dangerous man. Saving himself by the power of his seeing. And by his need to tell what he sees' (*P1*, 243). This is quite ironic, because the Cardinal himself is not unblemished and is far from the ideal of a truthful, upright clergyman. This is absolution given to a sinner by his own accomplice. Yet, it is the Cardinal's own degeneration that enables him to see Caravaggio's sins as forgivable. Despite the tone or intention of the speech, once these words are spoken, their power is registered, is present on stage.

Compared with the Cardinal, Caravaggio's priest-brother has an inflexible, more ordinary sense of morality, and thus represents the social and religious norms outside the painter's studio. The brother tries to convince Caravaggio to come back home and have children to continue the family, but when he discovers that Caravaggio turns down his suggestion because of his sexuality, he refuses to forgive him. Indeed, Caravaggio cannot be forgiven within the framework of traditional Church values. This juxtaposition of the Cardinal and the brother embodies what Joseph Campbell Calls 'the paradoxology of morality and the values of life'. . . . 'You cannot be so disobedient that God's mercy will not be able to follow you, so give him a chance. "Sin bravely," as Luther said, and see how much of God's mercy you can invoke. The great sinner is the great awakener of God to compassion. This idea is an essential one in relation to the paradoxology of morality and the values of life.'[47] But the fact that his brother's denial comes after the Cardinal's forgiveness makes Caravaggio all the more despairing, and Part One ends with Caravaggio cursing himself in the dark.

IV

If Part One, 'Life', is constructed by accumulating sensual imagery from Caravaggio's paintings of the 1590s, Part Two, 'Death', draws together the religious imagery from the later paintings. In the opening scene of 'Death', the stage direction says that 'Lena dries her hair. A pitcher of perfume stands on the ground near her' (*P1*, 256). Here McGuinness is again quoting *The Penitent Magdalena* [Plate 3]. When Caravaggio enters, wounded and bloodied after a fight on the street, Lena 'applies the perfume'(*P1*, 260) to Caravaggio's head. In doing so she copies Mary Magdalena with Jesus: 'There came unto him a woman having an alabaster box of very precious ointment, and poured it on his head.'(Matthew, 26:7) In Part One, Caravaggio is implied as the son of God when he appears in front of both Lucio and Antonio after they pray to God to send 'a man' or 'your son'(*P1*, 223), an implication deepened by the Whore: 'He looks a bit like Our Lord,' she says, 'Maybe it's the blood' (*I*, 41), though these lines are removed from 1996 edition. The religious atmosphere, though inflected by comical elements, is thickened when the Whore remarks on her vision: 'Suddenly he was standing before me. Suffused with a golden light. God love him, he showed me the big wounds in his side and his stomach. He let me put my fist into them. They were as big as your boot. I don't know how he survived the beating they gave him' (*P1*, 257).

This scene again is another quotation from a Caravaggio painting, *The Incredulity of Saint Thomas* [Plate 11]. According to St. John, Thomas was absent when Christ appeared to the disciples on the evening of the Resurrection. He returned later and was told of the return. Thomas said, 'Unless I see in his hands the print of the nails, and place my finger in the mark of the nails, and place my hand into his side, I will not believe'(John 20:25). The painting, which was drawn with 'surgical detail',[48] captures the very moment when Thomas put his finger into Christ's side after Christ appears again. Though it is the Whore who imitated Thomas's act in her vision, Thomas can be identified with Caravaggio, rather than with her. Caravaggio is 'in all the pictures'(*P1*, 284) he drew, as Lena later says. Hibbard's description of this painting and Caravaggio's belief in what he sees, his need for verification by the eye, explains the twist of this quotation very well:

Thomas was a scriptural example of lack of faith. Jesus said afterward, "Because you have seen me you have found faith. Happy are they who never saw me and yet have found faith" (John 20:24)[49] Paradoxically, Caravaggio was himself a Thomas; more than any other Renaissance artist he professed to believe only in what he saw.[50]

This reminds us of McGuinness's Caravaggio who, at the very beginning of the play, says that he paints with his hands 'as God intended the eyes to see and to see is to be God, for it is to see God'(*P1*, 208). This strange declaration typifies Caravaggio's arrogance and faith. For Caravaggio, seeing is godliness – yet he is branded as faithless because of this very tenacity of seeing, though, of course, he has earned this mark in other ways, too. This act of seeing brings damnation. At the end of Part One he says: 'I see clearly. I see this knife. I see the hand that carries it. I curse my hand. I curse my life. I damn my soul. Trust me'(*P1*, 255). As a painter, however, he cannot stop seeing.

Part Two, though religiously charged, does not edify or moralise like religion, and is a far remove from any Counter Reformation doctrine. Violence and death are still omnipresent. When Caravaggio kills a man, he gazes at the dead body. And, instead of mourning the man or regretting what he has done, he tells the Whore, who is alive and ugly, of the dead man's beauty: 'I didn't notice how beautiful until I saw his blood. It became him. Flesh and blood. Beautiful'(*P1*, 264). Caravaggio confesses to the Cardinal, at the end of Part One, his urge to kill young boys, and

1. *The Penitent Magdalena*. Rome, Galleria Doria-Pamphili

2. *David with the Head of Goliath*. Rome, Galleria Borghese

3. *Bacchus*. Florence, Galleria degli Uffizi

4. *Rest on the Flight to Egypt*. Rome, Galleria Doria-Pamphili

5. *Calling of St. Matthew*. Rome, Church of San Luigi dei Francesi, Contarelli Chapel

6. *The Taking of Christ*. Dublin, National Gallery

7. *The Lute Player*. Leningrad, Hermitage Museum

8. *St. John the Baptist*. Kansas City, William Rockhill Nelson
Gallery of Art

9. *Boy Bitten by A Lizard*. Florence, Fondazione di Studi di Storia
dell'Arte 'Robert Longhi

10. *The Musicians*. New York, Metropolitan Museum of Art

11. *The Incredulity of St.Thomas*. Potsdam, Schloss Sanssouci

12. *Boy with a Basket of Fruit*. Rome, Galleria Borghese

here we see its result. Even after the murder, because of which he
has to flee Rome, he cannot check his desire to look, to observe, an
act that somehow purifies violence and death into beauty.

The following scene shows how deeply Caravaggio and Lena
are entangled in each other's life. Lena, sensing, with profound
resignation, that their relationship will prove fruitless, urges
Caravaggio to leave, after telling him that their imagined son is
dead. Caravaggio now has to journey through a dark forest, a
forest very much like Dante's. 'Dante was', McGuinness said, 'a
key influence in the writing of the play'.[51] The very first lines from
Canto One of 'Inferno' in *The Divine Comedy* were quoted for the
production programme:

Our life's a journey and halfway through mine I found myself in a dark
forest when I lost my way forward. Oh, it's a tough job to speak of that
forest – wild and rough and thick. Just thinking about it puts the fear of
God back in me. Could death be any worse than that bitter place? If I am
to talk of the good I found here, well I must also tell of other things I
saw there. Don't ask me how exactly I entered here, I was full of dreams
at the moment I lost the true way.[52]

When Dante, as the protagonist of his own fiction, was lost in a
dark wood, he was 'so full of sleep' and 'left the proper way.'[53]
The 'dark wood' signifies the labyrinth of sin and folly, in which
the world is struggling. He, in his sleep, unwittingly 'arrived at
the foot of a hill . . . and saw the edges of its outline already
glowing with the rays of the planet which shows us the right way
on any road.'[54] This hill is equivalent to 'the Mountain of Heaven
as the opposite of the Cave of Hell'.[55] At the very beginning of his
long journey, Dante saw a hill as his goal, but was threatened by
three animals, symbolising pride, desire, and fear. Then Virgil, the
personification of poetic insight, appeared before Dante, who had
lost all hope of reaching the top of the hill, and said that he would
have to go another way. Heroes always go the long way round, as
Ibsen's Peer Gynt hears Great Boyg saying at the very start of his
own journey.[56] Virgil 'led Dante through the city of hell',[57] because
to see it is, as Virgil and Beatrice explain, 'an extreme measure, a
painful but necessary act before real recovery can begin.'[58] In the
labyrinth of Hell, Dante encounters the souls of people who were
once alive and from them learns the truths of human experience.

McGuinness's Caravaggio also aims at hills when he flees
Rome: when he is asked by Lena where he will go first, 'the hills'
is his reply. And this exchange is repeated twice, before and after
the dream scene in which Caravaggio sees the ghosts of his sister

and models. He first sees the ghost of his dead sister, Caterina, in the darkness of his own imaginary forest. The ghost reproachfully explains how she died: 'I died. Giving birth to my death. The child broke my body, Lello. I died cursing my son . . . they ripped me open to let my husband save his son . . . They cut him out and something spilt over me. I could not even squeal to stop, but I saw I was covered and it was black. It was my blood' (*P1*, 271).

This detailed description of her death in childbirth reminds us of Elizabethan and Jacobean revenge tragedies, where ghosts lay a duty of revenge on their auditors (Hieronimo, for instance, in *The Spanish Tragedy*, and King Hamlet). But Caterina's ghost does not. Her curse, instead, expands into a universal condemnation: 'I did not die cursing my child. I did not curse his father. I cursed all children and all fathers and I cursed God for creating woman' (*P1*, 271–2).

The despair she carries is deeper and darker than that of revenge tragedy ghosts. She does not demand revenge of Caravaggio, because she knows that revenge will not save her soul. Her curses are on the human race and on God, its creator, rather than on the people who took her life away. She takes Caravaggio's hand and says that the hand 'wants to stop'(*P1*, 272). Here, an ontological argument about the relationship between mind and body is developed between Caravaggio and Caterina: flesh and body want to stop, but mind goes on. 'Mind never stops seeing. I work. I paint. I paint well'(*P1*, 273). Caravaggio then summons his witnesses 'to prove that'(*P1*, 273).

The first witness is the ghost of the insane Cardinal, accompanied by his servant. The Cardinal, who was once Caravaggio's patron, cannot even converse properly. When Caravaggio kisses the Cardinal's hand, the Cardinal suddenly regains his professional eloquence, as if the kiss reminds him of his clerical vocation. In a mock sermon, the Cardinal advises him to 'paint no more. Pray', because Caravaggio only 'saw the evil'(*P1*, 274). Having listened to this, Caravaggio commands the Cardinal's ghost to leave; these words are not what Caravaggio wanted from his witness. However, the Cardinal continues:

Blessed be the hands that anoint me with iron. Blessed be the tongue that spits curses on my head. Blessed be the feet that walk the way to damnation. Blessed be the eyes that see the same damnation, for they have looked on truth and found it lacking. I have looked on God and found him lacking, Caravaggio. There's nothing there. Nobody there. Not even yourself, great painter. It comes to this. Nothing. No one.

Beware the sin of pride, my son. Beware the power of God. But do not believe. Do not believe. (*P1*, 275)

This is practically a black mass, the Cardinal having become a negative image of his living self. Contradictory images are abundant: the oil of anointment becomes iron, the source of a curse is blessed. And it is attractive and powerful, much as Lucifer, the light-bringer who rebelled against God, is sometimes more attractive than Michael, the leader of God's angelic army. At the same time, McGuinness catches the profound loneliness of a Lucifer, a Dracula, or a Caravaggio. Two characters in this play are part-avatars of the fallen angel. In the programme note for his adaptation of *Dracula*, McGuinness writes: 'The diabolic by necessity implies the divine, the heart and soul of christian cosmology.'[59] The Cardinal's alluring words allow us to think that even damnation can lead to salvation, to true faith. But this paradox is, of course, confusing, and confusion is what the Cardinal leaves behind, when he fades away after his strange sermon.

The next witnesses are the ghosts of the Whore, Lucio, and Antonio, the three models who posed for Caravaggio. The Whore was drowned, Antonio lost his beauty through venereal disease, and Lucio died of hunger. The ghosts throw misery, darkness, and despair at Caravaggio one after another, accusing him of being responsible for their despair, then, like the Cardinal, they too fade away. Then the ghost of his father, acted by Caterina, bids him live: 'the living mean more than the dead. You belong to them, not to me long buried. Go back. Live' (*P1*, 278). In confusion, Caravaggio tries to stab her, or father, the figure she portrays, but he can do nothing to a ghost with a knife. The only thing left to Caravaggio is to draw, using this implement. His hand cannot stop: 'This is how I die. How I kill myself. This is how I paint. Living things. In their life I see my death. I can't stop my hand. I can't stop my dying. But I can bring peace to what I'm painting' (*P1*, 279).

When his sister Caterina takes the knife away and tells him to raise his hand in peace, something miraculous happens on stage, as the stage direction indicates: 'He raises his hands. Light rises from his raised hands, drawing Whore, Antonio, Lucio from the darkness'(*P1*, 279). Writing the stage direction for this climactic scene, McGuinness must have had another of Caravaggio's paintings, *The Calling of St. Matthew* [Plate 5] in mind. The inspiration for the painting is to be found in a very short passage in St. Matthew's Gospel: 'Jesus saw a man called Matthew at his seat in the custom-house, and said to him, "Follow me"; and Matthew rose and followed him'(Matthew 9:9). In contrast to the act of doubting Thomas, 'Matthew's immediate acceptance of Christ's call was the significant act of faith'[60]

In the painting, Christ raises his right hand, inviting Matthew to join him. The light, actually streaming in from a source somewhere behind Christ, seems to emanate from his hand. According to studies on this painting, the right hand of Christ is a quotation from *The Creation of Adam* in the Sistine Chapel. The hand 'mirrors that of Michelangelo's inert Adam, who is about to be invested with life by God. Christ is the New Adam, and "as in Adam all men die, so in Christ all will be brought to life".'[61] We have seen several hands in the play: the musician's hand that plays the music, the priest's hand that blesses, and the artist's hand that paints and kills. Mirroring the posture of Christ in the painting, Caravaggio's hands are transformed, now able to relieve, heal, and redeem, echoing Christ, who says he can cast out devils 'with the finger of God' (Luke 11:20). He consoles the Whore, then dries her hands in his own. He remembers Antonio as a boy with a bowl of perfect fruit and wipes the disease away from his face. He then wishes that Lucio, whom he identifies with Bacchus, should live forever, and kisses him. (P1, 280) Through his hands, through the light they have acquired, the sensual episodes of Part One are sublimated into something divine and unblemished. In this way Caravaggio brings peace to what he paints. He retains, McGuinness says, 'some wonderful power that is innocent and strong.'[62]

Christ in *The Calling of St. Matthew* is breathtakingly beautiful. He has an aura of peace and serenity. His benevolent gaze also reveals the absolute solitude of the Saviour. For McGuinness's drama to work, it is essential that the actor playing Caravaggio on stage convey this beauty, serenity, benevolence, and solitude. This beautiful Christ is sexually attractive, too. The Christ of the Gospels, of course, never seduced anybody in the way the boys in Caravaggio's early paintings do. The charm and allure which radiate from Christ, however, are irresistible: Caravaggio's eye, perhaps, providing its explanation as to why Matthew followed Christ so readily.

So it is not Caravaggio himself but the Christ-figure, into whom Caravaggio is transformed, that invites Caravaggio's witnesses to sing out: 'Full, Father, as I speak, I see. As I breathe, I fire. As I love, I roar. I open my mouth. I change colour. Come to me, my animals. Open the cage of silence. Come from the forest of your frame' (*P1*, 280). The models, who accused Caravaggio, are now converted into real witnesses as to what and why he draws. Caterina sings out on behalf of the witnessess:

> Who is the bird whose song is golden?
> Dragon, breathe your web of fire.
> Steed, open your trusty mouth.
> Bull, charge with a beating heart.
> Lizard, change colour for ever.
> Hare, lie with the sleeping hound.
> Eagle, see with all-seeing eye.
> Hound, play with the wounded lion.
> Lion, roar your lament of love.
> Who is the bird whose song is golden?
> Unicorn, preserve the species.
> Unicorn, protect the species.
> Unicorn, preserve the species.
> Unicorn, protect the species.[63] (*P1*, 280)

As Jordan points out, the animals in the song are the very ones whose form Lucio and Antonio assumed for their mock fight in the Cardinal's palace.[64] Almost all of them are creatures of ferocity. Of the four evangelical beasts in Revelation, a lion, a calf, a man, and an eagle, three are present, representing the visionary animals Ezekiel saw. Here, however, the ferocity of these animals is subsumed into a bird's golden song, a paean to the human and natural world, which embraces tenderness and violence, sorrow and love. The image of a golden bird is not new to the audience. It appeared in Part One, when Caravaggio and Lena were playing word games, complementing each other: 'A bird moves through the forest. A golden bird, and the bird is golden because it carries the sun. The bird sees the tree and it feeds the tree with sun. The tree feeds the leaf, and the leaf loves the tree, and the tree cradles the bird and Lena is the bird who is the sun and the tree and the leaf, for the leaf is the fruit of the beautiful earth' (*P1*, 218). At the end of the game, this glittering imagery is destroyed by Caravaggio, who blows his nose into his hands.

But bathos is absent in this final scene in the dark forest. The stunning imagery of the unicorn in the song reminds one of 'The Lady and the Unicorn', a series of six tapestries made in 15th century, now kept in the Cluny Museum in Paris. The Unicorn, a term Lena repeatedly uses for Caravaggio, here combines itself, and thus combines Caravaggio (once again), with Christ: for the

Unicorn is seen, in Christian tradition, as the animal of the incarnation of Christ, and is often represented with the Virgin Mary at the moment of annunciation. An important similarity between Caravaggio and Christ is that both are childless. Jesus remained unmarried in order to serve God and the kingdom of God. 'For when they shall rise from the dead, they neither marry, nor are given in marriage; but are as the angels which are in heaven.' (Mark 12: 25) In the song, the Unicorn is encouraged to preserve and protect the species, implying generation.

The play does not end when Caravaggio heals and redeems his models, imitating Jesus. Even after the initiation in the visionary forest, Caravaggio is still 'scared of the dark' (*P1*, 281) and asks his father/Caterina to tell him a story, in which Caravaggio starts his life from his birth 'in the pit of his mother's belly' (*P1*, 281) all over again. His life, its glory and ignominy, remains as it was. And this is the condition that Caravaggio has to accept if he is to continue to live, implying that nothing changes, but implying also that existence is acceptance, and that there is a quiet joy to be had in such an acceptance. Caravaggio, as an artist, then reaches the recognition that 'only in painting can the light darken and the dark lighten' (*P1*, 282).

When Lena bids final farewell to Caravaggio, she describes her dream about the room where his paintings will hang on the wall. Lena, whose face is 'a bowl full of life' (*P1*, 218), and her story about the paintings affirm the life: 'I knew then somehow we'd won, we turned the world upside-down, the goat and the whore, the queer and his woman' (*P1*, 284). Finally, she orders Antonio to take his clothes off: she is going to make him model as *St. John the Baptist* [Plate 8],[65] which will be the last quotation of a Caravaggio painting in the play. St. John in the painting is beautiful, not an eschatological preacher with a cross of reeds but a proud warrior with a spear. When she has prepared her tableau of John the Baptist, Lena calls to Caravaggio:[66]

Well, Caravaggio, do you see him? Beautiful, yes? Can you hear me? Can you see us? It goes on and on and thanks be to the sweet crucified Jesus on. See? See. Do you see him, Caravaggio? Do you see? (*P1*, 288–289)

The play ends with Caravaggio's response: laughter from the darkness offstage. Is this the triumphant laughter of an artist whose creative works outlive their creator for four centuries? Caterina says, '[i]f he could paint, he could see and speak forever without dying' (*P1*, 281). And Lena: '[e]ven if you were gone from me, they [the pictures] were there and you were there with them' (*P1*, 284). Both of them foresee the immortality of Caravaggio's works of art. And now, on stage, he watches, from offstage, a living version, a tableau vivant, of his own *St. John the Baptist*. St. John and Caravaggio: each of them, in their very different ways, embodiment, agents, and seers of salvation.

3

'An Unhappy Marriage between England and Ireland': A Postcolonial Gaze at the Irish Past

The three plays dealt with in this chapter, *Mary and Lizzie* (1989), *Someone Who'll Watch Over Me* (1992), and *Mutabilitie* (1997), have much in common in the sense that all were written under the influence of postcolonial critiques of empire and its effects. The term 'postcolonialism' dates from the late 1950s, although the breakup of colonial empires began immediately after World War II. Franz Fanon's *The Wretched of the Earth* (1965) is now generally thought of as the first 'acknowledged intervening text in shaping postcolonial aesthetics and cultural theory'.[1] Postcolonial theory, which deals with the historical events of imperialism, colonialism and the aftermath of emancipation, has become a major area of cultural research in recent years. It focuses on the loss of identity, language, culture, sense of place and national integrity which the colonised have suffered during the process of dispossession.

Edward Said's pioneering *Orientalism* (1978), along with the responses to the book, marked a decisive change in the development of postcolonialism as a field of study. *Orientalism* offered a new set of questions about the role of the West and refined and subtilised theoretical understanding of both colonisers and colonised. In 1987, Said was invited as one of the guest speakers to the International Yeats Summer School in Sligo. His lecture on 'Yeats and Decolonization', which is now part of his *Culture and Imperialism*, had an enormous impact on intellectuals and academics in Ireland, and steered the whole debate of literary critique in Ireland, especially on Yeats, to a new course.[2]

Ireland is a unique case for postcolonial studies, since it is, as Seamus Deane notes, 'the only Western European country that has had both an early and a late colonial experience.'[3] Deane wrote this in 1990 in the introduction to *Nationalism, Colonialism, and Literature*, a collection of three pamphlets written by Terry Eagleton, Fredric Jameson, and Edward W. Said, originally for the Field Day Theatre Company in 1988. At that time, according to Deane, 'the idea that the situation in Northern Ireland might derive from a colonial crisis held little credence for the political and academic establishment in Ireland'.[4]

Postcolonialism is now a widely accepted field of study in Ireland. Declan Kiberd, for example, surveys the cultural and literary history of Ireland since independence in 1922 from this perspective in *Inventing Ireland*, published in 1996. There is, however, still a vast difference between theorising by critics and telling a story, engaging imaginatively with the past, which McGuinness has been doing since his first play, *The Factory Girls*, in 1982. His career in theatre *coincides* with the period during which postcolonial theory has evolved. For us, postcolonial theory throws light on some of the things McGuinness is about; but it does not finally explain his art. It helps, but the quicksilver detail of McGuinness's imagination always shoots ahead, into the awkward, intractable mysteries of human nature.

When he was asked in an open interview if *Mutabilitie* was the concluding part of a trilogy, that is the three plays covered in this chapter, McGuinness said 'No'. However, he conceded that the play was at least a companion piece to the other two.[5] In fact, all three deal with the warring relationship between Ireland and England, and were all first performed in London by English Theatre Companies – *Mary and Lizzie* by the Royal Shakespeare Company, *Someone Who'll Watch Over Me* by the Hampstead Theatre, and *Mutabilitie* by the Royal National Theatre.

The three plays differ in tone and structure, and in the reception each received: *Mary and Lizzie*, an experimental and surrealistic play about the Burns sisters who lived with Frederick Engels, perplexed the London audience; *Someone Who'll Watch Over Me*, a realistic chamber play about three hostages in Beirut, was well received and achieved international success, and is regarded as McGuinness's most commercially successful play to date; and *Mutabilitie*, a play (with songs and music) about three poets, Spenser, Shakespeare, and an early-seventeenth century Irish female bard, the File, is 'a conundrum for any critic', and received a 'lukewarm'[6] response in London reviews.

Despite their different tones and styles, the plays share an undercurrent theme: the unhappy relation between Ireland and England, a relation which McGuinness often chooses to view, to diffract, to see afresh, through the glass of mythology. Joseph Campbell says: 'Myth must be kept alive. The people who can keep it alive are artists of one kind or another. The function of the artist is the mythologisation of the environment and the world.'⁷ The function of McGuinness as an artist in Chapter One was the demythologisation of the world in which he lives, in order to close or bridge the sectarian divide; and this he accomplishes through the paradox of remembering the traumatic events within the context *of* myth, in its broadest sense. Here, McGuinness's role is to mythologise in order to heal what has happened in the past. Mythologisation and demythologisation do not contradict. In McGuinness's world, a world in which paradox swallows up fission, they can ultimately serve the same ends.

Mary and Lizzie

I

'Mary and Lizzie Burns were', McGuinness once said, 'probably the most important Irish people of the nineteenth century, in terms of world history'.⁸ He means that Engels could not have written *The Condition of the Working-Class in England* (1845)⁹ without them, and that the whole course of world history would have differed significantly without this book. But very little is known about these Irish immigrant factory girls who lived with Engels in Manchester, and who gave him 'safe passage through the dangerous poor'.¹⁰ McGuinness first came across their names when he was reading Edmund Wilson's *To the Finland Station*, in which Mary is introduced briefly as follows:

(Engels) was having a love affair with an Irish girl named Mary Burns, who worked in the factory of Ermen and Engels. . . . She seems to have been a woman of some independence of character, as she is said to have refused his offer to relieve her of the necessity of working. She had, however, allowed him to set up her and her sister in a little house in the suburb of Salford, where the coal-barges and chimneys of Manchester gave way to the woods and the fields. . . . Mary Burns was a fierce Irish patriot and she fed Engels' revolutionary enthusiasm at the same time that she served him as guide to the infernal abysses of the city.¹¹

Engels and Mary lived as 'a man and wife' until she died of a stroke on 7th January, 1863. Wilson writes that 'a few months after Mary Burns's death, Engels began living with Mary's sister Lizzy

[sic], more pious than Mary but still comfortable enough.'[12] On the relationship between Mary, Lizzie and Engels, McGuinness commented that 'it was very much a *ménage à trois* and quite an open one at that . . . it *was* very modern. Then again, Engels and Marx did argue for the abolition of marriage, and Engels lived up to his principles in this respect (though Marx didn't).'[13] Steven Marcus writes about this triangle, 'the character of Engels's relation with Mary Burns, and with her sister Lizzie, who kept house for the two of them while Mary was alive and took Mary's place after her death in 1863', noting that, 'nothing about it was simple.'[14] These are wonderful materials for the creative imagination, and out of them McGuinness conjures up 'the voice of the voiceless',[15] a voice heard in *Mary and Lizzie* when it was first performed at the Pit in the Barbican Theatre in 1989.

II

Mary and Lizzie Burns were just two of the many Irish people who crossed the Irish Sea to Manchester before, during, or after the Great Famine. McGuinness himself spells out the connection between this play and the Ulster plays we have already looked at in Chapter One:

The Irish just cannot get away from the effect that the past has on our present: that theme runs through *Sons of Ulster*, it runs through *Carthaginians* and it certainly runs through *Mary and Lizzie* – the girls are, if you like, the nameless dead who have come to tell the stories, to sing the songs of those who were never sung about. These plays are attempts to give what was lost a voice.[16]

However, in contrast to *Sons of Ulster* and *Carthaginians*, where transformation and transcendence happen in a more or less realistic world, Mary and Lizzie's story unfolds in dream-like, surrealisstic settings, borrowing its style, if not its concerns, more from *Innocence* than from the Ulster plays. Historical figures appear in *Mary and Lizzie*, and in *Innocence*, but neither are typical history plays.

In both the darkness the characters bear has the same tones, but the contexts in which they move are seemingly different. Narrative similarities do exist, though. Mary and Lizzie enter a forest, then descend into an underworld, where they explore the myth which brings insight, much as Caravaggio enters the shadowy, visionary forest for redemption. Both are experiments in how far a playwright can go, thematically and technically, in contemporary theatre. In film, much more is permitted in terms of sexual expression and violence. A screen can function very much like a Brechtian alienation effect: what happens in the film is distanced, leaving more room for its audience to accept what would be embarrassing or outrageous on stage. Compared to film, theatre, as a genre, is still to a great extent dominated by 'good sense', reflecting the tastes and attitudes of a middle class audience. Neither *Innocence* nor *Mary and Lizzie* fits easily into that audience's set of expectations. *Innocence* was a challenge to its Dublin audience in 1986: its iconoclastic, Church-baiting elements and its violent imagery, themes, and language provoked hostility. However, as argued in Chapter Two, it is also a very religious play. *Innocence* was an index of Irish society's tolerance level. In 1989 *Mary and Lizzie* tested an English audience.

III

McGuinness 'always wanted a fantastic form for the play, and what [he] found very liberating about *Peer Gynt* was that in it Ibsen can go anywhere and he can do anything, because Peer is such an extraordinary character.'[17] Peer is also famous as a storyteller and a liar, often making himself the hero of his own stories. Mary and Lizzie, female equivalents of Peer Gynt, have no intention of making themselves the heroes/heroines of their own tale, but like Peer, they also 'go the round way',[18] taking the heroic detour (a detour which Peer was instructed to take by the Voice of the Great Boyg).

   Mary and Lizzie questions and reviews the relation between Ireland and England. Its analysis or description of this relationship depends partly on an Irish reading of Engels's *The Condition of the Working-Class in England,* and by this means it is able to celebrate the lives of those history usually overlooks. Most London theatre criticism of the play was negative. For example, one critic said, when he saw Mary Burns practising oral sex on Engels, that 'the heart sinks at such banality, especially in a writer of McGuinness's talent'.[19] Many critics were at a loss and failed to pin down exactly the cause of their own irritation. Richard Allan Cave, whose impartial views on the play appeared in *Theatre Ireland,* summarises the situation accurately:

[L]ike nightmare, the play has a fierce clarity that disturbs precisely because it is so immediate. You can sense through their subsequent rhetoric how English critics get edgy and then rattled when a play exploits the devices of theatre to make an appeal to subliminal reaches of awareness in an audience. It is hitting below the belt, which is not fair, not British, not done.[20]

'Subliminal' is the keyword. What British critics only knew for certain was that they did not like the play. When one critic writes that 'Marx's marriage was exceptionally happy', and that 'even in the poverty of exile, he still played the good father taking the family off (on) jaunty Hampstead Heath picnics',[21] he reveals the utter irrelevance of his criticism of a play, which was not, nor set out to be, a biography.

The review in *Punch* is one of the most interesting responses, epitomising London's subliminal annoyance: Rhoda Koenig wrote that 'Frank McGuinness's *Mary and Lizzie* is as hopeless as Ireland'.[22] She lucidly conveys her malice and disgust, but is as dark as ditchwater on this apparent hopelessness. Perhaps, she is merely following an old tradition of *Punch*, which supplied numerous political caricatures and cartoons about Ireland to Victorian, Imperialist Britain, exaggerating the stupidity and recalcitrance of the Irish. Indeed, Thomas Kilroy might diagnose Koenig's attitude as the 'rigid stare of racism'. In the author's note to *Double Cross* (1986), from which this phrase comes, Kilroy says that:

Oppression disables personality. But it also profoundly diminishes the humanity of the oppressor. It creates grotesque distortions in an oppressed culture, inhibiting growth, development, change. But it effects a like rigidity in the invader, the conqueror, the would-be 'superior': that baleful, paralytic stare of racism.[23]

Postcolonial discourse tables the feelings of guilt of the colonisers or their descendants, and it is alive to the complicated, structured tensions that exist between occupier and the occupied. McGuinness is similarly alive to those tensions and rubs the audience's nose in their reality, their texture, in order to bring about an understanding between both parties. McGuinness's shocks are there to open the eyes. If success is measured as a comfortable consensus between audience and stage, *Mary and Lizzie* is a failure. It is, however, too good a play to be doomed by such a criterion. Its depth and its experimental richness demand our attention.

IV

The play consists of stories told by several storytellers: the

prologue, sung and recited by Lizzie and a chorus of women
(Scene One); a story about Mary and Lizzie's wandering, told
through the eyes of Lizzie (Scenes Two to Seven); another story of
Mary and Lizzie in the context of world history (Scene Eight); and
the epilogue, sung and recited by Lizze, Mary, their mother, and
another chorus of women (Scene Nine). Telling a story (stories) is
a recurrent concern for McGuinness's theatre.

The play's first story, the prologue, begins in Scene One (titled
'The City of Women') with a typical storyteller's opening: Lizzie
tells us that 'they say long ago in this country there was a city of
women who lived in the trees'(*ML*, 1). Among various images and
symbols concerning trees, de Vries says that 'sometimes the souls
of the dead enter trees, "living on" in those trees'.[24] The women in
Lizzie's story represent all the dead women and their collective
souls, clustered together since the creation of the world. This story
explores the archetypal depth of the female psyche and could be a
prologue to any woman's story, because whenever a woman tells
her own story, there is just 'all the one story'(*ML*, 4).

Lizzie describes how these dead women were once treated in
the soldiers' camp they were following, and how they suffered
from the ignominy of being outcasts from society. Once they are
introduced, these women immediately join in and sing as a
chorus. In contrast to the Attic tragedy, in which the chorus
members were 'interested spectators' with sympathy for the
fortunes of the characters, this community of women sing of their
own misery and hardship, but do not indulge themselves in self-
pity and lamentation: they retain their objectivity, much as do the
classical storyteller or Brechtian narrator, relating their misfortune
matter-of-factly.

Mary then enters the stage and says to Lizzie that they have
work to do, that is, to 'wander the earth' (*ML*, 2). Here, Mary
functions as a reminder of what the play is about. As its title
shows, it should be Mary and Lizzie's story. While Lizzie shows
her inclination to remain among the community of women and
hesitates to follow Mary's invitation to be together, another
character, a Pregnant Girl, with a bayonet, is introduced. This
character, an embodiment of womanhood, is to return to the stage
again and again throughout the play, whenever its dominant tone
becomes symbolic. When the Pregnant Girl asks one of the women
in the chorus (First Woman) how long she has waited for the man
who left her, she answers, 'How old is the earth? It must be
ancient. Old as the hills'(*ML*, 4). This answer alludes to *puella
senilis*, 'the woman who is as old as the hills', in Irish mythology. In

placing this story first, McGuinness excavates the women's history hidden in the depths of the prehistoric unconscious, and comes to terms with it, rather than revealing the misery that belongs only to one particular period in the history of the neglected.

This process shares similar characteristics with the presentation of incantation in Irish language on the English stage. The chorus of women sing in Irish: 'Sén trua nach mise, nachi mise,/Sén trua nach mise, Bean Phaídin'(ML, 1), meaning that 'it is a pity that I'm not Paddy's wife'. Mockery overrides lamentation in these lines. Even though very few in an English audience would know the meaning of these Irish phrases, the *tone* of the meaning is easily conveyed through facial and vocal expressions.[25] We can 'feel' the process of Irish history, rather than 'understand' it, as we listen to the sound of the first language of the country on stage, a language almost lost, despite the nation's official policy towards it after independence. At the same time, we can also feel McGuinness's ambivalent feeling towards the language. (Nuala Ní Dhomhnaill, who writes her poetry in Irish, was once told by McGuinness that 'you know as well as I do that Irish is the language of our humiliation and our pain'.) [26]

Urged by the First Woman to speak out, Lizzie sings a song about a woman and a soldier, about the pain and cruelty of love, but here again she, as a part of the chorus, does not betray her own emotions. The song, full of symbolism, leads the women into enigmatic exchanges. Asked by the Pregnant Girl if she had ever killed anything, the First Woman replies in riddles, which imply Mary has killed a child. In return, Mary plunges the bayonet that the Pregnant Girl has left on the ground into her body, but remains unbloodied; no harm is done to the body as long as she is in this dream-like underworld. Here, Mary once again acts as a reminder to Lizzie of where they should be: they have to go back to the world to which they belong.

After the chorus of women vanish, Lizzie ends Scene One, which started with her opening phrase, once again with her own words: 'kiss and tell' (ML, 5), inviting herself to tell her own story. She opens Scene Two again in a storytelling manner:

They say long ago in this world there were two women, Mary and Lizzie Burns. Why were they in this world? To wander it. Wander through time, through place, for that was their way, their story. This is the telling of Mary and Lizzie, and the ways they walked through lives together. (ML, 6)

In the story of two sisters, we are seemingly set up for a 'kiss-and-tell' exposé of their relations with Engels. But instead of scandal, she relates the story of their wandering, a telling whose style and content are dream-like and surreal, and out of which Scenes Two to Seven are constructed. It is not until Scene Seven (titled 'Manchester') that we actually see Engels with Mary and Lizzie. Prior to that in Scene Six (titled 'Bed'), we find Engels and Marx, two giants of history, jabbering to each other in a big bed like a comic duo, very much like Morecambe and Wise, the British stand-up comics.

Engels and Marx are just two characters in Lizzie's story; others, with even more dream-like qualities than the bed-time revolutionaries, include the Old Woman (Mother Ireland), who invites them to the underworld, the Magical Priest, her son, who threatens them, (but his threat cannot be realised since their energy surpasses his), their dead Mother, whom they meet at the Feast of Famine and who sends them to England because Famine is coming to Ireland. On the shore of England young Queen Victoria welcomes them, and they finally encounter Frederic Engels and show him the poor of Manchester. Lizzie ends the story of their wandering at the point where they have just met Engels, in Scene Seven, bringing to a close the dramatic narrative, the great wandering, begun in Scene Two:

Years ago in this country they say two women met a man and they went walking through Manchester. . . . They showed him the poor and they showed him their father and they showed him their race and themselves to him, the two women, Mary and Lizzie Burns, sisters in life, sisters in love, living with Frederick Engels, for they believed in the end of the world. Listen to the world changing. Listen to the world ending. (*ML*, 32)

In the play's first production at the Pit, the interval came after this phrase, enjoining us to 'listen to the world ending', and the following scene stands largely outside the framework of Lizzie's story of wandering. In Scene Eight (titled 'Dinner with Karl and Jenny'), Mary and Lizzie are, therefore, depicted in the context of world history, that is, outside the context of their own mythical journey. They are 'remembered by a line in (Engels's) life. Frederick Engels lived with two Irishwomen, Mary and Lizzie Burns' (*ML*, 47–8). This is another story of Mary and Lizzie's added to the play.

McGuinness sets a deliberately realistic and prosaic tone in this scene, in which Mary and Lizzie emerge from obscurity in history. There are no experimental devices to soften what Engels's two 'mistresses' say and do. When they gatecrash a tea party at the Marxes', Jenny, Karl's wife, who represents Victorian middle class morality, cannot accept the vitality and vulgarity of these two wild Irish immigrant sisters. Mary and Lizzie, invaders of the table and bourgeois propriety, interrupt everything Marx says:

Marx: To the successful analysis of much more composite and complex
    forms there has been an approximation –
Lizzie: Why?
Marx: Because the body –
Mary: Body?
Lizzie: I like the body.
Mary: Yes.
Marx: As an organic whole –
Lizzie: Legs.
Marx: Is easier to study –
Mary: Tits.
Marx: Than are the cells of that body.
Mary: Body.
Lizzie: Legs.
Mary: Tits.
Lizzie: Frederick's more of a tits man than a leg man. Which are you,
    Karl? (ML, 33)

Mary and Lizzie's discourse is a very basic example (or parody) of *Ecriture féminine*, a form of feminine writing sometimes called 'writing the body': 'It describes how women's writing is a specific discourse closer to the body, to emotions and to the unnameable, all of which are repressed by the social contact.'[27] The fluidity and spontaneity of the language has a subversive impact, going against the grain of logocentric ideology, which is one of the reasons why Marx and his wife, Jenny, detest the two sisters.

In contrast to Mary and Lizzie, Jenny stands for an 'upright', middle-class ideal, and opposes them in order to protect it. But she also represents another voice of the voiceless, being a victim who has lived in the shadow of her husband, Karl, 'who cannot feed his family but who would feed all mankind' (ML, 38). She becomes 'indisposed' (ML, 35), but maybe this is because she was, to borrow from Humm, 'made mentally ill by the social construction of pathology in the home and family'.[28] For Marx's part, not only does he reject the Burns sisters, but he also rejects his wife and 'turns from her' (ML, 39), regarding her as a ' wicked witch' (ML, 27).

As someone oppressed by the self-serving machine of

patriarchy, Jenny could have shown sympathy and solidarity with the Burns sisters. Instead, in a fiery, almost hysterical vein, she reads out a poisonous passage about Irish workers from Engels's *Condition of the Working Class*.

Drink is the only thing which makes the Irishman's life worth living. His crudity which places him but little above the savage, his filth and poverty, all favour drunkenness. The temptation is great, he cannot resist it, and so when he has money he gets rid of it down his throat. (*ML*, 40)

McGuinness regards these remarks of Engels's as 'the most racist statements imaginable about the Irish and the condition of the working class'.[29] It might, however, be worth comparing this remark with his observation on German workers. Before he came to Manchester, Engels knew the lives of the mill-workers in the industrial town of Barman, where he was born. Wilson writes:

The workers got drunk every night; they were always fighting and sometimes killed one another. When they were turned out of their grog-shops at closing time, they would go to sleep in the haylofts or stables or fall down on people's dungheaps or front steps.

The reasons for this, Engels wrote, were quite plain. All day they had been working in low-ceilinged rooms, where they had been breathing more dust and coal smoke than oxygen; they had been crouching above their looms and scorching their backs against the stove. From the time that they had been six years old, everything possible had been done to deprive them of strength and enjoyment of life. There was nothing left for them but evangelism and brandy.[30]

The similarities in the recorded behaviour of the Irish and German mill workers may help us to revise Engels's comments on the Irish as an observation on class, not on a nation's character. But it is difficult for Mary and Lizzie, and also for McGuinness, to excuse Engels's lack of sympathy. McGuinness says that, 'when they do actually hear what he's written about their people, and all that the people have endured . . . that's the death of their love for him.'[31] After the two sisters learn of his 'betrayal', this slight against their nation, Mary gives Jenny a stone, Marx a straw, and Engels the book wrapped in rags, all of which were lifted from the cauldron and given to her by the Pregnant Girl at the Feast of Famine in Scene Four. Mary's feelings for each of them are expressed through these items: a stone of hardness for Jenny, a straw of triviality for Marx and the ideology he constructs (trivial, at least, from the Burns sisters' point of view), and the rags for the despair of the working class about whom Engels writes. The wisdom of the book is wrapped in despair. She finally casts a spell on Engels: 'Through you be I remembered, live when I die. Fade' (*ML*, 42). The play nevertheless goes on. With the reappearance of the Pregnant Girl at the end of this scene, the play again becomes rich in symbolism. In order to understand better the final scene, the epilogue to the play, I would like to return in detail to the wanderings of the two sisters through Scenes Two to Seven.

V

When the Old Woman opens the earth with her key[32] in Scene Two (titled 'the Earth Opens'), Lizzie recognises it as a grave. Neumann is useful here, for he says that 'when she is angry, the Goddess . . . can close the wombs of living creatures, and all life stands still'.[33] In addition to a key's ability to open, there is, of course, its ability to close things, to lock them up. In this imagery of the engulfing underground, the Old Woman's priest son, who declares that he looks upon both Catholic and Protestant faiths with new eyes, is confined. This priest, thus, mockingly, represents Christianity, encapsulating sectarian schizophrenia in himself. Even though the Christian Church claims a history and tradition going back at least 2000 years, it is merely a young son to a much older, religio-mythical sensibility, which here the Old Woman represents. Seen this way, the difference between Catholics and Protestants seems trivial.

When Mary and Lizzie meet the Priest in the underworld in Scene Three (titled 'the Magical Priest'), he tries to overwhelm them with his eloquence:

Shall I spell out the faith of the future? Christ is amongst us with a new commandment. Hate one another as I have hated you. Jesus it was who tempted Satan, promised him the throne of Rome. (*ML*, 9)

The Priest is totally serious, but his muddling up of good and evil sounds absurd. Mary and Lizzie's energy (which is drawn from a reservoir of womanhood) surpasses his, which is wasted through nonsensical mock-theology. Their power finds its ancient and nature-given symbols. They nearly eat the priest in this scene, very much like female spiders devouring their mate. In fact, McGuinness, spelling out this parallel, has the Old Woman call them 'two spiders' (*ML*, 10); moreover, she presents them to her son, who wants a cobweb, an unmistakable symbol of female entanglement. 'Female dynamism', Camile Paglia says, 'is the law of nature. Earth husbands herself'.[34] Mary forces the Priest to marry her to herself and Lizzie forces him to marry her to her mother. *The Oxford English Dictionary* gives a figurative meaning of the word 'marry': 'to enter into intimate union, to join, so as to form one.' Mary marrying herself and Lizzie marrying her mother strongly underline and confirm female self-sufficiency and the matriarchal principle.

Lizzie's mother is attended by six women, when Lizzie summons her at the opening of Scene Four (titled 'the Feast of Famine'). All six of these women, six ghosts, died in childbirth, just as Lizzie's mother died giving birth to her. This imagery of death in labour continues a concern from *Innocence*: death and birth are two sides of chthonian reality. Yet we are impressed by the festive, celebratory mood of this scene, by the baroque music and the women's 'elaborate, jewelled costumes' (*ML*, 14) – another McGuinness paradox: joy in the midst of death, for which we should have been prepared by the scene's title.

During this 'Feast', the Pregnant Girl brings a cauldron, into which the women throw a stone, a book, rags, a spoon, a straw, and a bone. The fact that nothing edible is put in this cooking utensil represents, on one level, the misery of the Great Famine in Ireland. At the same time, however, according to Irish Mythology,[35] a cauldron is a symbol of re-birth and regeneration. The items put into the cauldron are also rich in symbolism. Each stands for an aspect of the human condition: a stone of hardness, barrenness, and petrification; a book of wisdom and also of the rigidity of the patriarchal principle; rags of 'poverty, despair, and self-deprecation';[36] a spoon of 'the female principle' or 'androgyne (female bowl and male handle)';[37] a straw of triviality; and a bone of death and resurrection. And all this symbolism is crystallised into a song, sung by the mother:

> Soup of stone and bread of straw,
> Eat the rat, the field, the haw.
> Bread of bone and head of rags,
> Eat the dead of starving hags.
> Head of stone and empty the spoon,
> Eat the stars and belly's wound.
> Remember the feast, remember the famine,
> Famine feast and feast of famine.
> Times of want, times of plenty.[38] (*ML*, 17)

As mentioned, the imagery evoked is not just metaphor or exaggeration but also has a certain historical validity. When these items, and their negative connotations are stirred in the cauldron, the paradoxical phrase 'the feast of famine' suddenly takes on new reality. This is one of the most powerful moments in the play, in which symbolic, surrealistic elements merge with reality to produce some alchemical meaning.

When the music turns into a reel, a pig, 'dressed as a Victorian getleman', appears. In contrast to the symbolic representation of the famine, the pig recites his poem:

> We'll call the butcher empire and the knife we'll call its greed,
> And it cut the throat of Ireland, leaving it to bleed.
> But what care for the Irish, aren't they dirty pigs?
> Leave them in their squalor to dance their Irish jigs. (ML, 19)

In this sequence, McGuinness, who so far has been careful to avoid direct expression, throws caution to the wind: his criticism of the British Empire now becomes blatant, too blatant for an English audience to accept at the time. This gentleman pig has a horrific importance and is to some extent based on historical truth. Some people who openly show their bitterness against the British Empire regard the Union Jack as the 'butcher's apron', and the empire as 'the place where the sun never sets and the blood never dries'.

In 1986 McGuinness wrote a review of Michael Longley's *Collected Poems, 1963–1983*:

Love and joy, thank God, are plentiful in this poetry, but they are often tinged with fear, for if Longley's feet are anywhere, they are solidly on this earth, and his and our's so easily turns into nightmare ground, releasing from its graves hideous realities masquerading as dreams, as the poem "Nightmare" tells.

> In this dream I am carrying a pig.
> Cradling in my arms its deceptive grin
> The comfortable folds of its baby limbs,
> The feet coyly disposed like a spaniel's.
>
> I am in charge of its delivery,
> Taking it somewhere, and feeling oddly
> And indissolubly attached to it –
> There is nothing I can do about it,
>
> Not even when it bites into my skull
> Quite painlessly, and eats my face away,
> Its juices corroding my memory,

The chamber of straight lines and purposes,
Until I am carrying everywhere
Always, on a dwindling zig-zag, the pig.

The pig will not be killed, and Longley knows it.[39]

What McGuinness wrote about Longley's poetry applies also to
the gentleman pig scene from his own *Mary and Lizzie*. Both
worlds are strikingly similar. Unfortunately, in comparison,
McGuinness's pig loses its nightmarish power by virtue of the fact
that it is staged in too realistic a manner. If McGuinness could
have somehow retained the ambivalent tone he admires in
Longley's poem, this gentleman pig would have had a most
ironical impact and the balance of the play would have been
different.

In the end, the pig's throat is slit with a bayonet by the Pregnant
Girl, as the pig describes it in his own poem. When the pig runs
off squealing, the symbolism is deepened and ramified: the
Pregnant Girl gives all the items in the cauldron to Mary and
Lizzie, for 'they'll be useful one day'(*ML*, 19). To Lizzie's 'what
for?', she replies: 'That would be telling' (*ML*, 20). This enigmatic
answer, contrasted with the pig's overt remarks in his poem,
implies that the outspoken way is not the female way to heal the
wounds of the past. At the end of this scene, the mother licks her
own palm and touches her daughters' foreheads, complaining that
she 'shall have to do everything for them' (*ML*, 20). In effect, this is
a good luck charm against evil or misfortune, and under the
mother's magical protection, Mary and Lizzie then swim across
the Irish Sea.

When they reach the English shore, in Scene Five (titled 'Passing
the Time with the Queen Victoria'), Mary says that it is 'time for a
man' (*ML*, 21). Instead, they meet young Queen Victoria, who
carries a 'bucket and spade'.[40] She is about to build the empire
with the spade and store the wealth in the bucket. But once the
bucket is full, she has to empty it: this bucket is 'an attribute of
Fortune with her wheel of buckets',[41] meaning that the wheel of
Fortune always turns, 'alternately filling and emptying'.[42] Victoria
anticipates the future of her kingdom, which is to empty colossal
wealth accumulated in its glory:

What is England like? . . . I can tell you one thing. It isn't content. So it
roams the world, looking for contentment. And finds it nowhere. For no
one wants it . . . I worry for poor England when the wandering's over.
Where will it go then but into itself, and what will it find. A tenement.

The England that was wont to conquer others now makes a conquest of itself. Some third-rate isle lost among her seas. How shall we cope? By lying, I suppose. (*ML*, 23–4)[43]

This is a shrewd statement about the rise and fall of an imperial nation whose glory is no longer there: it can only survive by 'lying'. When she is about to leave, Queen Victoria says, 'forgive me', not, 'excuse me', the normal polite form of farewell. If this is a symptom of 'an unconscious sense of guilt',[44] as Jordan suggests, Mary nevertheless forgives her, saying: 'She'll get over it' (*ML*, 24). Later in *The Bird Sanctuary* (1994), this clemency for Victoria is touched on once again: an aunt and her gay nephew are remembering a family myth about Queen Victoria calling at their house during her visit to Dublin in 1849, and a beautiful old woman who lived in the house forgiving the Queen, saying 'all sins are forgiven' (*Bird*, 7).

In the following scene (titled 'Bed'), Marx and Engels are found in bed together. Their exchange works as comedy – and as a revelation of significant differences in their characters. Engels thinks that laughing 'lightens the load'(*ML*, 27), whereas for Marx 'the load is not to be lightened. Not to be lifted. The load's there to be carried' (*ML*, 27). In contrast to Marx's logical and rational attitude, Engels is sympathetic and emotional. The difference, though caricatured and heightened by their dialogue, was there in the real Marx and Engels. Wilson writes:

What is to be noted in Engels from the beginning is his sympathetic interest in life. Marx's thinking, though realistic in a moral sense and though sometimes enriched by a peculiar kind of imagery, always tends to state social processes in terms of abstract logical developments . . . he almost never perceives ordinary human beings. Engels's sense of the world is quite different: he sees naturally and with a certain simplicity of heart into the lives of other people.[45]

One could argue that the scientific, rational, somewhat prosaic attitude of Marx towards the world enabled the construction of the whole system of Marxism, (which could never be called 'Engelsism'). According to Engels in the play, Marx is always arguing like the father Engels remembers. With this affinity between Marx and Engels's father, McGuinness is pointing out the patriarchal elements in Marx. Marx's sleepwalking on stage is also symbolically indicative. Scientific studies show that sleepwalking occurs only in deep sleep when dreams seem essentially absent.[46] Even in his sleep, Marx's mind (that is, the mind of McGuinness's

Marx) totally rejects irrational explanations, shuts out dreams, refuses messages from the unconscious. McGuinness is deliberately underlining Marx's abstract and rigoristic nature, which is set against Engels's more human qualities.

In contrast to Marx's rejection of dreams, Engels admits to a fear of the dark and of dreaming, because 'the dream might come true . . . you know the way you walk for miles through somewhere you know, but you see nothing, for you're lost inside your own head? I do that. I'm lost. I'm lonely. In a funny way it's why I love the poor. I think they're lonely too' (*ML*, 27). Mary, one of the poor he thinks he loves, says: 'We're the dark. We're the night' (*ML*, 42). Mary and Lizzie, it seems, represent the darkness that Engels fears. Even though he is to disappoint Mary and Lizzie, as we have seen, with his observation and writing on the Irish poor in his book, here, he accepts what he does not understand with a sense of awe. Instead of rejecting or ignoring this darkness emblemised by both women, he learns even to love it.

As the argumentative inclinations of the father are attributed to Marx, so the benevolent inclinations of the mother are attributed to Engels, emphasising his communion with his own inner femininity. Engels sings about his parents:

> My father's in the house,
> He eyes my mother. (*ML*, 28)

This sexually-charged gaze summons up an Oedipal desire in Engels to kill his father, which Engels describes as an impulse of 'war', rather than 'murder'. Engels sees his father in the same way as the Old Man in Yeats' *Purgatory* 'dreams back' the night when he was begot. Instead of killing his father (who is already dead), Engels focuses on Marx, whom he supports financially. He says: 'I'll send you money, Karl. It's his for the taking. My father's, that is' (*ML*, 28). The money then, which enables Marx to live and write, is inherited capital: and Engels is pointing this out to Marx, this perverse reliance on the very thing Marx abhors, and in pointing it out, it is as though Engels is punishing him for the shadow of the father which stalks through Marxist reason. Engels's father haunts his own son and 'the whole of Europe' (*ML*, 28), just as Marx's work haunts the world as a mixture of conscience and guilt.

We, however, have to keep in mind that the two of them are in bed for the whole of this scene with two 'polystyrene busts of Marx and Engels's'[47] looming above them. These busts are a Brechtian device: beneath them, two actors, in the style of

Morecambe and Wise, are parodying Marx and Engels, in order, as McGuinness said, 'to crack the statues'.[48] Engels teases Marx about his circumcised penis, saying that for 'two men so much into materialism, it seems to me like a waste of good skin' (*ML*, 25). Marx does not understand his joke and replies: 'Frederick, at the time it happened I had not as yet evolved my political theories'(*ML*, 25). Engels constantly makes fun of the po-faced Marx, and together they are the archetypal comedy duo, the funny man and his stooge.

Scene Seven, in which Mary and Lizzie meet Engels in Manchester, is mostly sung: another dramatic device. One of the characters, the sisters' father, is, following the convention of American minstrel shows, 'half-naked, dyed brown'(*ML*, 29). We are to take this as an ironic nullification of living conditions in Manchester – just as the real misery of Africans in America was hidden by the sugar-coating of the minstrel shows. This is Lizzie's version of 'the condition of the working class' through the eyes of the people who belong to that class. This musical interlude marks the end of the sisters' wanderings.

VI

Scene Nine, the epilogue to the play, which follows the scene at the Marxes' tea party, returns to the tone and mood of the prologue. While we hear voices from the past in the prologue, the first voice in this scene is heard from the future. Like the Irish chanting in Scene One, Russian is spoken by a boy, but this time it is immediately repeated in English by the Pregnant Girl. We learn, through these imagistic phrases in English translation, of a Russian mother, who is thirsty and bleeding, and a father, who is shot dead: the boy has come from the future to haunt Mary and Lizzie with the fruits of Marx and Engels's theorising, the collapse of the Soviet Union.

Soon the boy disappers, leaving Mary and Lizzie at a loss where they are. Then the chorus composed of the same women as in the prologue, begin to sing about the earth, about women and their children, and about human hearts. Here, the past, the present, and the future converge into the song. After the song, the Pregnant Girl gives birth on stage, but not to a baby. She cuts her belly open with a bayonet and takes out a wooden box, which is empty. She lets this box of emptiness, the emptiness from her empty womb, 'fall into the cauldron' (*ML*, 47). Into it too go the bone and the spoon, which Mary and Lizzie were left with after giving away the

stone, the straw, and the book in rags in the previous scene. The
bone symbolises death and resurrection, and the spoon the
androgyne (the female bowl and the male handle).[49] The bone, the
spoon, and the empty box in the cauldron convey powerful
images of regeneration.

The play then goes further back to the symbolism of creation
myths, which generally 'present a symbolic view of birth'[50]
according to Walker. The mother appears to Mary and Lizzie
again, and says:

Shut your mouth. I'm thinking. Sing to me . . . That's how the earth
became. That's what I learned here. God didn't make the earth. We sung
it. He heard us and joined in. We did it together, creation. There's no
difference between God and man, or woman for that matter. Isn't that
interesting? Will we head home? Do you want to see me create the
earth? (*ML*, 48)

This creation myth, which posits that both women and God sang
together to make the world, is very different from the canonical
Biblical creation, and different, too, from the feminist
interpretation of creation, that a goddess or Mother made the
world from the darkness and that God then usurped it.
McGuinness's women are given pre-eminent status as the ones
who started the creation, and 'Creation/birth', Walker says, 'was
inseparable from the figure of the Mother.'[51] They, however, allow
God/man to join them in singing together. The images here do not
exclude, but instead stress harmonious coexistence between
women and God/man in the creation of the world.

After giving her version of creation, the Mother sings a song
about the Lagan, the river which runs through Belfast city: 'When
Lagan streams sing lullabies,/There grows a lily fair'(*ML*, 49).
McGuinness follows in the tradition of medieval poets, who 'tend
to set the ancient myths in familiar places'(*S*, 37), as Michael says
in *Someone Who'll Watch Over Me* when explaining the story of *Sir
Orfeo*. Because it concerns healing, the importance of transcending
the old pains, it is necessary that people understand the
symbolism of the song on an individual level, a level where they
can feel grounded.

When Mary, Lizzie, and the Mother continue singing, 'No rest
have I nor liberty,/For love is lord of all' (*ML*, 49), the song
promises a deliverance that is both sublime and pathetic. At the
very end of the play the three women repeat a phrase, 'so be it',
which is a translation of *amen* as usually used in the Old
Testament. 'So be it' is uttered three times, emphasising their

agreement with, their confirmation of, the world through which they have to journey. It should be noted that 'in the speech of Jesus in the Gospels, *amen* often appears not as a closing response but as an opening affirmation of the validity and seriousness of what follows.'[52] Which means that this 'so be it' also means agreement and confirmation that comes after: life goes on when the curtain falls.

Women's inclination for wanderings is explained by Cixous as follows:

A boy's journey is the return to the native land, the *Heimweh* Freud speaks of, the nostalgia that makes man a being who tends to come back to the point of departure to appropriate it for himself and to die there. A girl's journey is farther – to the unknown, to invent. [53]

This catches the difference between Peer Gynt and the Burns sisters. Peer comes back home, where Solveig has been waiting for him for years, and where he will probably die, whereas Mary and Lizzie come back home to the earth, where the magical cauldron belongs, and will start all over again.

VII

McGuinness does not polemicise in *Mary and Lizzie*, does not overtly seek to restore the rights of the oppressed and neglected, or to accuse the oppressors in history. Rather, he looks forward, affirming the shared aspects of the Irish and the British:

We are both complex people and there is a complex relationship. There have been terrible misunderstandings between the Irish and the British, but we also feel very close to each other. We do, after all, have a shared language and a shared history.[54]

The two countries also share culture in many ways. The English comic tradition, for instance, is a part of English culture which McGuinness enjoys and loves. Though the sense of humour sometimes differs between the two countries, there is still common enough ground for shared laughter.

Pantomime is one sub-genre of this comic tradition. In addition to her Irish and mythical aspects, the fact that the role of the Old Woman was acted by a male performer at the Pit tangibly demonstrates the male, devouring aspects hidden behind the female face. Yet, this kind of cross-dressing reminds us, too, of the English pantomime dame. In Christmas pantomime, a peculiarly English theatrical form, whose uncertain origins go back to the early eighteenth century, it 'became traditional for a young actress to take the part of the hero, or principal boy, and a comic actor to portray an old woman, or dame, for comic relief.'[55]

Queen Victoria is also acted by a male performer, just like a pantomime dame. Maybe this reflects the popular perception of the Queen in her later years as a monstrous old lady, who, like the Queen of Hearts in *Alice in Wonderland*, transcends the distinctions of sex. As the representative of the oppressors, Imperial Britain, this stage figure could easily fall into bitter caricature. But she is rescued from such a fate by the stage directions, which stipulate that she be acted as 'a young woman', who has just acceded to the throne. The dissonance between a naive young woman and the awe-inspiring imperial monster acted by a man causes laughter, as do the bucket and spade she carries. The gentleman pig in Scene Four is yet another typical pantomime touch: a humanoid visitor from the animal kingdom often referred to by pantomime actors as a 'skin part'.[56] Peter Holland comments on the essence of this theatrical tradition for children, and for adults who used to be children:

The concept of panto as designed for children was and is a convenient fiction, a protection of the adults both from the embarrassment of admitting their pleasure in folk tales but also from the open avowal of the vulgar sexuality of panto humour. For panto is quintessentially English precisely in its exploration of that comedy, the comedy of ridiculousness of the sex.[57]

The sexual undertone of pantomime, this very English theatrical form, combines with McGuinness's dark fantasy: the dark can be in tune with the comic. Pantomime gives McGuinness another framework. He uses pantomime characters without ever descending into inhuman caricature. When he describes this method as 'a homage to the very English conventions of drag artist and pantomime dames,'[58] he describes the play's nature, its ability to deal with very serious matters in a comic vein.

Someone Who'll Watch Over Me

I

McGuinness dedicated *Someone Who'll Watch Over Me* (1992)[59] to Brian Keenan,[60] who was taken hostage in Beirut by fundamentalist Shi'ite militiamen in 1985. Keenan became international headline news along with his fellow hostages, John McCarthy, Terry Anderson and others.[61] The western media actively campaigned for their release and Keenan was finally freed in 1990. When interviewed in *The Independent*, McGuinness, however, made it clear that 'this play is nothing to do with Brian's life; there are parallels with what he suffered – but it isn't his story.'[62]

There are various parallels between *Someone Who'll Watch Over Me* and *An Evil Cradling*, Keenan's autobiographical work, which was published a year after the play's first performance. Keenan himself wrote in a review of the play's Dublin production in 1993: 'The opening – shallow lights on a man chained and leaning on a radiator, choked me in its immediacy. Like seeing an old photograph and instantly recalling unwanted memories I sat frozen but with a part of me melting.'[63] The hostages are enclosed in a small, dark cell, and they are in the dark, too, about why, exactly, they have been kidnapped. They are not sure whether they are waiting for death or release. McGuinness's three hostages try various means to relieve the boredom and kill time: in their imagination, they write letters to their families, shoot new movies, drive a car through the air, play a tennis match, remember horse racing.

An Evil Cradling records a comradeship between more or less like-minded individuals, between sophisticated, university-educated men of the world. Keenan writes how he felt when McCarthy touched his foot at the moment they, both of them blindfolded in a car, first encountered:

I took some reassurance from it and I am sure that the man who touched me was reassuring himself. I fumblingly put my hand upon his and patted it gently. It was a strange first human touch conveying such warmth and companionship in such desperate circumstances.[64]

Of course, there were cultural differences between Keenan, a protestant from the Belfast working class, and McCarthy, a man from the English middle class, differences which were sometimes intensified by their confined living space. There was, however, an understanding that they were unconditionally on the same side: they were allies against the men who took them as hostages. Keenan writes:'I was reassured by this stranger whom I had instantly befriended and who had returned my friendship so warmly. We spoke about the conditions that we had experienced in our separate cells. The terror seemed, as we talked about it, to become less extreme.'[65] There was no room to heed their distinct Irishness or Englishness. The absurdity of the situation in which they were caught made a process of deepening companionship inevitable and natural: Keenan, who happened to be an Irishman, met McCarthy, who happened to be an Englishman, and they began with the mutual understanding that they were friends.

II

Keenan describes a clumsiness, hesitancy and sense of complexity in his shared life with McCarthy. But McGuinness's three hostages are a different matter. That complexity is straitened, crystallised, into the cultural stereotypes that each hostage carries. There is no quick overcoming of difference by comradeship; but, we shall see, McGuinness uses these cultural stereotypes in order to unbuckle them, in order to show the deeper human reality that lies between them.

When the curtain rises with Ella Fitzgerald's 'Someone to Watch Over Me', we see Adam and Edward chained to the wall of a cell. Adam, a doctor from California, and something of an American fitness-freak, is doing energetic press-ups. Through his conversation with Edward, an Irish journalist from Dublin, we gather that Adam has been in this cell for four months, and Edward for two. In this first scene, the sheer volume of Edward's speech overwhelms Adam's, Edward talking three or four times as much as the American. Here Edward conforms to the stereotype of the talkative, glib Irishman. He speaks endlessly: of his favourite Irish mare, Dawn Run, the winner of the Gold Cup, (a creature he would have liked to marry!), of BBC Radio 4's *Desert Island Discs*, (Edward says he would have to include Ella Fitzgerald's 'Someone to Watch Over Me' in his favourite eight records), of his weird sexual experience with a man at home in Omagh whom he once mistook for a woman, and of the time when Glasgow Celtic won the European Cup. All these reminiscences are familiar to Adam, since they seem to have been repeated so often during their confinement.

When Edward criticises Adam for failing to admit that money brought him to Lebanon, Adam, who takes the role of a patient listener, finally bursts out: 'I want to crack your fucking face open. I'm going to fucking kill you. If I've to listen to you much longer, I will kill you' (*S*, 5). Of course he cannot kill Edward. For a start, he is a doctor: killing is something that runs against his own nature. But from his outburst we immediately sense the strain that confinement has on them and catch the scent of insanity that hangs about people who have been unjustly, unaccountably confined. Edward says: 'I do know that the cool's going to crack, it has to, and we'd better both be prepared for when it does'(*S*, 6). Each man has responsibility for his own sanity, but they can cooperate with each other in their attempt to keep sane. Edward continues:

Whatever else about this place, we're in it together, we have to stick it out together. We'll come out of this alive. One favour – let me be able to do my worst to you, and you be able to do your worst to me. Is that agreed? (*S*, 6)

Edward's rather unexpected suggestion 'to do one's worst to one another' does not mean physical violence, but rather, a deliberate desertion of good manners, the adoption of verbal abuse as a survival mechanism. Verbal violence is a safety valve for their depression, a means to cope with their absurd situation. This verbal violence is proposed by Edward, which thus reminds us of another stereotype: the 'violent' and 'wild' Irishman.

In Scene Two Michael, an Englishman, joins them. At the opening of the scene, he is lying on the floor, having fainted. When he comes to and speaks, his middle-class British English jars comically with the others' voices.

Michael: I'm terribly sorry, but where am I?
Edward: So it's yourself, is it?
Michael: Pardon?
Edward: Do you recognize me? We were at school together.
Michael: I don't think so.
Edward: Eton, wasn't it? Or Harrow? (*S*, 9)

Michael, who speaks public-school English, is another stereotype. Having got used to the bawdy English of Adam and Edward, strewn with cursing and abuse, Michael's polite language strikes us as something out of a textbook. We now have three different voices on stage – American English, Irish English, and British English.

When Michael introduces himself to his fellow hostages as an Englishman, Edward responds with a sarcastic remark: 'Of course you are'(*S*, 10). Edward is just following the 'doing one's worst' convention established in the previous scene; it is, however, suggested that there may surface, at times, an unconditional Irish enmity on the part of Edward towards Englishmen. Michael, in these exchanges, becomes a target of Edward's mockery and ridicule. And when this happens, the abuse is not a tool for sanity, but a mark of real conflict. The relationship between Edward and Michael begins with this open and stereotypical hostility. Adam, the American, mediates between them. It is said that McGuinness started the play with an idea based on the old joke-pattern: *There was an Englishman, an Irishman and an American.* This pattern gives McGuinness an opening template through which stereotypes can be explored and interrogated. He presents us with a stage Englishman, a stage Irishman, and a stage American; and once he has set them up, he allows them, as we shall see, to discover the truth and the myth of their national peculiarities.

III

In a pre-production interview, McGuinness said that 'the warring relationship between England and Ireland' is his personal obsession:

It's like a desperately unhappy marriage which is either going to go on being desperately unhappy or something is going to happen and heal it. The play exposes the wounds[66] and continues the wounding, then comes the healing or the admission of wounding.[67]

This unhappy relation comes alive on stage from the moment of Michael's arrival. When Michael says that he wants to see 'a movie', Edward raises an objection to this American usage of the term and says:'Do the English not call them films?' Michael, a disciplined and self-controlled Englishman, is perplexed about how to react to this bullying and simply replies: 'I just call it a movie. Why do you object?'

Edward: It just sounded strange.
Michael: Oh, sorry.
Edward: Why are you sorry?
Michael: That I didn't call it a film, if it offended you.
Edward: It didn't.
Michael: Then why did you bring it up?
Edward: Something to say. (S, 14)

We can see how differently these two men approach one another: Michael is innately polite and pleasant whereas Edward, on the contrary, goes for the jugular.

Here is another example of this bullying:

Michael: I imagine being an actor is quite a boring life.
Edward: Yea.
Adam: Yea.
   (Silence)
Edward: Aye, boring.
Adam: Yea.
Edward: No.
Michael: No.
Edward: What do you mean, 'no'? You've just said yes.
Michael: I was agreeing with you. I thought you were agreeing with me.
   So I said no.
Edward: You say no when you're agreeing with someone?
Michael: If they've said no, yes.
Edward: Yes or no, what is it?
Michael: What?
Edward: Shut up.*(S, 14)*

Michael is serious; he does not mean to be funny here. And the more serious he is, the more absurd the situation becomes. This absurdity through these monosyllabic exchanges makes us laugh, but it also deepens the awkward rift between Michael and Edward.

When the three of them write imaginary letters home in Scene Four, they are, in fact, not writing to their family but addressing their cellmates, since they have no pen and paper. By now Michael has realised that Edward's verbal attacks always target him. In the letter Edward writes to his wife, he describes his two cellmates. After a lengthy explanation about Adam, Michael is mentioned as 'an Englishman. Enough said.'(*S*, 24) When he finishes writing to his mother, Michael, who is now paranoid about this kind treatment from Edward, invites yet another onslaught: 'Oh go ahead, Edward. Start straightaway'(*S*, 24). As a childless widower, Michael only has his mother to write to: Edward's asking about his own children in the letter to his wife sounds like malicious showing off. Edward, however, does not choose to write to his wife merely in order to get at Michael. Even though Edward enjoys writing with barbed brevity about Michael, his humour has other targets, too: he begins his letter to his wife with 'Dearest wife, what is your name again?'(*S*, 23); or in postscript under his signature, Edward, he writes, 'What do you mean, Edward who?'(*S*, 24) Nonetheless, Michael's annoyance is far from groundless.

The unhappy relationship between Edward and Michael,

standing in for England and Ireland's, culminates in Scene Five. Michael and Edward personify the very different historical attitudes of the two countries to one another: the Irish have always considered England a cause of their sufferings, whereas Ireland has just been one of many problems for England. Michael means no harm when he says that 'Hiberno-English can be quite a lovely dialect'(*S*, 30), but we cannot miss his unconscious ethnocentrism, which inflames Edward's feelings against England. In *The Bird Sanctuary*, Marianne remembers her father saying that 'the best speakers of the English language are well educated Dubliners . . . you are Irish and you can outdo the English, that is our revenge. You must love the English language, and we must speak it beautifully. (*Bird*, 31)' The children who were brought up by this father also know that they just sound like the English. Edward, displaying ambivalence towards the English language, personally accuses Michael of being responsible for eight hundred years of colonisation of Ireland. Michael's reply is that '[t]here is not much historical validity to that charge'(*S*, 30).

When the Irish Famine arises as a topic, the different attitudes toward it are made even clearer. For many Irish people the Famine is one of the most traumatic wounds in their history. When Edward says it happened yesterday, he is expressing a psychological truth. E. Estyn Evans writes that: 'It is hard for an Englishman to comprehend the Irishman's view of the past, for all time appears to be foreshortened into the living present.'[68] Evans then quotes Dr Lloyd Praeger: 'We Irish can never let the past bury its dead. Finn McCoul [*sic*] and Brian Boru are still with us . . . the Battle of the Boyne was fought last Thursday week, and Cromwell trampled and slaughtered in Ireland towards the latter end of the preceding month.' Many Irish people, and Edward is one of them, regard the Great Hunger as a very recent event. But for his English counterpart, Michael, it was 'a dreadful event' which took place a hundred and fifty years ago. Michael, irritated by Edward's continual attacks, then says:'I am a little troubled by the Famine. Could it be you only had your silly selves to blame?' and he innocently continues with a Marie Antoinette-like remark: 'You left yourselves utterly dependent on the potato. Why didn't you try for a more balanced diet? Carrots are delicious. What about bread and cheese?' (*S*, 31).

Obviously Michael is unaware of the strong argument that 'famine' is something of a misnomer for this catastrophe, because food was plentiful in Ireland in the period 1845–50. Ireland continued to export wheat, barley, cattle, sheep and pigs to

Britain. Only the potato crop, on which poor peasants were utterly dependent, had failed. To this ignorance, Edward can only make a monosyllabic reply, 'Jesus', which Michael responds to with: 'That's typical. That is so Irish' (S, 31). These exchanges finally provoke an uncharacteristic outburst of anger from Michael. 'I have done nothing to offend him. Yet he attacks me. . . . If your intentions were to annoy me, you have succeeded admirably'(S, 31). We can understand the hostility of Edward as the oppressed, or at least a descendant of the oppressed, towards Michael. But we can also understand Michael's bewilderment and irritation at being directly accused as the oppressor, or again, as a descendant of the oppressors. The gap between both characters is so great that it seems unbridgeable. If only they could each begin to understand the other's viewpoint – but this seems very unlikely.

But Adam, as a third presence, a mediator between two hostile parties, might help to bridge this gap. By dramatic means, McGuinness shows how a third party might remove the sterility of oppositional hatred by offering another voice, another way of speaking. Michael and Edward apologise, or pretend to apologise, to each other for the sake of Adam. Adam says: 'For as long as you are here, I am here. OK?'(S, 32) Because of the existence of Adam, Edward and Michael's reciprocal enmity gives way to an uneasy truce. Each of them then invites the other two to his country and home, to Peterborough, Dublin and San Francisco.

In the imaginary drinking session which follows, Edward tells a joke, disguised as an anecdote about a rucksack, which might have contained a bomb or firearms (a more common event in Northern Ireland, perhaps, than in England or the US). When Edward says that he opened it, Michael asks what was inside, which is exactly the response Edward needed for the joke to work, for he says 'mind your own fucking business', which is repeated several times in the joke itself. At this point, their relation slightly changes: Michael is still a deadly serious Englishman, very slow to understand what is going on around him. He needs Edward's explanation: 'Michael, it's a joke'(S, 37). It is a joke about the Troubles in the North, told by an Irishman, who, out of the three, has the most right to make a joke out of them.[69] This is typical Irish gallows humour. Here, nobody is really laughing at anybody else. And we see there is no harshness in Edward's remark: Michael begins to enjoy the fun with his cellmates, being a part of the joke but not exactly a target of ridicule. At the end of this scene, Michael orders a vodka martini, which the others have been drinking all the time, instead of his usual sherry (that index of somewhat antiquated English middle-class taste). The three men sharing the same drink hints that real change might yet be possible. This imaginary drinking session ends, after Adam's singing of 'Amazing Grace', with a 'thank you' from each hostage. Adam's 'thank you' are his last words on stage. When Scene Six opens, he has gone, presumably to his death. And it seems that the stability of the triangle has gone, too. Edward and Michael bury him metaphorically. This imaginary funeral is their first acknowledgement of a shared wound, to which, in retrospect, the vodka martini's now strike us as a sad prelude.

In the opening of Scene Seven, Michael pretends to be one of the audience in the 1977 Wimbledon Women's Final between Virginia Wade and Betty Stove, jerking his head from side to side. Then an imaginary match is played by Michael as Virginia and Edward as Betty. When Michael shows his enthusiastic support for the English woman, Virginia, who actually won the 1977 match, Edward automatically sides with the Dutch woman, Betty.

Edward: I'm just feeling sorry for poor wee Betty Stove.
Michael: Poor wee Betty Stove is six foot and weighs twelve stones.
Edward: Her mother still thought of her as poor wee Betty.
Michael: Her mother is irrelevant. Virginia is playing to win and is going to win.
Edward: That's unfair.
Michael: That's history.
Edward: To hell with history, I'm rooting for Betty. (*S*, 43)

By now they have become used to Adam's absence. They have had to in order to survive. The relationship is less hostile, though they are still not the closest of friends. And Edward still senses or imagines himself to be on the loser's side, for it is difficult to discard the learned habits of the oppressed. After enjoying the imaginary match and a hilarious interview with the Queen (acted by Edward), they come to a conclusion:

Edward: Who won the 1977 Wimbledon Women's Final?
Michael: An Englishwoman won it.
Edward: I rest my case that there is a God.
Michael: Well done, Virginia.
Edward: Well done, Virginia.
Michael: Poor wee Betty Stove.
Edward: There always has to be a loser. In every game, a loser.
Michael: Yes, that's the history. (*S*, 46–47)

From this point on, England's complaints about the unfairness of history cease; he is now able to admit that in every game there is a loser and a winner. And, for his part, Michael now shows more sympathy for the loser.

In the next, the last scene, Edward will be released but Michael will have to remain a hostage. Edward combs Michael's hair, then gives the comb to Michael. In return, Michael combs Edward's hair. This is a re-enactment of a Spartan military ritual, which was described earlier by Michael: 'Before the Spartans went into battle, they combed each other's hair. The enemy laughed at them for being effeminate. But the Spartans won the battle' (S, 50).

The combing of hair prefigures a possible unity between England and Ireland. Edward and Michael bury an old historic enmity with this restrained and touching act of union. They do not embrace in an demonstrative manner before they part, but that little display of affection, which reminds one of animal-grooming, stays with us. With the image of two men combing each other's hair, McGuinness makes us hope for, believe in, the chance of change between people, in which politics might be overridden by a recognition of a shared humanity.

The play started with three stereotypical characters. Eventually, Michael and Edward slough their stereotyping, their national masks, and become individuals; and by turning to the personal, the self under the mask, a solution to hostility is proffered. Each of them becomes someone who cares for, watches over, another. *Someone Who'll Watch Over Me*'s rather straightforward framework gives McGuinness room to expound the unhappy relationship of England and Ireland. This is the 'exterior' aspect of the play. Let us now focus on its 'interior', on the inner journey undertaken by the characters.

IV

Adam, sensing that he is soon to die, asks Edward to look after Michael when he is gone, as though making a will. And Edward, who platonically, though unconsciously, loves Adam, takes this seriously. Edward responds with: 'If the boys out there bump you off, I won't be long after you at the pearly gates' (S, 29). Orpheus, in the classical myth, descends into the underworld to retrieve his bride Eurydice, who has been killed by a snakebite. Sir Orfeo, the Middle English version of Orpheus, which is told by Michael in the play, also goes down into the underworld to rescue his wife. Sir Orfeo succeeds in his mission, whereas Orpheus fails. Unlike the archetypal Orpheus-myth and its variations, here, in a tale of suffering at the hands of largely incomprehensible powers, McGuinness has a man following another man, not his wife, into the underworld.

The pearly gates, the gates of heaven as described in the Book of Revelation are a famous metaphor for death. Barbara Walker explains the history of this metaphor:

(It is) a Christian borrowing from the cult of Aphrodite Marina, the Sea-mother Mari, to whom pearls were sacred. Her own body was the Gate of Heaven, through which all men passed at birth (outward) and again at death (inward). Various yonic symbols of the Goddess were said to be bordered with pearls, including even the Celt's sacred Cauldron of Regeneration.[70]

Edward's imagery of the pearly gates leads us to the region explored in *Mary and Lizzie*: the underworld of ancient mythology. The Cauldron is another key word connecting these two plays: it is a big pot at the bottom of the sea or of lakes, or it is a wide gravel way equated with 'the Great Mother's cosmic womb'[71] and it evokes another queen of the Underworld, Hel in Norse mythology,[72] the etymological source of 'hell' in English. The early 'hell' seems to have been a uterine shrine or sacred cave of rebirth. 'Though Christian theology gave its underworld the name of the Goddess Hel, it was quite a different place from her womb of regeneration. The ancients didn't view the Underworld as primarily a place of punishment. It was dark, mysterious, and awesome, but not the vast torture chamber Christians made of it.'[73] The image of hell as a place of eternal torment was introduced by patriarchal religions like that of Zoroastrian Persia. When this patriarchal hell entered Christian theology, it became dominant.

There is a labyrinthine complexity of imagery at work in McGuinness's play: the pearly gates as the celestial entrance means at the same time the nether yonic gate to Cauldron-womb. This cosmic womb of regeneration is then equated with ancient 'hell', through the name of the queen of the Underworld, Hel. And this version of hell itself becomes a patriarchal place of eternal torture. In this mythological entanglement and cross-threading, the masculine and feminine components of both Edward and Michael are first confused and then, possibly, brought into a new equilibrium.

When Adam has gone in Scene Six, Edward refuses to eat for three days as a way of protesting about his disappearance. By means of the hunger strike, an action frequently taken by Irishmen to protest against perceived or actual injustice, Edward threatens to end his life. In this way, he tries to go through the metaphorical pearly gates, as he promised Adam he would in Scene Five. Sir Orfeo, in the Middle English verse romance, went into the forest 'to lead a living death' and entered hell. Edward also leads a living death. In torment, in a hell on earth, he accuses Michael, who does not seem to suffer from Adam's death as much as he does: 'You want him dead. You feel safer with him dead. One of us down, and no more to go. With him dead there'll be a big outcry and we will be saved. Isn't that it?' (S, 40)

However, Michael's understanding of Edward seems here to surpass Edward's ability to understand himself, for he says: 'You condemn yourself out of your own mouth. It isn't me who wants him dead. It's you, isn't it?'(S, 40). Michael has glimpsed Edward's unacknowledged desire for Adam's death, and knows that this desire is somehow bound up with 'a sense of sacrifice' that Edward is working out in his unconscious. Some psychologists argue there is nobody, who has not, at some time, and in a deep, unacknowledged sense, wished for their nearest kin's death, a wish which cannot be admitted on a conscious level. In order to integrate the two split selves of himself, Edward then follows Michael's advice to bury Adam by means of words:

He was gentle. He was kind. He could be cruel, when he was afraid, and while he was often afraid, as we all are afraid, he was not often cruel. He was brave, he could protect himself, and me, and you. He was beautiful to look at. I watched him as he slept one night I couldn't sleep. . . . He was innocent. Kind, gentle. Friend. I believe it goes without saying, love, so I never said. He is dead. Bury him. Perpetual light shine upon him. May his soul rest in peace. Amen. (S, 41)

Edward, who has the most aggressive and masculine personality of the three, reveals his love for Adam when he mourns. Men sometimes react with defensive hostility to homosexuality and femininity in other men, feeling, perhaps, that these traits put their own integrity at risk. But a salutary effect is appearing in Edward's defensiveness. In his admission of a hidden and subtle homosexuality lies a chance for him to re-order himself, to re-integrate something inside him that until now has remained unspoken.

With this new self, Edward has to re-encounter, and come to terms with, his dead father, of whom he once told: 'I didn't know him until it was too late' (S, 4). As a son, Edward paid little heed to his family: he was too busy. An imaginary drive through the air on Christmas Day takes Edward (and Michael) over to England

and then to his father's grave in Ireland. Fantasising that he is
before the grave, Edward relives the last conversation he had with
his dying father, who asked if he would go to hell. Edward
remembers that he replied: 'There's no such place as hell, Da' (*S*,
55). For Edward, this is no longer true, and he has returned to his
father to ask for help, admitting that 'there is a hell, Da. And I'm
in it' (*S*, 56). So far, he has always been the one to encourage his
cellmates, doing his worst, leading by belligerent example, but
here, thrown into despair, he begins to cry. And it is now Michael
who encourages Edward, forcing him to laugh. Their roles are
reversed: Edward passive and weak, Michael now positive and
strong. Michael even (and very untypically) uses impolite
language to cheer up Edward: 'Laugh, you bastard, laugh'(*S*, 56),
he says. Edward, with Michael's encouragement, can now
empathise with his father's anxiety about hell: his despair amply
compensates for the gap between his father and himself.

Michael, a widower, has his own ghost, too: his wife, whose
death, in keeping with the myth of Orpheus, led him to the
spiritual underworld, to the cauldron-womb, a symbol of
femininity. When he realised that he was not able to bring his wife
back, he became entrapped in it: Michael, who has the least
masculine personality of the three, has fallen into a more
'effeminate' life, busying himself with such 'womanly' pursuits as
making a pear flan. As he self-contemptuously defines himself, he
is a 'pansy little Englishman'(*S*, 24). Since he gave way to
femininity inside himself, which the shape of a pear often
suggests, Michael lost impetus in his life and then his job.

Before her death I was full of ideas for publications. Nothing terribly
exciting. Mostly on English dialects. Anyway, after the incident, I simply
read the Old English elegies and the medieval romances, and I taught as
best I could. I published nothing. I'd lost my wife and my ambition. (*S*,
22)

So he had to come to Lebanon for a university post; and it was in a
market in this city that he was kidnapped, while looking for pears,
with which he intended to make a flan for a party. The pear flan,
which symbolises his feminine aspect, is the immediate reason for
his being taken hostage. He has to regain his 'ambition', the
positive part of masculinity, once again by re-establishing his
relation with his wife, and with another ghost, his dead father.

Michael's father was a war prisoner for many years: this
experience made him a deeply reticent man. Michael remembers
the conversation with his father about Spartan warriors and tells

to Edward what the father said: 'When (Spartans) have pain, they show it by controlling it. Don't be afraid of pain. Don't be afraid of controlling it' (S, 50). This is a lesson from a father to his son, a lesson contrary to what the 'imperialist' children had been imbued with: they had been told not to show fear, 'even if you're a coward' (S, 50). This attitude might originate from the notion of 'the white man's burden', a notion which is still, perhaps, part of the British mentality, now being out of context. Michael's father is saying that it is unnecessary to grin and bear it: rather, it is necessary to admit freely that you are often very frightened, and this admission is the very thing that makes you become truly brave.

Michael remembers another conversation, this time, in his imagination, with his father. When he was reading an Old English poem, *The Wanderer*, he heard the voice of his dead father. Michael, in lament for his dead wife, identified with the protagonist of the poem, who 'sits alone in a desolate, frozen landscape, remembering when he had friends, when he had dreams, and now he is deserted'(S, 50–1). One line haunts him: *Oft him anhaga are gebideth*, which means that 'a man who is alone may at times feel mercy, mercy towards himself' (S, 51). This is also the voice of England. He feels both for his father and England, and says:

We long for our dear life, lamenting great loss – my father is dead – but accepting fate. *Wyrd bith ful araed.* In the same poem. *Wyrd bith ful araed.* Fate is fate. When I read 'The Wanderer', I feel possessed by my father. I feel for him, and for England. I love my country because I love its literature very much. I am proud to have taught it. That pride and, yes, I mean pride, is the reason I can sustain my sanity here. (S, 51)

Michael, like Edward, comes to an understanding of his dead father, through the reading of poetry which is something to do with his profession.

This acknowledgement of the father is how both Michael and Edward come to terms with their inner selves. Before he leaves, Edward says to Michael that he is 'the strongest man'(57) he knows. McGuinness says that this is 'a gigantic admission for an Irishman to make'.[74] And Edward continues: 'I'm not.' And we have to come back to that powerful symbol of two men combing each other's hair at the closing scene.The brave Spartan warriors, who were, at the same time, effeminate, become again a vital image where masculinity and femininity meet in the depths of human integrity. When left alone, Michael's body convulses and then he regains control, as if following his father's advice: 'Don't be afraid of pain. Don't be afraid of controlling it.'

Mutabilitie

I

Edmund Spenser,[75] who is regarded as one of the greatest poets of the Elizabethan period, wrote most of *The Faerie Queene* in Ireland. He came to Ireland as a secretary to Lord Grey, who became Lord Deputy of Ireland in 1580, and Spenser stayed there for eighteen years. This experience led him to write *A View of the Present State of Ireland*,[76] a prose dialogue between Eudoxus and Irenius, who discuss how to make the Irish subordinate to the Tudor State. It is 'a piece of practical advice for the English government'[77] detailing how Ireland's reform might be accomplished and its crisis ended. Recently, this non-literary aspect of Spenser as a public official in Ireland, or 'undertaker' of the Munster Plantation, to be more precise, caught the full intellectual attention of academics under the influence of the postcolonial theorising: he is regarded as a pivotal figure to show 'the involvements of culture with expanding empires',[78] as Said put it. Edmund, one of the three main characters in McGuinness's *Mutabilitie* (1997),[79] is based on this person.

It is interesting to compare various commentaries on *View*, often quoted in *Mutabilitie*, from different periods of history. Henry Morley, the editor of *Ireland Under Elizabeth and James the First*, published in 1890, wrote: 'Spenser's *View* . . . would add breadth and depth to the record of the great struggle under Elizabeth, and join to it a good man's endeavour to interpret its significance and show the way on to a happier future.'[80] Written at a time when the British Empire was in her prime, Morley's phrases ('a good man's endeavour' and 'a happier future') reflect the confidence or arrogance of an Imperial mentality. Obviously 'the struggle' here is that of the English to subdue the Irish: the Irish standpoint is seen as totally irrelevant.

Things had changed about forty years later, in 1934, when W. L. Renwick wrote a commentary for his edition of *A View of the Present State of Ireland*. He admits that there are two standpoints to be considered, the English and the Irish, though this editor still believes, to borrow Seamus Deane's phrase, in 'the autonomy of cultural artifacts':[81]

Our concern here is not with Ireland's rights or wrongs, nor with belated apology, condemnation, or moralizing, but with one man's surroundings and experience, which interest students of literature because that man was a great poet, and students of history because his is the best statement of official opinion at a difficult period. The two interests are not mutually exclusive . . . Our concern is with Spenser, and this commentary, accordingly, is not argumentative, but illustrative.[82]

McGuinness would be at one with Renwick on keeping literary aesthetics and 'belated' argumentation apart, were it not for the fact that McGuinness's project – to heal 'the warring relationship between England and Ireland' – entails a moving forward; and that to make progress, it is impossible not to be 'argumentative' about a figure like Spenser.

Andrew Hadfield and Willy Maley, the editors of the latest edition of *A View*, published in 1997, quote from Edward Said's *Culture & Imperialism* (1994):

[I]t is generally true that literary historians who study the great sixteenth-century poet Edmund Spenser, for example, do not connect his bloodthirsty plans for Ireland, where he imagined a British army virtually exterminating the native inhabitants, with his poetic achievement or with the history of British rule over Ireland, which continues today.[83]

Inspired by Said and the postcolonial theorising he did so much to nurture, the re-reading and re-evaluation of Spenser are well under way, of which a collection of essays edited by Patricia Coughlan, *Spenser and Ireland: An Interdisciplinary Perspective* (1989), Andrew Hadfield's *Spenser's Irish Experience: Wilde Fruit and Salvage Soyl* (1997) and Willy Maley's *Salvaging Spenser: Colonialism, Culture and Identity* (1997) are examples.

And there are non-theoretical revisions, too. Robert Welch's novel, *The Kilcolman Notebook*,[84] for instance, and McGuinness's *Mutabilitie*, are radical re-*creations* of Spenser by Irishmen. Though these creative writings try to show the literary depth of Spenser as a poet, they acknowledge, too, that anyone who reads Spenser from an Irish point of view is likely to be appalled by the gap between the beauty and elaboration of his poems and the hatred and atrocity of his political writings. McGuinness once commented on Spenser's *View*: 'It is quite a harrowing document because it is a very clear articulation of the absolutely ruthless policy of colonisation and conquest on the part of the Elizabethan authorities. And it projects deep disrespect for Irish culture.'[85]

There is 'disrespect', certainly, but at the same time, it is clear that Spenser did love the Irish landscape, 'his spiritual home as well as his "real," emotional home in Ireland, for Arlo Hill (a setting for *Two Cantos of Mutabilitie*) is both a type of Eden and a favorite mountain near Spenser's Kilcolman estate'.[86] McGuinness sees Spenser as a man 'haunted by images of the starving Irish' with 'a tremendous sense both of guilt and of moral righteousness'.[87] Any creative writer who looks carefully at Spenser is likely to emerge with a complex picture of the man. The better they write, the more contradictory Spenser appears – evil remains pure evil only as long as it is depicted in a shallow or stereotypical manner, as long as Spenser is seen as an enemy standing exclusively on the other side.

Declan Kiberd wrote about this kind of complexity between England and Ireland in the opening chapter of *Inventing Ireland*, which deals with Spenser:

[Spenser] marvelled at the capacity of Ireland to enforce a gentle man to violence, a violence which "almost changed his very natural disposition". Already this seductive island was manifesting its fatal tendency to convert even the most rational and cultivated of Englishman into arrant tyrants. This tyrannizing may have owed much to the remarkable *similarity* of the two opposed people. The Irish . . . actually looked like the English to the point of undetectability; their poets were court poets, whose duties were, like those of Spenser himself, to praise the sovereign, excoriate the kingdom's enemies, and appeal in complex lyrics to the shared aesthetic standard of a mandarin class. . . . It was perhaps, a subliminal awareness of this resemblance which distressed Spenser, as it would so many of his contemporaries and successors.[88]

In view of this 'resemblance', it is ironically fitting that Kiberd here quotes Spenser's *View* from the *Field Day Anthology of Irish Writing*, which included Spenser as an 'Irish' writer.[89] Kiberd's emphasis on 'similarity' between the Irish and the English, for all their differences and oppositions, suggests a change in Anglo-Irish relations, including, on the Irish side, an understanding of English distress at a psychological level. Through this mature, lenient reaction to their past, Kiberd believes that some sort of parity has been established between the Irish and the English, the colonised becoming equal, or vying with, the colonisers, and that the coloniser and colonised now exchange meanings within the same, mutually agreed, field of terms and historical references.

II

The congruence of the Irish and the English, and the subliminal distress this similarity causes the English, are two of the major concerns of McGuinness's *Mutabilitie*. In order to underline these concerns, McGuinness compares and contrasts two court poets, Edmund, who belongs to the winners' side, and the File, an Irish bard and wise woman, who speaks for the losers. Edmund praises Queen Elizabeth: 'She is the fairest creature to tread God's earth. All who look at her do so with awe and obedience . . . Beams of light spread from her like the sun's rays. When she speaks, the birds of the air sing to her accompaniment. When she walks, flutes sound through the air' (*M*, 6). Breaking into verse, he continues:

And she herself of beautie soveraigne Queene
Fair Venus seemed unto his bed to bring
Her, whom he waking evermore to weene.
To be the chastest flowre, that ay did spring
On earthly braunch, the daughter of a king. (*M*, 6)

The Faerie Queene, Canto I, Stanza 48, is the source of these lines. Edmund's admiration of the queen turns back again into prose: 'In her eyes lie the most precious jewels of all, for they are the mirror of her soul, and it shines like the most beautiful diamond. This is Gloriana. Elizabeth' (*M*, 6). There is no doubt, in the play's context, about Edmund's intention of approbation. However, McGuinness's mischievous trick is at work in this quotation: in the original context of *The Faerie Queene*, the narrator is talking of neither Gloriana, nor virtuous Una, the beloved companion to the knight, Redcross in Canto I, but of a false Una, who is about to tempt Redcross to 'unwonted lust' in his dream. McGuinness attributes this impure, voluptuous image to Queen Elizabeth, as the File later depicts her to the Irish in the wood: 'Elizabeth announces her virginity to the world and proclaims it to be a sacred decree. So sacred that when she lies with a man, as she must, she does not offer him her jewel for pleasure, she offers instead –' (*M*, 14). This is McGuinness's subliminal curse on Elizabeth in clever disguise: it is a playful ploy, which captures the complex psychology of the contemporary Anglo-Irish relationship.

The surface of Edmund's remark, however, still reflects the image of the immaculate queen. When the File praises the Irish Queen, likening her glory to the sun, she sounds similar to Edmund:

Your glory is eternal as the sun. . . . Night shall not darken the greatness of your name. . . . It shall live for ever. Most valiant warrior, most true knight, most loyal in the faith of Christ, Maeve, queen of all, most loved, most loved, most loved. (*M*, 31–2)

The File, as her name suggests, belongs to the Irish literary tradition of Filidh, a class of poets 'whose first duties were to praise their patron, to preserve their genealogy and to be learned in history and literature, as well as to master their craft'.[90] She and Edmund/Spenser resemble each other both in the way they praise their sovereigns, and in the way they curse their enemies. Spenser curses Ireland in *The View*, and the File curses Queen Elizabeth, her kingdom's scourge, saying 'Elizabeth, Elizabeth, you rhyme with death'(*M*, 80). The resemblance is deepened by the fact that both of them are court poets without a proper court. 'Deprived of a court, a learned man who had somehow lost his full entitlements'.[91] These are Kiberd's words on the Irish historian and poet, Seathrún Céitinn (Geoffrey Keating), comparing him with Spenser. The File has lost her court and dignity, and Edmund himself is craving to return to the court in England.

William (Shakespeare), Spenser's contemporary, younger by about twelve years, is added as the third poet to the play, as the antithesis of these two court poets. William's appearance in Ireland is a totally fictitious invention by McGuinness.[92] Unlike Edmund and the File, William can come and go wherever and whenever he likes. Unbounded by Nation or politics, he is at liberty to praise whoever he loves, often comparing her (or him) to 'a summer's day'(*M*, 23). It is only when this sonnet (No. 18) is quoted that the audience can identify this William as Shakespeare, because his surname is never used in the play. It is suggested by the behaviour of the other two poets that William should praise his patrons and Queen occasionally, to improve his prospects, but he is in a far freer position than the court poets.

III

Mutabilitie is set in 1598,[93] Spenser's final year in Kilcolman Castle as the Sheriff of County Cork, by which time he had accumulated considerable property. Spenser, after seeing 'the late wars of Munster', wrote of the misery of the Irish in his *View*:

they were brought to such wretchedness, as that any stony heart would have rued the same. Out of every corner of the woods and glynnes they came creeping forth upon their hands, for their legges could not beare them; they looked like anatomies of death, they spake like ghosts crying out of their graves; they did eate the dead carrions, happy where they could finde them, yea, and one another soone after, insomuch as the very carcasses they spared not to scrape out of their graves; and, if they found a plot of water-cresses or shamrocks, there they flocked as to a feast for the time, yet not able long to continue therewithall; that in short space there were none almost left, and a most populous and plentifull countrey suddainely left voyde of man and beast; yet sure in all that warre, there perished not many by the sword, but all by the extremitie of famine, which they themselves had wrought.[94]

This is the very situation that the Irish experience.

However, McGuinness made it clear that 'the play is a metaphor for 1998'.[95] There is, therefore, symbolic timeliness in the fact that *Mutabilitie* opened at the Royal National Theatre in London in late November, 1997, and ran in repertory until February 1998, by which time McGuinness had been working on it for twelve years. McGuinness said, in an open interview held at the National Theatre, that *King Richard II* was in his mind when writing *Mutabilitie*.[96] On his return from an unsuccessful expedition to Ireland, Richard faces a rebellion by Bolingbroke,[97] later King Henry IV, whom he had sentenced to six years exile. What captured McGuinness's imagination was probably not these fragmented references to the relation between England and Ireland, but the political impasse for which both Richard and Bolingbroke are responsible. Their actions inflict on England a wound that will fester for generations. Taking into consideration that *King Richard II* is set in 1398, another two hundred years of retrospective expansion is added to McGuinness's concerns: the play is about 1398, 1598 and 1998 all at the same time. The File cries out:

We have fought for centuries . . . We approach the end of this century . . . Let it be an end to war . . . Or must it continue for another hundred years? . . . And another hundred years? . . . And another hundred years? . . . And another hundred years? (*M*, 58–9)

Her cry is also McGuinness's, and it appeals to everyone involved in the situation in Ulster at the end of the twentieth century.

IV

The play moves between two settings, Spenser's castle, and the woods where banished Irish people live after the wars of Munster.

Hugh, the Irish King's son, and the File act as spies in Edmund's castle. Ben, an English actor, who is taken hostage by the Irish, analyses the situation and explains to Richard, his fellow-actor and fellow-hostage: 'If I'm reading this story right, the king, so-called, has lost his kingdom and his mind, and the good lady wife's gone off her rocker to keep him company . . . The File moves between two camps, ours, and this one. She's up to badness'(*M*, 35).

The King is called Sweney and his lady wife Maeve. There are legendary Irish monarchs called Sweney (Suibne) and Maeve (Medb), but they are not supposed to be Spenser's contemporaries. *Buile Shuibne*, 'Frenzy of Sweeney', probably written in the 1670s, is related to the battle of Mag Rath (Moira) in the early 7th century. Suibne was cursed by a cleric named Rónán, and fled insanely into the wild woods, leaping from tree to tree like a bird. In *Táin Bó Cuailnge*, 'Cattle Raid of Cooley'), the central saga of the Ulster cycle, Medb, Queen of Connacht, fought against Ulster to take the great brown bull of Cooley, and was 'the goddess of Tara whom every successive Tara King married symbolically'.[98] These epics have been translated and retold by several Irish writers and commonly read since the Irish Renaissance: Flann O'Brien's *At Swim Two-Birds* (1939) and Seamus Heaney's *Sweeney Astray* (1983) are inspired by *Buile Shuibne*. Lady Gregory's version of *Táin Bó Cuailnge* is included in *Cuchulain of Muirthemne* (1902) and Thomas Kinsella translated it as *The Táin* (1970). Both Suibne and Medb, well known figures in Irish mythology, are regarded here as indices to Irish culture and order before Tudor colonisation.

When McGuinness introduces these legendary characters, Sweney and Maeve, the different conception of Kingship and Queenship held in England and Ireland is underlined. Even though they apply the same word 'Queen' to Elizabeth of England and Maeve of Ireland, the implications of the word are very different. Queen Elizabeth is the symbol of a modern unified nation about to expand her empire, following in the footsteps of Spain, whereas Queen Maeve is a legendary character, closer to the image of warrior and goddess.

An Irish king is described as follows:

Kingship, the pivotal institution of early Irish society, has its own rich mythology woven into the legends of famous kings . . . and embodying many reflexes of Indo-European ideology. Though part of the heroic tradition, the emphasis here is on wise leadership and good judgement, and on the physical and moral qualities that ensure or endanger the prosperity of land and society.[99]

McGuinness's King Sweney has gone mad: this madness enables him to survive the turmoil of the wars of Munster but is also the very thing that 'endangers' the prosperity of his tribe. Having lost his competence to rule the kingdom, he speaks to birds: 'Good birds, you know nothing of a kingdom lost. You are kings of sky and stars, I am lord of river and forest, but river and forest do not heed my command' (*M*, 86). The ruler should be wise and good in judgement for the fertile and beautiful land. His wife, Queen Maeve, 'most valiant warrior, most true knight' (*M*, 32), therefore, takes command of the tribe, the role of decision-maker, on his behalf.

In this forum – the wood and Spenser's castle – the differences, and the similarities, between England and Ireland are played out. Edmund boasts that he treats Hugh and the File as his children, and then, continuing in this patronising vein, says: 'To remain safe in this castle, there is one rule to obey. You have proved yourselves to be good, obedient creatures. I see in your behaviour the benevolent future of your unfortunate Irish race' (*M*, 8). King Sweney, having lost his kingdom and his sanity, still acts as Edmund does. When Annas, his daughter, asks him for the release of the two hostages, he replies:

Where? Into the darkest forest? That would be cruel, Annas. They would be lost for ever without our protection. Here, they are safe. They have milk to drink and berries to eat. We share our plenty with them. Without our kingly generosity they would surely starve to death. (*M*, 15–6)

Both the English and the Irish are benevolent enough to protect those who do not belong to their tribes: if, that is, they are obedient. Kiberd writes that '[Spenser] wished to convert the Irish to civil ways, but in order to do that found that it might be necessary to exterminate many of them.'[100] This Irish king feels more or less the same about his hostages, and he eventually orders that they be killed. By showing this parallel between the Irish and the English, McGuinness suggests that the ferocity found in Spenser's political writings is not a personal trait but a universal human defect.

V

The File and the other Irish expect William, 'Bard of Avon' (*M*, 55) to be their saviour: 'A man shall come from the river and he shall speak [their] stories, he shall sing the song of songs' (*M*, 55). The File's reasoning for this is that 'bard' and 'Avon' are two of the very few words in English that originally came from Irish, 'bard' and 'aibhne', which mean 'poet' and 'river' respectively. Bolstering this apparent connection, William, during a fever, also reveals his Catholic faith, which is the almost universal Irish faith. 'He is the epitome of English culture', said McGuinness, 'and he's the great connecter between Protestant England and Catholic England because he has those two wires fused in his theatre'.[101] Showing his affection for Hugh, an Irishman, William invites him to speak and sing in his own language, which Hugh refuses, quoting Seamus Heaney's phrase, the 'government of the tongue': 'We had lost power to govern our lives and part of that curse was the loss we accepted over the government of our tongue. We do not break our vows. I will not sing nor speak to you in Irish, Englishman' (*M*, 68).

Instead of speaking or singing in Irish, Hugh's bare foot moves towards William's and their feet touch and rest together (which reminds one of Michael and Edward's mutual grooming in the last scene of *Someone Who'll Watch Over Me*). Hugh and William are irresponsibly drunk in these exchanges, still this touching of feet could be read as the beginning of an Englishman's understanding of an Irishman's loss of country and language. In the previous scene, however, Ben and Richard mockingly speak of William's love affair with a Welsh man. Ben mimics William: 'Speak to me in your language, sing to me in your language' (*M*, 63). For Ben, this is just a favourite ploy for William when he seduces a man whose native language is not English. Despite Ben's remark, the touching of feet in this scene still holds good, affecting us as a powerful communication or understanding between two distinct parties.

William is also a coloniser. Along with his fellow actors, Ben and Richard, he comes to Ireland seeking new opportunities, full of ambitions. Richard says that 'Ireland's opening up' (*M*, 36), and Annas, who is in love with Richard, regards him as 'so innocent', because he 'wished to obtain land . . . to be a farmer' (*M*, 27), revealing her own innocence. She does not recognise the usurper in Richard, under the disguise of a humble would-be farmer. It is, according to Ben, William who first thought of coming over to Ireland. William the coloniser is revealed through the conversation with Edmund, most of which comes from Spenser's *A View of the Present State of Ireland*. William, who, like Eudoxus, hardly knows Ireland, questions Edmund, who, like Irenius, has lived there for a long time: 'This country of Ireland that you have now lived in and know is by repute a goodly and commodious soil. I wonder why no course is taken to turn it to good use and to turn that nation to better government and civility' (*M*, 45). This is a verbatim quotation of Eudoxus's opening question in *A View*. Edmund then explains a few things about Ireland, outlining the Brehon laws, describing the bards, and the role of the church, quoting all this time from *A View*. William responds with a very simple outsider's view:

William: We have started to conquer, we have conquered–
Edmund: We have started to go mad.
William: Let me assist you in the continuation of that conquest. (*M*, 52)

In contrast to Edmund, who anticipates a political quagmire which will last for four centuries, William is optimistic and asks Edmund to 'get [him] a job in the civil service' (*M*, 50). By the end of this exchange we know that the File and her compatriots are mistaken, that William is not an almighty saviour.

When asked if he was a soldier, William says:

I have been . . . I have also been a king and his queen and a boy and his girl and a lover and a clown, all these trades come naturally to me when I sit alone and sometimes I hear sweet airs in the fire, throw water on the fire, let the ashes sing – (*M*, 20)

Here, through William's acting career, through his sarcastic but lyrical remark on his experience, the possibilities of theatre are suggested. There in the theatre, you can be anybody, transcending barriers of gender, class, or profession. Theatre is represented as a new way for the Irish to reverse and transform the misery of their state. At the beginning of the play, however, William is tired of life in the theatre and is about to give up his career. It is the File, who has not even seen the theatre, who believes in its possibilities:

You wish to turn away from the all-consuming theatre, why? . . . I have imagined this place . . . Is it not now a sacred dwelling? Is it not a temple where the remembered dead rise from their graves? . . . Sins are forgiven there . . . Cries are heard . . . Prayers are answered . . . Is it not there that your race now speaks to God? Is that theatre not your country's true place of reformation? . . . Are you not a priest in this new religion that may attach itself most secretly, most devoutly to the old abandoned faith? (*M*, 56–7)

She keeps asking questions but William does not reply. Through her imagination, the theatre is consecrated as a holy place, a place in which prayers are offered, and some form of hope is given. She asks him to give her the theatre, to make a gift of it, 'as the theatre is God's gift to a Catholic who must speak in the language of a Protestant'(*M*, 59), a request which William does not (or does not want to) understand. Maybe she imagines too well what theatre might be, and the heights it is capable of reaching; these expectations discomfit William, who knows all about theatre's squalor, vulgarity, and wretchedness, qualities which are, of course, also sources of its vitality. Ben and Richard's comic-relief, even in their darkest misery as hostages, reflects this aspect of the theatre.

The File, who has not seen a play staged in the theatre, forgets to include laughter in her own imagined theatre. However, laughter is not dismissed in this very sombre play; indeed McGuinness never forgets it in any of his work. When Elizabeth, wife to Edmund, asks how Irish people respond to death, the File answers that: 'It's a habit amongst us, a custom, to laugh when we should cry' (*M*, 66). Elizabeth thinks they are 'a mad race' (*M*, 66). This black, defiant laughter became part of the tradition of the Irish theatre in the future. Many Irish plays written since the Irish Revival are, broadly speaking, tragicomedies. Synge and O'Casey belong to this tradition. Behan, too. In Beckett's *Endgame* (1958), Nell says: 'Nothing is funnier than unhappiness, I grant you that.'[102] In Tom Murphy's *Bailegangaire* (1985), a laughing competition is held about unhappiness. This laughter, which is by no means innocently joyful or pleasurable, becomes rather disturbing, and causes the heart to bleed.

In this play, another type of laughter is introduced, which seems to borrow from Wilde. When accused by Hugh of not saying 'Amen' after a Protestant prayer, the File said: 'I did not think it polite to listen to the Protestant at prayer' (*M*, 23). This reminds one of the opening scene of *The Importance of Being Earnest*. When asked if he heard Algernon's piano playing, Lane, the butler, replies: ' I didn't think it polite to listen, sir.'[103] Or, in the final scene, the File, teasing Hugh for taking so long to bathe, says: 'It shows signs of vanity . . . Apart from your vanity you are quite perfect, and I dislike perfection' (*M*, 99). This again reminds us of another character in Wilde's play, Gwendolen, who, when told that she is quite perfect, replies: 'Oh, I hope I am not that. It would leave no room for developments, and I intend to develop in many directions.'[104]

The Importance of Being Earnest is often regarded as a typical example of English humour, in spite of the fact that Wilde was born and brought up in Dublin.[105] In letting the File utter these

Wildean remarks, McGuinness underlines the link between the Irish and the English sense of humour, with Anglo-Irish writers like Wilde acting as an intermediary. As McGuinness said, they, the Irish and the English, 'do, after all, have a shared language and a shared history'.[106]

In Act IV, after acknowledging the fact that both Hugh and William lost their own sons, William sings to his own dead boy:

Your cat's asleep before the fire.
Wonder, child, what does it see,
There are no powers that are higher,
Lord, what fools we mortals be.

The cat, it plots to steal the cream
And holds its putrid, perfumed breath.
Sweet child, it's all but strangest dreams
Until they end in darkest death.

A black cat speaks to me at times
And makes my art a witch of craft.
I call that cat by your soft name,
And then I hear the spirits laugh. (*M*, 74)

At the very bottom of William's (and McGuinness's) views on life and theatre, which are condensed here into a song, lies acceptance that human beings are mortal. But William never becomes pessimistic. Through the eyes of a mischievous cat, he sees the world as 'strangest dreams'; which, for each of us, will 'end in darkest death'. The breath of the cat, which is 'putrid', and at the same time 'perfumed', reflects his view of the theatre: it is not a sacred temple, it sometimes stinks, yet, at its best, it has a sublime sweetness. William's reliance on cats[107] is comically remarked on by Ben and Richard in the previous scene. When Richard compliments William on his writing, William replies: 'Don't thank me . . . It's the cats. They communicate a feline energy, a leonine power, they're my inspiration'(*M*, 36). Richard remembers their exchange, saying: 'What kind of man thinks a cat writes his plays?'(*M*, 36). Yet, the cat makes his art 'a witch of craft', with which he entrances the File and Edmund. He urges the File to 'gain the gift' (*M*, 74), and shows her what this gift, the magic of theatre, can do, arraying before them, as a performance, not of the Fall of the Irish, but that of Troy, enacted by the Irish. The woe of Troy, the sorrow of Cassandra, the agony of Hecuba, are just variations on the torment of the Irish experience.

But this magic of telling a story on stage, of transformation, does not stop the Irish killing their hostages, Ben and Richard, or Maeve ordering Hugh to kill her and the king – theatre has little power, it seems, to change reality. William, who came from the river, sets off for England, his home, along the river, leaving behind no solution for the people with whom he has been briefly involved. Ultimately, the File and William do not understand each other, though they are in awe of, fascinated by, each other. McGuinness was once, asked 'what can a play ever do?' and replied:

Well, nothing practically. Nobody laid down a gun after seeing *The Plough and Stars* or *The Silver Tassie*, but theatre can tell a story . . . Also for me, theatre can register your conscious commitment to the historical reality of your country and the responsibility you bear to that future. And I can say that I got involved, not in the narrowly reduced sense of that phrase, but I don't think you can let what's happening to your country pass by without saying 'I notice it, I see it.[108]

Admitting its limitations, McGuinness still believes in and expects something of the theatre. In *Mutabilitie*, he carefully represents a kind of history of the theatre, from Greek tragedy through the medieval Mystery Cycle (in which Ben and Richard took part as actors), to a Wildean comedy of manners, and thus reveals the versatility of the medium.

VI

As in Part Three of *Sons of Ulster*, four scenes are sectioned and run intermittently in the latter half of Act III. There are two scenes in the castle, between the File and William, and between Edmund and Elizabeth; and there are two scenes in the woods, one involving Sweney and Maeve, and the other Annas and the two hostages, Richard and Ben. As discussed before, the File tries to convince William to give the Irish the gift of theatre, of speech. But William will not, saying 'that is only [her] dream' (*M*, 60). Annas tries to convince Richard to take her to England, away from her parents, declaring that she would die for him. Richard replies he would not do the same for her. Sweney expresses a desire for his own death, despite his fear of it; Maeve encourages him to live because they have yet to avenge their dead. Elizabeth urges Edmund to leave Ireland, but he says he cannot. In each scene, somebody is pleading for something, but every plea is rejected in one way or another. As in *Sons of Ulster*, there are interplays of powerful resonance:

File: Sins are forgiven there.
Sweney: They died for my sins.
File: Cries are heard.
Sweney: I pray to God for forgiveness.
File: Prayers are answered.
Sweney: He is tired too and no longer listens. (*M*, 56)

The File in the castle and Sweney in the woods speak to William and Maeve respectively, but neither of them is answered by their immediate partners. Instead, each plea is met from another space. The File continues: 'Is it not there that your race now speaks to God? Is that theatre not your country's true place of reformation? (*M*, 56). The File, the bard, seeks the power of theatre in order to save her tribe.

In the last scene of Act III (which was followed by the interval in the first performance at the National Theatre), the words of all nine characters converge into one notion, that of death:

Edmund: Will you consent to sleep with me tonight?
William: That is only your dream. You will wake from it. As I have.
Elizabeth: I will consent to die with you tonight.
File: When I die, I will waken and find it was not a dream.
Hugh: File.
Edmund: Elizabeth.
William: It is a way of dying, yes.
Annas: I would die for you.
William: This dream, this theatre.
Richard: I would not for you.
Niall: Annas.
Elizabeth: We will die in Ireland.
File: But the dead have risen before.
Maeve: We must avenge our dead.
File: The dead will rise again.
Donal: My lord, my lady, vengeance.
Maeve: We will see the English dead.
Edmund: I will not die in Ireland.
File: In this your theatre you will make our dead rise, William. You will
    raise our Irish dead, Englishman. (*M*, 60–1)

Death is not just the end of human life: the dead will rise from their deaths; and that is another recurrent theme in McGuinness.

This imagery of death underlines the notion of the 'mutable' earth in the play.

VII

The play's title, *Mutabilitie*, is taken from Spenser's *Two Cantos of Mutabilitie*, 'a fragment of an apparently never completed "Legend of Constancie", which first appeared in the 1609 folio edition of *The Faerie Queene*.'[109] The *Cantos* begin with the desire of Mutabilitie, the personified power of change, to take Jove's place and be recognised as governor of the heavens. Her claim is not without legitimacy, because she is the granddaughter of the great Earth and the daughter of Chaos. She also believes she has power over everything which is subject to change under the moon. In the court held on Arlo Hill, great dame Nature, who is 'ever young, yet full of age', acts as judge. Mutabilitie calls as witness the Months, the Hours, Day and Night, and finally Life and Death. She even claims that the gods themselves are subject to change. Yet, Mutabilitie never wins. Things, Nature says, are not changed from their first natures, though 'by change their being do dilate' (VII vii 58). Mutabilitie is obviously the intruder against the Order of Heaven; however, she is depicted not as a villainess but as a beautiful and attractive woman with a 'louely face, in which faire beams of beauty did appeare' (VII vi 31). For Zitner, 'the *Mutabilitie Cantos* are both surprising and inevitable in their spirit of almost continuous gaiety'[110] and he pertinently notes that:

In short, seasonal change embodies God's unchanging will. . . . Even Death, though composed of negations, is neither an illusion nor merely the end of something. This is perhaps the central point the *Cantos* make about mutability: change does not put an end to prior states nor is it their goal. Mutability is only the means by which the unchanging essence of things is revealed.[111]

Time is a one-way flux, yet also cyclical. Understanding of this, which means a reconciliation between two notions of time, helps us not to lament the changes and mutations of our world.

McGuinness's King Sweney is, however, overwhelmed by the notion of change:

Change and chance have befallen us. This mutable earth is now our lot. Brother earth, greetings from your mad king. We race, we rant, we dwell in darkness, until we dim to death. Is the lord listening? Is he in heaven or is he in hell? Oh god of change and chance, revenge me. (*M*, 34)

As long as Sweney sets his past glory as the measure of the world's order, the only thing left for him is to forsake that world and to seek revenge, which will lead him nowhere.

On the other hand, the File, who understands the mechanism of change, advises Elizabeth to change her affections: 'Turn your hatred of Ireland to love of it, then it may be your husband's love will turn to hatred' (*M*, 42). To Elizabeth's charge that this 'is the thinking of a fool', the File replies:

A fool? Perhaps I am. But it is thinking which pays homage to the principle of change, and change controls this earth and all its workings. I am proof. Once no man nor woman would dare call me fool. I once had servants, washerwomen, I too have suffered change in these late wars of Munster – (*M*, 43)

We can see that though she is able to accept the principle of change she is still full of lament. She sings a song of mutabilitie:

The gods possess a power strange,
For all things turn to dust and change,
Mankind, the sky, the rivered sea
Sing of mutabilitie. (*M*, 43)

She continues, singing that men and women flower, wither, and die, and that by dying bring exile to an end. Even for the File, it takes time to transform acquiescence into reconciliation.

In Act IV, Scene 2, two scenes again play in juxtaposition, but here the effect is very different. In one, the File is explaining how she lost her child:

They took the child. The child was taken from me. It had been snowing heavily that night. We were hiding in the mountains. We had lost our homes. We trooped across the hills, seeking any sanctuary. So many of us at first. As I was with child, I was not expected to survive. I did. It did not, the child. We buried it in the snow. It now has melted, of course. The snow, the child. I was called upon to weep. I did not do so. Instead I was determined from that moment to join with the English. We had lost. You had won. I decided to serve the winning side. (*M*, 71)

And in another, Hugh explains the same incident to William, but not with the full-blown bitterness of the mother's version:

I have only once seen hanging. It was a child. The mother twisted its neck. It was my child. I watched it happen. I let it happen. We were hiding in the mountains, seeking any sanctuary. So many of us. Dashed its brains out, she did. She had sworn to survive. It didn't, the child. Spilt like milk on the winter snow. (*M*, 71)

What matters here is not which version of the story is true, but that pain (here, the agony of losing a son) admit of different tellings. The File, the mother, was reluctant to strangle her son, but had to do so to survive. She has the responsibility of the wise woman for her tribe. In this scene it is left unclear who actually killed the child; maybe she says 'they took the child. The child was taken from me', because she cannot face the reality of what she has done. Hugh, the father, cannot sympathise with her agony, and accuses her of infanticide. It seems that after this event, all that ties them to one another is their tribal loyalty, their allegiance to their king and queen, and maybe their mutual hatred.

They are, to some degree, reconciled after Hugh kills the king and the queen, his parents. Looking at his bloodied hands, Hugh asks the File to defend him against the accusations of his sister, Annas: 'File, plead for my life. Plead for my life. In the name of our lost love, I plead you, save my life. I plead in the name of our lost child' (*M*, 96). This the File, who has killed her own son, does. But instead of trying to convince Annas that Hugh's act was done under the direct instructions of his mother, the queen, who had to be obeyed, she makes a conciliatory move, praying that the dead monarchs' souls may rest in peace. This is the only way to lift the curse that Annas, nearest kin to both the deceased and the murderer, casts upon Hugh. The File, the bard, says:

I knelt where my lord and lady loved arm-in-arm in death. I kissed their hands and feet. I saw the light of eternal rest in their faces. The grave itself did weep, and in that weeping I heard their sweet voices speak. They say, repent, repent for your revenge. Leave the world and its desires. Renounce the kingdom. Walk as beggars through the earth. Or there is no consolation beyond the grave. Repent. Be penitent. Be pilgrims. (*M*, 96)

Like a medium, the File speaks through the voices of the dead king and queen to the Irish. If they, the Irish, can repent, and renounce the kingdom of Ireland and its cause, to which they have so far been bound, there may be a tiny possibility of consolation.

Donal, the Catholic priest, obstinately refuses to accept this message. He tries to convince Hugh that he should keep the fight going as the new king:

'Drink the warrior blood of your dead. Restore the order of our laws, our customs, our religion. Through your power, your valour, and through prayer – prayer – through prayer – through faith – we will win – we will – through God –(*M*, 97)

This injunction is charged with the authority of the masculine principle, law, and tradition: his speech here and elsewhere is suffused with abstract words of power –'deed', 'order', 'laws', 'customs', and 'religion'. However, as indicated in McGuinness's careful punctuation in the text, he stumbles over the words which imply a spiritual element, 'prayer', 'faith', and 'God'. The contradictions involved in fighting in the name of God and religion are encapsulated in this Catholic priest. Hugh rejects the priest's words: 'Poor priest, look at you. Look at us. We are nothing. My sister, I will live with you in eternal destitution' (*M*, 97). To make atonement for his parricide, Hugh knows that a life of penance, his own style of penance, is necessary and he decides to wander the earth. This reminds us, perhaps, of Mary and Lizzie's wandering, which eventually brought them to regeneration.

In the final scene, there is a remarkable feeling of peace and serenity which encompasses the Irish who live in 'eternal destitution'. This difference of tone, literally created by stage effects, music, lighting and so on, indicate a shift in possibility in the future that might be moved into. The stage direction says: 'A river. The Irish move with a new freedom. Hugh bathes in the river, watched by the File. Annas and Donal prepare a frugal meal. What clothes cover them do so with ease' (*M*, 99).

Giving up everything, the kingdom, and all its duties, is the only way to gain 'a new freedom' and 'ease', though both Hugh and the File continue to 'think of the life before' (*M*, 99). Niall, Hugh's brother, finds Edmund's son, who was lost in the confusion when the castle was set on fire. The child recognises Hugh and the File as servants from the castle, and explains what happened to him. Then he apologises for having frightened the File. 'I'm very sorry too' (*M*, 100) is her reply. This exchange of apologies is significant, carrying echoes of Queen Victoria and Mary in *Mary and Lizzie*. There, when Queen Victoria says 'forgive me' to the Burns sisters, Mary comments that 'she'll get over it' (*ML*, 24). Even though Mary implies forgiveness in her remark, her knowledge of the reasons for the queen's guilt makes her unable to respond to this apology directly. In *The Bird Sanctuary*, the Queen is obliquely forgiven by a woman in black, who says that 'all sins are forgiven' (*Bird*, 7).

The child in *Mutabilitie* is frightened and distressed at losing his parents and their protection, but is still able to think of the others. The File is also able to show sympathy, without patronising him. McGuinness seems to suggest that this mutuality is an essential requirement for a new understanding. The Irish decide to foster the child.[112] 'There's a tiny glitter of hope, a spark of humanity that can't be entirely extinguished', McGuinness commented on this final scene, 'but yes, it acknowledges that we're living in dangerous times. And ongoing events, particularly the breaking of the ceasefire, certainly fed into it.'[113] So it is significant that in the play (and this is not mentioned in the text), there are still arems lying on the stage. And that Donal regards the child as 'a hostage' (*M*, 100), and is also reluctant to give him any milk because 'there is little' (*M*, 101). But the File takes command of the situation and orders him to 'fetch our little milk' (*M*, 101) for the boy, and in doing so takes the play one step closer to whatever it is that is promised by this scene's tranquil, hopeful atmosphere.

When McGuinness was asked why he made the File a woman, he answered that she just happened to be. However, the contrast between the female File and the male priest, Donal, is dramatically effective, and significant. The mechanism of this mutable earth shadows the archetypal conflict between male and female principles, and bears strong resemblances to the *I Ching*, "The Book of Changes", an ancient Chinese text, one of the Five Classics of Confucianism. This envisages the world as a system involving the conflict between *Ying* and *Yang*, the male and female principles.

McGuinness said he had 'enormous faith in Tony Blair', the British Prime Minister elected in 1997; but we should not forget Mo Mowlam, who was the Northern Ireland secretary of his Cabinet in the peace process at the time the play was staged.[114] As McGuinness said in an interview, Blair and Mowlam have each had to 'deal with dangerous fire, and it's going to be very hard to reduce all that'.[115] But there is a change in Ulster's mood, a consensus now that peace can be secured and made permanent, and that surely owes something to the fact that people are listening to Mo Mowlam's female voice, which carries in it, unmistakably, a female principle. The File, a female court bard, comes into play when we put the male principle aside for a time in order that reconciliation take hold.

4

'The Voice of the Voiceless': Representation of Women's Reality and the Eighties in Ireland

In order to understand McGuinness's plays it is necessary to know something about their settings and the context in which they were written and produced. The three works discussed in this chapter, two stage plays, *The Factory Girls* (1982), *Baglady* (1985), and one television drama, *The Hen House* (1990), demand this kind of contextualisation – the context itself being Ireland in the late Seventies and Eighties.[1] All of these works are about Irish women, written by a male playwright in the persona of a woman, but none of them has been positively included by feminist critics in their discussion of Irish feminist drama or film.[2] The reason is, perhaps, simple: McGuinness is a male writer. But what is feminist theatre or film? Is it of women for women by women, meaning that men are always less competent than women to represent women's reality? The more avowedly feminist critics would say yes.

Feminist criticism, at least in the form we know today, dates from the 1970s. During the first phase of development of this relatively young field, feminist critics aimed to overturn the negative and stereotypical representations of women which cropped up in texts by male writers. Traditional systems of representation tended to distort, silence, and oppress the reality of women's lives, to objectify women through the male gaze. Kate Millet, in her *Sexual Politics* (1970), for example, criticises the insidious operation of traditional patriarchal systems, analysing texts by male writers. She argues that sexual politics is based in misogyny, which leads to women's oppression both in society and at home. When this kind of approach is adopted, the works of male authors, 'canonised' in literary curriculum, become targets of attack.

In the second phase, labelled 'Gynocritics' by Elain Showalter, the focus shifted to female writers, who posssess their own body of values, methods, and traditions. Showalter writes: 'To see women's writing as our primary subject forces us to make the leap to a new conceptual vantage point and to redefine the nature of the theoretical problem before us. It is no longer the ideological dilemma of reconciling revisionary pluralism but the essential question of difference.'[3] These are, in a way, effective tactics to reveal the inequalities of women in culture and society and to rediscover neglected women writers and evaluate them in a female literary tradition.

But might this shift espoused by Showalter not have a debilitating effect on feminist criticism? I am tempted to imagine the reaction of certain feminist critics to the works in this chapter if they had been written by the woman called Fionnuala McGonigle,[4] Dido's nom de plume in *Carthaginians* when he writes *The Burning Balaclava*, the play-within-a-play. These works might then be acclaimed as pioneering examples of feminist theatre/film in Ireland. *Is* the sexual identity of the writer so important? When asked whether *The Factory Girls* is 'a feminist play', McGuinness was very careful in his use of the word, 'feminist': 'I've great respect for certain feminists and the challenge they present to our own ways of thinking, but I don't think any man has a right to call himself a feminist.'[5] Elsewhere, he insisted that Irish theatre needed women playwrights:

There's a crying need, a desperate need for more women playwrights. Women's names spring immediately to mind in other forms of literature. There is Mary Lavin in the short story, Elizabeth Bowen in the novel, Eavan Boland in poetry and there are many more names. I think and intend no disrespect to any woman playwright in saying that it is difficult for any woman to find an audience for her work here. There's nothing like greater numbers of women playwrights emerging and uniting to lessen that difficulty.[6]

It is true that women were, and to some extent still are, underrepresented in the decision-making bodies in Irish theatre business: fewer female playwrights, fewer directors, and fewer members on the boards and managements. Even actresses face difficulties in finding places in the theatre, because there are, on the whole, fewer female than male roles. Charabanc, an 'all-women theatre company', was founded in Belfast in 1983, in order to create works for them. At the same time, a strong objection was raised by the women who worked in the Irish theatre against such labels as 'women's theatre' or 'all-women theatre company'. As Eleanor Methven, co-founder of Charabanc points out, few people regard or mention McGuinness's all-male *Sons of Ulster* as 'men's theatre', whereas Charabanc's all-female *Lay up your ends* is referred to as 'women's theatre'. They need equal employment opportunities, but they are 'adamant that their work should not be ghettoised as 'women's theatre'.[7]

If they do not want to be 'ghettoised', women should not monopolise 'women's theatre', either. *The Factory Girls* is a powerful representation of Irish women, and so, in their own ways, are the other two plays discussed in this chapter. We will, therefore, look closely at these works, focusing on their depiction of women's experience, and on the social context in which they were written.

A main incendiary to 'the Troubles' in Northern Ireland, which began in 1968, was the treatment of Catholics, then rated as 'second-class citizens'. Northern Ireland was a largely Protestant state:[8] it has been its raison d'etre since partition in 1922, and how, in many ways, it defines itself in opposition to the Catholic Republic of Ireland. However, the problem of gender lies athwart this opposition: women on both sides of the border, or on both sides of the sectarian divide, were oppressed. In the North, the campaigns for equality of Catholic and Protestant seldom widened to include equality of man and woman. Both men and women demonstrated for civil rights. We can see in photographs taken at the time how many women and children took part in civil rights marches. Yet, Bernadette Devlin,[9] commenting on the women who were behind the Free Derry Wall in the film *Mother Ireland*,[10] said that 'even though they had demonstrated, women were still coming home and cooking. Women were still being oppressed at home.' The wall, on which the slogan, 'You Are Now Entering Free Derry', was written, and is still there today, was supposed to be a symbol for freedom, but women were nonetheless oppressed behind it. With reference to the Irish historical context, it has often been pointed out by commentators that nationalism does not go together with feminism. Irish nationalism, it is argued, is a patriarchal ideology rooted in traditional Catholicism, subordinating women and excluding them from the official version of Irish history. The Civil rights movement, consisting mostly of Catholics, seems, if Bernadette Devlin is correct, to have inherited this aspect of Irish nationalism.

McGuinness does not directly mention this kind of oppression of women, but in his first play, *The Factory Girls,* set at a time of recession in Donegal, it is hinted at in various ways. It is a play about five women, aged from sixteen to sixty, who work for a local shirt factory and go on a wild-cat strike. Examples of gender inequality and unkind treatment by the Church include a husband demanding a clean shirt for Sunday while his wife is on strike, and a priest not supporting the striking women when asked to say Mass for them. In Derry/Londonderry and part of Donegal, the area where McGuinness came from, many women were employed in shirt factories, and were often the breadwinners of the family. McGuinness's own mother and aunts worked in shirt factories in Buncrana.[11] As a novice dramatist, McGuinness tried to record this culture in which he grew up: 'It's part of a culture of work', he said, 'and all cultures need to be recorded'.[12]

This is also a play about freedom. In the 1996 published version,[13] Rebecca, named after Rebecca West from Ibsen's *Rosmersholm,* quotes from Olive Schreiner:

'I saw a woman sleeping. In her sleep she dreamt Life stood before her and held in each hand a gift – in the one Love, in the other Freedom. And she said to the woman, Choose. And the woman waited long and she said, Freedom.' I heard the woman laugh in her sleep. (*P1,* 89)

Schreiner's *Woman and Labour* (1911) is widely acclaimed as a 'bible' of the women's movement and McGuinness's quotation reflects his interest in women's issues. It should be noted, however, that he quotes not from her 'political' writings but from 'Life's Gifts', an allegory collected in *Dreams and Dream Life and Real Life.*[14] Allegories arouse more powerful, more emotional responses than theories. The passage from Shreiner was originally an epigraph to the 1982 and 1988 publications of the play, where it is slightly longer than the above quotation. After the woman choses Freedom, it continues with: 'Life said, Thou hast well chosen. If thou hadst said Love, I would have given thee that thou didst ask for; and I would have gone from thee and returned to thee no more. Now, the day will come when I shall return. In the day I shall bear both gifts in one hand.' And then, the final line: 'I heard the woman laugh in her sleep.'[15] The message is simple but powerful. There is no such thing as 'Love' without 'Freedom'. Moreover, it is instinctively difficult for women to choose 'Freedom' first. Though McGuinness knew very well that it was quite improbable that a woman factory worker like Rebecca would know, would get access to, such a book,[16] he still wanted her to voice the decision for Freedom. He also made the final line of the quotation Rebecca's own: it is Rebecca herself who 'heard the woman laugh in her sleep'.[17]

McGuinness made another alteration in the 1996 version at the very end: he has Rosemary say to Rebecca, 'Come on, Rebecca, waken.' Rebecca replies: 'I have, woman, I've wakened' (P1, 89). Coincidentally, the word 'waken' echoes what 15–year-old Ann Lovett, who died giving birth in an open-air grotto in 1984, used to shout after nightfall in the street of Granard, Co. Longford: 'Wake up, Granard.'[18]

In the South, religion was, and to some extent still is, a force for women's oppression: a list of constitutional bans, proscribing contraception, abortion and divorce, was evidence of the dominant role of the Catholic Church in the state. During the years 1982 to 1985, when The Factory Girls and Baglady were staged in Dublin, women's issues began to take on a new urgency. When the Pope, John Paul II, visited Ireland for three days in 1979, he appeared to make an enormous impact on Irish society. In his sermon at Knock, the Pope emphasised 'a long spiritual tradition of devotion' of Irish people to the Virgin Mary. He then addressed the Virgin herself: 'We entrust to your *motherly* care the land of Ireland, where you have been and are so much loved. Help this land to stay true to you and your Son always'[19] (emphasis added). People involved in the pro-life amendment campaign, which was launched in June 1981, must have greatly been encouraged by the Pope's words in Ireland. In retrospect, it seems that his visit and the pro-life amendment campaign, which culminated in the triumphant referendum in 1983,[20] ironically led to the uncovering of the long-hidden secrets of 'this holy Ireland', which included such phenomena as 'unmarried mothers',[21] domestic sexual abuse, abortion, and infanticide.

Twenty years later, in The Irish Times, Patsy McGarry assesses his visit as 'a failure': 'If his intention then was to stem the 'filthy modern tide' threatening to overwhelm the country, it is hard to disagree. He may have put starch in the resolve of the bishops and some of the faithful to resist the contraceptive culture, divorce and abortion, but it was to no avail.'[22] He then lists the changes in Ireland following his visit: 'Contraceptives became available here on prescription in 1979 itself, with condoms available to all over-18s from 1985. The introduction of divorce was held back in a 1986 referendum but became legal in 1995. Abortion was banned in a 1983 referendum, but there was the X case in 1992. It was followed by the right-to-travel and information referendum, which was passed in 1992 also, and which allowed abortion where 'the life, as distinct from the health, of the mother' was at risk.'

Margo Harkin,[23] a film director from the North, (who, in 1998, made a BBC documentary on McGuinness, 'Clear the Stage'), remembers the widespread impact made by the death of Ann Lovett, which was reported on 31 January 1984:

Ann Lovett is the one that affected all of us: that a fifteen year old was sexually active, that she gave birth alone, and that she was found next to the grotto, the place of the Virgin Mary who has been the role model for many Irish women. (She certainly was for me when I was growing up.)[24]

Ann Lovett's death next to the statue of the Virgin was very symbolic: she must have craved the 'motherly care', as the Pope had put it, of the Virgin. However, in 'The Statue of the Virgin at Granard Speaks', a poem by Paula Meehan, the Virgin's care was absent. Meehan's Virgin says: 'I did not move,/I didn't lift a finger to help her,/ I didn't intercede with heaven,/ nor whisper the charmed word in God's ear.'[25]

On the 14th April of the same year in which Ann Lovett and her baby died, another baby was found dead on the White Strand beach, three miles from Cahirciveen, Co. Kerry. According to Nell McCafferty, 'his neck was broken and he was stabbed twenty-eight times in the neck and chest.'[26] This came to be known as 'the Kerry Babies Case', and McCafferty records the story of 25 year old Joanna Hayes, who was suspected of the murder of this baby – a crime which, it was subsequently discovered, she had never committed. In *A Woman to Blame: the Kerry Babies Case*, published just after the official inquiry closed, McCafferty relates how, in contrast to the protected privacies for men involved in the case, this investigation displayed for public scrutiny a woman's most intimate sexual history and inflicted a public humiliation on her and her family.

The following year, 1985, was the year of the moving statues. The first sighting of an animated Virgin Mary was in Asdee, County Kerry, in February. Then Marian statues throughout the Republic began moving. This included one in Ballinspittle, Co. Cork, where, typically, thousands flocked and miraculous cures were reported. A woman from Cork, for example, who had been completely deaf for nearly twenty years was reported to have recovered her hearing during her visit to this particular statue. McCafferty suggests that these phenomena were 'a direct result of Ireland's highly publicised debates surrounding female sexuality, divorce, and abortion.'[27] Angela Bourke regards these phenomena as 'the end of a thirty-year period during which the position of Irish women had changed almost beyond recognition: between the Marian year, 1954, during which most of the grottoes were built or planned, and 1984, women had indeed moved.'[28] In the introduction to *Seeing is Believing: Moving Statues in Ireland* (1985), Colm Tóibín catches the general atmosphere of that year:

The Kerry Babies Tribunal, the bad weather, the Air India crash, the death of Ann Lovett, the national debt, facts and divisions which came to light during the Amendment debate, unemployment, the hunger strikes in the North, boring television programmes in the summer, the failure of Garret FitzGerald to improve the lot of anyone in the country, simple piety, nostalgia for the happiness and harmony induced by the Papal visit, fear that the church has moved too far away from things of the spirit and too far into the public domain, simple curiosity, the feeling that more sin is being committed than ever before, the sense that things cannot go on as they have been going, the need to pray in the darkness in the company of others.[29]

Baglady was written and staged in this climate. It was a pure coincidence, McGuinness said, that the Kerry Babies and Ann Lovett cases, and the public debate which ensued, should occur while he was writing and rehearsing the play. He admired the courage of Maureen Toal, who played the title role for the first performance at the Peacock, because society was not, he believed, ready to accept the themes of *Baglady* at that time.[30] In a heart-rending monologue, Baglady tells us, in an oblique manner, of her rape by her own father, of the birth of a child, and of a subsequent infanticide.

Baglady looks not only into the evils perpetrated behind the closed doors of the family home, but also into the homelessness which is often the only recourse of the abused. In the first study ever carried out on homeless women in Ireland, *But Where Can I Go: Homeless Women In Dublin*, Stanislaus Kennedy reports that there were nearly 400 homeless women in Dublin in 1983, and that 'some became homeless after a family death, family disruption, desertion, violence at home, rape or incest.'[31] McGuinness need not have been quite so anxious about *Baglady*'s audience: the play was well received. One review even said that 'the Mason-McGuinness combination is a most interesting one, both for Irish theatre and for *Irish society* (emphasis added).'[32]

Of course, McGuinness's trepidation was not without foundation. A year later he was to face the hostile reaction of the Irish audience to the scene in *Innocence* (1986) where Caravaggio acts as a pimp for the Cardinal, acquiring rent boys for him. Yet, this scene acquired, in retrospect, a prescience, foretelling the Catholic Church's scandals in the Nineties, when case after case of priests' sexual abuse of boys came to light. According to *The Irish Times*, about fifty priests or brothers were either convicted or awaiting trial on charges of child abuse by the end of the decade. 'When the social history of our time is written', said the editorial, 'the early months of 1996 will figure as a period of stark revelation, a final drawing away of the veils from a darker, hidden Ireland. These days and weeks have marked a convergence of suppressed grief, of buried secrets and of enduring pain.'[33]

The last work dealt with in this chapter is *The Hen House*(1990). This television play is loosely based on an actual event in Co. Down in 1956, which came to be known as 'Patrick Murphy case', a case with which Seamus Heaney, too, engaged, in his poem 'Bye Child'. Mrs Margaret Murphy, a 45–year-old widow, was sentenced to nine months' imprisonment when she pleaded guilty to wilful neglect of her seven-year-old son, Patrick. She had kept her illegitimate son in a henhouse outside for almost all of his life until he was found. The child was discovered 'after children at play had told their parents that they had seen a young "Tarzan" and when a child's father had watched and called in the welfare authorities'.[34] He could neither walk nor speak when he was taken to a Belfast welfare institution. Mr Basil Kelly, counsel for Mrs Murphy, commented: 'This woman had already suffered much. The full glare of publicity has been shining on her private life, and it is fair to say that gossip and distortion will always follow her. She had had to confess to a mistake she made in her past life, and there is another factor which is even more hurtful, she had had to plead guilty to a crime that any mother would be ashamed to admit.'[35]

Baglady and *The Hen House* could not have been written in the Seventies or Sixties. People were not then ready to confront their own darknesses without its pitching them into an irremediable negativity. 'There's a lot of people who could find what happens in *King Lear* deeply offensive', McGuinness said, 'but yet it is in some way healthy because Shakespeare found the language for these terrors and one feels less alone in fear when someone has voiced them in a way that we can all hear.'[36] McGuinness himself seemed to find the language and voices for certain terrors, to tell the stories of Irish women.

The Factory Girls

McGuinness attended a writer's workshop in Galway in 1980, organised by the Irish Arts Council, and this is where he started writing his first play, *The Factory Girls*. Patrick Mason, who, in 1982, was to produce the play at the Peacock Theatre in Dublin, ran the workshop. As mentioned before, McGuinness wrote the play to record the culture in which his mother and aunts had worked, and he dedicated it to them. It is interesting to note that another dramatist from Donegal, Brian Friel, wrote a play – *Dancing at Lughnasa* (1990)[37] – in memory of his mother and aunts, and that he, too, dedicated the work to them. Both plays, Friel's and McGuinness's, evince deep affection for the women who surrounded and cared for the playwrights when they were boys. They listened to the speech, the sharp exchanges of their mothers and aunts, the humour, joy, bile, and infelicity of these women's words. Each play brings to life what are already vivid memories of the past.

Bringing such loved people to life is 'a political act', according to McGuinness, whose favourite playwright is Ibsen: 'Because his politics have a passion and they're not just based on intellect.'[38] *The Factory Girls*, however, is not propaganda: McGuinness certainly deals with the industrial background to the play, but the foreground is the sustained vigour of the women in the face of suffering.

Shane McGuinness, the playwright's younger brother, relates an event that occurred when his brother was preparing to write the play:

One day Frank held a shirt up in front of Mum, and asked her what did she see. I thought he was going off his head, what did he think she saw? As it turned out he was only seeking information for his first play, *The Factory Girls*. Mother was an examiner in the local shirt factory and knew all about shirts.[39]

McGuinness transformed what his mother told him into one of the play's most memorable exchanges: that between Rohan, the young Catholic manager of the factory, and Ellen. For Rohan, a shirt is 'a simple piece of coloured cloth, stitched together . . . a unit of production that I need to see go out this factory quicker and in greater numbers' (*P1*, 36–37). Ellen sees it differently:

Let me tell you what I see. I see a collar. Two cuffs. Eight buttons. Eight buttonholes. Bands. A back. Two sides. A lower line. When I look closer, do you know what else I see? A couple of thousand stitches. Why do I see it? I've been trained to see it. ' (*P1*, 37)

Ellen, a woman in her fifties, is the leader of the strike, and is thus the person with whom the factory management wants to negotiate. When she is called into their office, she asks instead that Rohan, and Bonner, the union man, come down to the shop floor to explain the situation to all of them. There, the manager suggests that voluntary redundancies will be necessary and he urges the women to accept a new production quota. The women are unwilling to accept either redundancy or a new quota. Eventually, Ellen instigates and leads the wild-cat strike. With supplies of food and alcohol, the five women occupy Rohan's office.

Ellen always takes the lead, but the other four are far from docile followers. From Una, the eldest, who is in her sixties, to Rosemary, who is sixteen, the sharpness of their talk is the only weapon they have.

Ellen: Your skin can take it(smoking), dear. It's hard to ruin a Brillo pad.
Una: It's better than being shaped like a Dettol bottle.
Ellen: What's that supposed to mean?
Una: I don't know, but I'm glad it annoyed you. (*P1*, 19)

This is one of many examples of their spiky, quick exchanges, by which they liven up their somewhat dull, routine work and support each other. There is little real bullying or harassment. They are enjoying themselves.

During the occupation of Rohan's office, however, the situation begins to change: they are made anxious by various threats over the phone. Una receives a call from her seventy-year old sister, Susan, who is, in a pub, drunk. The women have teased Una for being taken care of by her 'big sister', but now they overhear the telephone conversation only to learn that it is Una who actually minds the older sister, and that her solidarity with them means that this sister is now without her care. Rohan calls them, warning them to leave, suggesting that they will bring blame and bad fortune on themselves if they continue. The women phone the parish priest, asking him to come and say Mass for them, only to be refused. The church gives no help or support. Before putting down the phone, Una says: 'I'd just like you to know, father, I think you are very very cruel' (*P1*, 66).

Under the pressure of these threats and anxieties, the bond that links the women seems to slacken. Vera is deeply disturbed by the fact that her two little children have measles. She cannot decide whether she should stay on with the other women or leave to take

care of her children (and her husband, another big child). Ellen
suggests that she 'slip out well on in the night and come down
early in the morning', adding that: 'I know how you can worry
about them. Didn't I have to go through it too? (*P1*, 69)' Ellen has
suffered the loss of three children from TB: she understands very
well Vera's distress. But Vera intentionally misinterprets what
Ellen says, implying that her own children might die as Ellen's
did, and that Ellen might have been somehow remiss in her duties
as a mother.

McGuinness once said that the play is 'challenging to all the
internalised prejudices we have about women. The convention
about women that they're bitching, that they're snobby, that
they're too concerned about their physical appearance. This is
more true about men. These conventions have been transferred to
women by men.'[40] In the play, 'bitching' and bullying never last
long. Vera is immediately ashamed of her reply to Ellen and
apologizes; and Ellen responds with a terse, yet clement, 'All
right.'

Una then opens a bottle of whiskey and they take turns to sing.
A strike, usually a grim, serious business, becomes a joyous
session which banished the women's anxieties. But it cannot last.
They begin to face up to the threats within, which, in a way, are
sometimes more ominous than the threats without. Ellen
remembers the blouse in which she was married: 'I burned it. I
burned it every stitch. After the burials (*P1*, 80).' It seems that the
burnt blouse symbolises the curse she cast on herself when her
three children died in quick succession, the burning itself
standing for the emptiness and self-hatred that followed their
deaths. Una, who has supported Ellen since her tragedy, says: 'I
heard you cursing your own life. The curse has been lifted. Fight
on(*P1*, 86).' In reply, Ellen mentions the smell of the room they are
in, and says that she wants to get out into the fresh air. She
continues:

But how could I get rid of the smell of myself? A nobody that has
nothing, beaten the day she walked into this godforsaken factory.
Would I have been somebody if I never set foot in it? It would have
taken luck, and I never chanced my own. A wasted life. Heartbreaking
isn't it? Another martyr for old fucking Ireland. Well here's one martyr
that's going to be carried to her grave squealing. (*P1*, 87)

She then leaves the room for the toilet and does not return to the
stage. It is hard for anybody to admit that she/he is a nobody and
has nothing, but this moment of self-reflection, no matter what its

accuracy in Ellen's case might be muddied by bitterness, startles the other women into realising that seeing oneself, looking into oneself, is a way forward. Their wild-cat strike brings them nowhere, if we mean success narrowly defined. Rebecca, however, insists that some facets of oppression can be changed, or that such a change can be at least attempted. The important thing for her is the attempt: it is a beginning, which makes things easier for all women who come after.

When Rosemary tells Rebecca her dream of running away from the threat of redundancy and the boredom of work and joining the circus, Rebecca tells her to 'steal a horse and release the gypsy in your soul, Sonja?' (*P1*, 45), referring to Rosemary's favourite story about a gipsy girl, Sonja and her pony. Near the end of the play, when Rosemary says she would fall in line, do what everybody else does, Rebecca again says: 'Steal a horse and get out. Get away as far as you can (*P1*, 88)', conveying the romantic, heroic image of a gypsy girl galloping free of everything mundane, unmagical, into a kingdom of freedom. However, Rebecca's fairy-tale sensibility should be read in tandem with her tough, prosaic line, 'how dirty can you fight?' (*P1*, 82). Rebecca suggests that they should go to any lengths in order to win the fight.

As McGuinness said, there is 'no hard and fast resolution to the story'. The fact that he twice rewrote the final scene reflects this. In the final version, the play ends with Rebecca saying: 'I have, woman, I've wakened.' (*P1*, 89)

Baglady

'I saw somebody drown once'(*P1*, 385). This is how the Baglady starts her bleak monologue, underlining her position as onlooker. But immediately after this, she says: 'I was carrying them in my arms' (*P1*, 385), putting herself in the picture of what she saw. She is the observer and at the same time the one observed. The Baglady then repeats once again: 'I saw someone drown. I saw' (*P1*, 385). These repetitions are then combined with a conjuction, 'but': 'But I didn't tell', she says, implying that if one sees something, one's instinct is to tell someone about it. 'But' she didn't tell in the past: 'now' the urge is too strong not to. She continues: 'Tell me now. Tell me to the water that took you.' Her way with words reflects her inner confusion, the sudden change of position from teller into listener her instability. She is the teller, the listener, and the told all at once; and she is the observer and the observed. These complications, which will define the dramatic structure of the play, are set forth in the very first eight lines of her monologue.

Then she begins to sing: 'Who's at the window, who? Who's at the window, who? (P1, 385)'. This imagery of a window, which is to recur frequently in her monologue, somehow mediates, refracts, contains the relation between the Baglady, the observer, and what she observes.[41] The window has been a key symbol of our way of looking at the world since the Fifteenth Century, which was when the linear perspective system – which, at first, literally viewed the world through a window-like frame – was born. Linear perspective has greatly influenced the way the world is framed intellectually, and how distance is perceived or imagined: since the Fifteenth Century, we have been looking at the world through a window. Filippo Brunelleschi explained 'the concept of a single vanishing point, toward which all parallel lines drawn on the same plane appear to converge, and the principle of the relationship between distance and the diminution of objects as they appear to recede in space.'[42] Stephen Heath, a literary and film theorist, argues that this window is still inflecting, controlling our style of perception: 'What is fundamental is the idea of the spectator at the window . . . that gives a view on the world – framed, centred, harmonious'.[43] With this framing device of the window, the spectator gains a rationalised means of perceiving the world.

A spectator, standing in front of a window, must remain still if linear perspective is to work:

The cost of such fixed centrality is the marginal distortion which ensues when the observer's eye is not correctly in position in the centre of the perspective projection but pulls to the edge. Anamorphosis is the recognition and exploitation of the possibilities of this distortion.[44]

Anamorphosis, a by-product of the linear perspective system, plays 'havoc with elements and principles; instead of reducing forms to their visible limits, it projects them outside themselves and distorts them so that when viewed from a certain point they return to normal'.[45] While she speaks, the Baglady, walks around the stage, as if trying to find that particular angle to create an anamorphosis of her world. Analogous to the relation between the perspective projection and anamorphosis, the Baglady's world wavers between 'appearance' and 'reality'.

Later, she tells of the room made of windows: 'In our house there's a room made from windows. I'm not allowed in, even to see out of it. But I can see it clearly. That's where they sleep, my mother and father. The room only appears when they're lying in it. They can change the shape of our whole house. They have magic' (*P1*, 395). The amorphous nature of this room embodies, as it were, the Baglady's anamorphosis of her world.

The Baglady evokes herself looking through the window in her own song; but in that song she is a child. Outside, a bad man is watching her through the window. The song, 'Who is at the window, who?', is often sung in Donegal[46] by parents to make their children behave at bedtime. The message of the song is obvious: as long as children are good and on the inside, they will be safe. The terror lurks outside, in the form of the bad man. But the audience soon realises that the Baglady is not at all safe in the room: her monologue is about the terror within. The confusion of this terror, both within and without, is conveyed in the following passage:

Sometimes you could look into the window and see your face. It moved, not like your face in the river swallowing you for ever. You could take your face out of the window. I looked through my face one day in the window and I saw my father and my mother. My mother wasn't there, and my father was moving. He called me by my name. It was my mother's. My mother. (*P1*, 388)

The Baglady watched her own face through the window. There she also saw her father and mother. But immediately after this, the presence of the mother is denied. Her father then called her both by her name and by her mother's name. Where was the Baglady? Was she outside, looking into the window at herself, her father, and her mother? Or did she just see herself and father? Or was she inside and looking at the reflection in the window, which functions as a mirror in the dark of night?

As discussed in Chapter Two, storytelling or narrative can function as a contemporary theatrical technique to reveal a character's hidden thoughts and feelings, 'while at the same time concealing them as fiction or at least distancing them as narration'.[47] Commenting on Beckett's *Not I*, Kristin Morrison says that, 'the character's attempts at evasion and disguise are particularly poignant'; and that 'telling a "story," providing an "account" of something, becomes a dramatisation of the character's struggle simultaneously to face and to avoid a deeply personal issue.'[48]

Even though McGuinness denies the direct influence of Beckett on his plays, especially when it comes to his female characters, saying that 'certainly the power women in the play (have), that's not due to Beckett',[49] the resemblance of *Baglady* to *Not I*, in light of Morrison's comment on the latter, is obvious: the Baglady always shies from involvement with what she tells, trying to disguise herself as a distanced narrator. She is a victim of twin desires: for confession and for concealment, as we have seen in the discussion about storytelling in *Carthaginians*. The Baglady wants to tell us what happened to her, but she has difficulty doing so. Reality still sneaks away, out of view. The urge to 'tell', which the Baglady evinces at the very beginning of her monologue, is immediately replaced with another, childish meaning of the word: 'I'll tell my father what you call me'(*P1*, 385). This kind slip into another semantic is continually distorting her narrative.

By introducing this 'you', who seems to speak ill of her, the Baglady pretends that she is a good little child under the protection of her 'respectable', 'decent' father. She is dependent on this image of her father, which is nevertheless an appearance, summoned up by her contorting words, an anamorphosis. 'He never touched me', she says, 'never raised his hand, never. I haven't a bad word to say against him. He played cards but he deserved respect' (*P1*, 386). There is something suspicious here: why should a daughter repeatedly underline the fact that her own father never touched her? This is one example of her concealments. The more she tries to hide about her father, the more our attention is directed at him. Again, theatrical distortion serves to emphasise a hidden meaning, triggering specific intuitions and guesses.

Her concealment is not lost on the audience, whose guesses, as they listen, harden into expectations. McGuinness regards this kind of expectation as very much in the Irish storytelling tradition. In reference to *Baglady*, he said:

I don't rely on traditional narrative structure. I generally like people to know well beforehand what is going to happen. And I think that is part of the Irish tradition, the storytelling tradition, which is the great tradition in Irish. Its strangeness can be emphasised only by hearing. The wonder can grow through repetition.[50]

The Baglady's discourse is littered with hints about what is to come. Her father's cunning, for example, sneaks out in her use of the word 'cards', again in combination with the conjunction 'but'. He played card games, and at the same time manipulated whatever or whoever was around him. Still, he deserves respect.

'Cards' are important factors in the way the members of this family relate to each other and to the world. The Baglady tells us that her mother told fortunes, that 'she could read people's cards' (*P1*, 388). When the Baglady handles the deck of cards later in the play, she reads them as her mother did; and she 'manipulates the cards as characters' (*P1*, 393) just like her father.

The Baglady starts fortune-telling with a deck of cards, which provides her with the means to keep the story going: she can retain a position as an objective third person for her story and feel less pain when she tells it. Fortune-telling usually forecasts the future. The Baglady, however, relates the past. The cards she draws personify the characters of her story. We gradually understand, through the way she questions each card, that the king of diamonds represents her father, the queen of hearts her mother, the queen of spades the Baglady herself, and the ace of spades her son.

When she speaks of the queen of spades, the Baglady describes herself as if she were somebody else: 'A black lady. Bitter. The quiet card. This one keeps her counsel because she's angry, and no one knows that anger's source. She has the face of a corpse' (*P1*, 392). This is actually her self-image, which reveals her sense of guilt. Next, the Baglady turns to the queen of hearts, her mother, a figure who knows the secret in her daughter's heart, but will not speak of it. The queen of hearts also had a son, who was taken from her; the Baglady obscurely hints that history has repeated itself, that she and her mother are, in a certain dark sense, just the same. This could be a delusion on the Baglady's part, a product of her agony, but it still chills with a breath of unverifiable truth. Finally, the Baglady tells her father's story:

Some night he turned into a black dog and took himself out walking . . . one day this dog grabbed the man's daughter by the throat. She went hysterical but the dog wouldn't let go. It chained her up. Then one night the dog changed back to the man. When he spoke to his daughter she thought he was the devil. He said she was his wife. He'd come back for her. She got such a shock she jumped that hard from her chain that she tore her head away from the rest of her and all that was left behind was her skin and bones. The man whistled for his dog and it came running. He set the dog on his daughter's body and it ate all that was left of her. (*P1*, 394)

At last, she identifies the man with her own father: 'I know now for sure that's my father' (*P1*, 394). However, even after this painful recognition of her father's sexual abuse, she accuses not her father but herself, condemning herself as a dirty little child. The only way to get out of this impasse, to keep going, is to adopt her father's voice, which assumes the tenderness of a parent, soothing his crying child: 'Stop that crying. Hear me? Stop it. Be a good girl. Your daddy does it for your own good. You can be a bad girl. You have to do as your daddy tells you. Don't you? Stop that crying' (P1, 396). This apparently caring father then shows her her mother's wedding ring and promises to buy a ring and a white dress for her own wedding. He has, he believes (or at least, wants her to believe) the right to be father to a bride: 'You'll be crying when your daddy gives you away at the altar . . . They say if a girl sleeps with a wedding ring in her bed she will have lovely dreams about the man she'll marry, the house they'll have and their children, boys and girls together' (P1, 396).

In this hypocritical disguise, her father controls her as he wishes:

She did as she was told. And she could keep a secret. A big secret. And because she could keep secrets, her father gave her a golden necklace. He trusted her with his life. When she kept her mouth closed, the necklace shone like the sun and she was beautiful, very beautiful. But if she breathed a word of their secrets, the necklace grew black, blacker, and it tightened about her throat, thighter and tighter, twisting her face up, so she hardly had a face and she couldn't breathe again until she said she was sorry. (P1, 396–7)

Her father's prohibition on telling binds her like the *geis* of ancient Irish mythology. If she tells, she will be a bad girl and suffer torment. If she does not tell, she will also be tormented. She is caught, racked between two impossible courses of action. Yet she eventually finds something almost like, symbolically akin to, a solution: she performs a ceremony to bury her agony and her long-dead son. The Baglady winds the chain into a heap, as though building a cairn for the dead. She conducts a symbolic funeral for her unbaptised child, whose body was, it seems, thrown into the black river, because, in Christian tradition, unbaptised children should not be buried in consecrated ground. On the chain heap, which stands for her bind, she drops the queen of hearts, the king of diamonds, and the queen of spades – her mother, father, and herself. So now, the family are attending the funeral, and at the same time, they are buried in the cairn, with the child who sprang out of sin. The ace of spades, which represents her son, is then torn in pieces and dropped into a red lemonade bottle. This is a version of water-burial, the red liquid symbolising her own blood. The Baglady shakes the bottle and pours the contents on to the chain heap as though purifying her son's grave. She then places the bottle, the coffin, on top of the chain.

This is a strange mixture of pagan and Christian burial. She still tries to follow the Christian tradition, the tradition by which she was so harshly rejected. The Baglady alludes to the involvement of a priest, who here takes the form of the knave of clubs: 'A man in black came to the house and said she was a liar. But he forgave her because he took her with him to the house of God' (*P1*, 398–9). The priest, and the nuns, 'women in black, who washed her in fire'(*P1*, 399), hold out no prospect of real salvation for her. They represent the negative aspect, the hypocrisy of the (Irish) Church. In *Dolly West's Kitchen*, McGuinness shows us how children born out of wedlock were treated in convents. Anna, a servant girl to the Wests, tells of her experience in such a place: 'Could it be any harder than the back of the bitches' hands that reared me? Dear kind nuns? More like mad women.'[51]

The anger McGuinness feels towards church institutions and their hypocrisy is clear here. When he was asked to write on sustenance for the soul, he responded with qualified spleen:

They celebrate the human body and the human mind in all our changes and contrariness, our sorrow and our secrets. If they're holy it's because they are angry and even in despair, they are never resigned. Their hatred of women is hateful, so they are not perfect, and that gives them the edge that saves them from being sacred. They are in no way heroic, but they try to be truthful – that's as good a criterion for prayer – to God, to man, to woman – as any I'd expect.[52]

Despite the anger he feels, or because of it, the end of the play is marked by poignant Christian terms and imagery. The Baglady's son was said to be 'nailed' to a river, alluding, of course, to the nailing to the cross. This analogy, however, just underlines the difference between 'the Father and the Son', and that unholy father of her own and his offspring. The play ends with the Baglady's harrowing prayer:

With this ring, I thee wed. This gold and silver, I thee give. With my body, I thee worship. And with all my worldly goods, I thee endow. In the name of the Father and of the Son of the Holy Ghost. (*P1*, 399)

This bleak metaphor of a wedding ceremony shows how strongly the Baglady is grasped by Catholicism. She lives by its mythic motifs – the cycle of Christ's coming into the world, suffering, dying, resurrection, and return to heaven – in order to cope with the death of her son and of her own past.

The Hen House

The Hen House, a television play commissioned by BBC Northern Ireland, was transmitted in September 1990 and received both the Prix del'Intervision and the Prix de l'Art Critique at the 1990 Prague International Television Festival.

It is based loosely on the 'Patrick Murphy case', which occurred in the mid-Fifties, and McGuinness accurarely depicts the bleakness of rural Ireland at that time. Lily, a widow, hides her illegitimate son in one of the hen houses in her farm yard. The child is discovered by one of the McCloskey's twin boys. The McCloskeys are her neighbours, and it is hinted, as Marin McLoone[53] points out, that Mr McCloskey, a local shop-keeper, is the father of the child. McCloskey reports the matter to the local police. The boy is taken into public care and Lily is arrested.

Under interrogation by a young policeman Lily is unable to give a convincing reason for doing such a thing to her son. It is obvious, however, that she was ashamed of his illegitimacy and did not know what to do with him when he was born. The classroom scene, in which a schoolmistress punishes even minor misbehaviour on the part of her pupils, exemplifies the intolerance of this society. Lily is also a victim of this intolerance. This poor mother is not entirely lacking in any motherly care or affection for the boy. She continually addresses him, though in a murmur, and though we never see him. When a letter with some money arrives from her daughter in London, she says to this unseen entity that it is from 'your big sister'. She then buys a box of chocolates for him and puts it in the hen house. When she cooks a meal, she does so for two, for herself and for the son. On her bed a set of child's clothes is spread,[54] as though he is lying there with her – there is a yearning for intimacy but it is always displaced, expressed through objects rather than direct touch. Everything implies that it is only in her imagination that Lily can live cheek by jowl with her son.

Although the Baglady has difficulty in coping with her own story, she manages to tell it and to bury her son in her own way.

Lily does not have a voice to tell her own story. But through the bleak scenery caught by the camera, we somehow hear the voice of the voiceless. This silent voice is eloquent enough to convince the viewers that a sombre but certain hope creeps into the last scene, where the child spreads out his arms, as if showing clemency to his mother.

5

The Families at War: McGuinness's Irish 'Comedy of Bad Manners'

I would like to describe the two plays in this chapter, *The Bird Sanctuary* (1994) and *Dolly West's Kitchen* (1999), as McGuinness's Irish 'comedy of bad manners'. This is a term McGuinness used when discussing the works of Brecht and Jane Austen: 'For some strange reason Brecht always reminds me of Jane Austen. Theirs is a comedy of bad manners.'[1] The comedy of manners was originally a theatrical genre which flourished in England during the Restoration period. It makes play with the social codes of the upper-middle and upper classes; their witty and sophisticated exchanges are its characteristic features. Those who supplied London's theatres with such plays were often Dublin-born Anglo-Irish playwrights: William Congreve, George Farquhar and Richard Brinsley Sheridan. Another of that clan, Oscar Wilde, revived the tradition towards the end of the Nineteenth century. These plays are based on their amused but acute observations of English manners and conventions. It is ironic that despite his origin in Ireland, Wilde's comedies are often thought of, especially by non-Irish critics, as perfect examples of 'English' humour. Such an opinion overlooks, among other things, the importance of the outsider's eye for these comedies.

The troubled relation between Ireland and England is, as we have seen in Chapter Three, one of McGuinness's main concerns. And his way of dealing with it is subtle, even-handed, entailing rather more than simply labelling Ireland the oppressed and colonised, England the oppressor and coloniser. He knows there is also a very complex, even subliminal, relation or exchange between Irishness and Englishness. This is what Declan Kiberd tries to explore and decipher in Oscar Wilde in *Inventing Ireland*: 'The man who believed that a truth in art is that whose opposite is also true was quick to point out that . . . every sensitive Irishman must have a secret Englishman within himself – and *vice-versa.*'² From this standpoint, this chapter shares something with Chapter Three. There, in our investigation of Englishness and Irishness in *Mutabilitie*, we came across many quotations from Wilde's *Importance of Being Earnest*, even though McGuinness's play stands some distance from any comedy of manners.

McGuinness greatly admires Wilde and once expressed his own desire to be a part of that Irish tradition of a comedy of manners:

I don't know if you can see Wilde as influencing you as a playwright because the perfection of *The Importance of Being Earnest* is so self-contained and so rightly narcissistic that I don't think that it's in any way something that you can do anything other than stand back and gaze in amazement at. In my last play, *The Bird Sanctuary*, I very much tried to extend my own repertoire by writing a play which would be part of the Irish tradition of wit and that would go back to Farquhar, Congreve and Sheridan, with Wilde as the apex of what I was trying to achieve and ally that style to a contemporary series of dilemmas. I enjoyed doing that immensely, actually, and there would be, probably, the prime influence of Oscar Wilde in my theatre.³

Placing himself as an inheritor of the 'Irish tradition of wit', McGuinness is able to investigate and dissect a complicated contemporary series of dilemmas to do with the family: love and hatred; the relation between Irishness and Englishness; and (homo)sexuality.

The Bird Sanctuary (1994)

The Bird Sanctuary was staged at Dublin's Abbey Theatre in 1994, one hundred years after Wilde began writing *The Importance of Being Earnest*. *The Importance* is set in London and the English countryside, whereas McGuinness's play is set in Booterstown, a posh suburb of Dublin. It is a play about the Henryson family who own a big house overlooking the Booterstown bird sanctuary, about love and hatred within the family. The eldest member of the family, Eleanor, is a successful painter who has lived as something of a recluse in the house for three years, with her artistic disorder. She has been busy with her huge painting of the sanctuary: if she does not paint the bird sanctuary, she believes, it will be ruined by global warming, pollution, and the construction of a road. Her sister, Marianne, is a successful doctor in England, married to an Englishman. Their brother Robert has a son, Stephen, who, as an assistant, helps Eleanor paint. Stephen's mother Tina, unable to deal with her son's homosexuality, has thrown him out of her home. The play opens when Marianne comes back from England to the house to discuss the possibility of selling her share in it.

The big house is another persona of the play: both Eleanor and Marianne address it as 'dear House'. It was built just before the Famine in 1843, so it represents the wealth of the Anglo-Irish ascendancy in Dublin of that time. There is a family myth about Queen Victoria's recognising its beauty when she visited Dublin in 1849. So the story goes, the queen knocked on the door, but there was no proper welcome. Instead, she was greeted by a forbidding presence: 'And seeing the queen's sorrow, the woman of the house, a beautiful old woman dressed in black, opened at the door. This woman said to the queen of England –All sins are forgiven' (*Bird*, 7). The Henrysons are not the descendants of this beautiful woman in black, since they only obtained the house in 1929. They were 'the nouveau riche of the Free State'⁴ who were not affected by the Great Depression of 1929. McGuinness makes it clear that a complex history lies behind Irish prosperity of the 1990s. The house has been witness to Ireland's changes for over a century and a half.

When the play was staged in 1994, Ireland had just begun enjoying a new prosperity: the ignominious label applied to the Republic in the Seventies, 'the weakest member of the European Economic Community', was fading away. In May 1993, there was a very symbolic meeting in London between the British and Irish heads of state, Queen Elizabeth II and Mary Robinson, the first in seventy-one years of independence. 'The commentary on it', says Kiberd, 'in the British press was fascinating because there was a kind of envy of the Robinsonian persona built into a lot of it, particularly in the broadsheet press. Here was this modern woman, who had been elected on her own merit and had all these virtues and was articulate, beside this perfectly decent other woman who was just there because of, basically, inheritance.'⁵

The overall tenor of this Ireland is one of new affluence and confidence, and it is this very mode which makes a comedy of social manners again possible. Reflecting this new wealth, the prices of Eleanor's paintings are, according to her sister Marianne, 'ridiculously high' (*Bird*, 19). This painter has the artist's licence to shock people, as Wilde had. She is full of Wildean remarks, twisted though they are by her own logic. Despite her own claim to recluseness, she loves an audience and parties. Eleanor's favourite party piece, when the drink is flowing, concerns her

abortion and miscarriage – neither of which she ever had: 'Do you
know I'm one of the few Irishwomen to admit in public that I've
had an abortion. That, and a miscarriage' (*Bird*, 61). When Stephen
asks whom she most detests, she replies: 'I hate your mother. I
detest my sister. I ignore your father. But I like you, a little. Until
you turn against me. As you will, I hope' (*Bird*, 6). Her reason for
hating Stephen's mother, Tina, is just 'pleasure', a resonance of
Jack Worthing's 'Oh, pleasure, pleasure',[6] the pleasure that brings
him to town. Eleanor says: 'Pleasure, pure pleasure. How did you
spring from the loins of those two? I'm quite convinced the
hospital gave them the wrong baby' (*Bird*, 6).

New affluence, however, does not automatically bring
happiness to the Henrysons. As Tina says:

> More money being made. Not much happiness, but more money. Plenty
> of money. Less happiness. When there was less money, people were – I
> don't know – people were together, together in their misery, you know.
> Now they're alone in their misery. Aren't they? (*Bird*, 21)

Misery and unhappiness haunt the people in this light comedy:
Robert is 'a failure', for a doctor's son, something of a disappoint-
ment; Marianne's marriage to an Englishman is a failure, they are
on the verge of divorce; Stephen is a failure for his parents because
of his (homo)sexuality; their dead father was also thought a failure,
because he married their mother, a servant girl. The domestic
discord for the Henderson family is generalised in Eleanor's
remark: 'Families fight. All families fight' (*Bird*, 62). One characteristic of her wit is that it seems to revolve around hatred, which is,
ironically, the very thing that ties the family together; as she says:
'in this family, hate like love, is only a figure of expression' (*Bird*,
44). This kind of open admission of hatred seems actually to free
up, to facilitate, communication in the family: people become freer,
compared with hidden and oppressed hatred.

In addition to private conflict within the family, conflict between
Englishness and Irishness is revealed through Marianne's marriage
to an Englishman. As a professional Irishwoman living in England,
she has to go through what Wilde had to; as Kiberd explains:
'Wilde had discovered that an Irishman only came to consciousness
of himself as such when he left his country'.[7] With this
consciousness of his being Irish, Wilde, 'wearing the mask of the
English Oxonian', was 'paradoxically freed to become more "Irish"
than he could ever have been in Ireland'.[8] Marianne is different:

There are many many times I pass as an Englishwoman, and this helps me in my practice in Kent, where it is so important to build up a trust between patient and doctor . . . but after the trust is built up, I find it lost again, for I am an Irishwoman who sounds like an Englishwoman, and this undermines my trust in myself. (*Bird*, 31)

Eleanor does not have this problem, because she is an Irishwoman living in Ireland. According to Marianne, 'she doesn't give a shit about anyone' (*Bird*, 31). When Marianne points out that the room looks like a pig sty, she can light-heartedly joke: 'This was our parlour, dear. Don't the English believe we keep pigs in our parlour?' (*Bird*, 13). As a successful artist with wealth, she can nonchalantly joke about their poor past in Irish history. Eleanor still has a sharp eye for what has been going on in her sister's marriage and perceives in it the subtle work of Englishness clashing with Irishness. 'It's the terrible attraction of the Irish for the English, and the English for the Irish. Together, they behave as expected. She's mad, he's cruel, that's the way. They should never have married, but they are. And it's gone on so long, they're set in their ways' (*Bird*, 57).

Marianne's version of her strong sense of displacement is different. She remembers how her English husband would, in a joking manner, call her 'the Irish navvy', 'the Irish maid', or 'the Irish skivvy', and how deeply this hurt her:

We would be serving drinks before dinner, and if someone needed more ice or tonic, he'd say ask the Irish maid. All these years I've tried to fit in and through thick and thin I've made wonderful friends, but I didn't really belong there, although in general I loved people. And the older I get, the more I'm aware I did not belong there, yes. And I've wasted my life there, working my fingers to the bone. (*Bird*, 33)

In return, Stephen, tells a nicely twisted lie to lift her heart:

I'm having an affair with your husband. He visits Ireland secretly. I insisted we stay in the finest suite of the Shelbourne Hotel. We make love. I humiliate him each time. I make him do as he doesn't wish to. He obeys me. Then I call him my English maid. My English skivvy. And if he does not obey, if he is not my English maid, then he will know the strength of his Irish navvy. (*Bird*, 34)

Here, the metaphor about the relation between the two countries – that of weak lamenting Hibernia being raped by England – is reversed. Stephen, Marianne's gay nephew, is punishing, in his imagination, his English uncle-in-law.

In order to resolve this unhappy marriage, a fairly-tale device is introduced. Marianne's choice is to keep her husband, rather than to leave him, since, as Eleanor says, the Henrysons marry for life when they marry (*Bird*, 57). Marianne secretly asks Eleanor to use her power of witchcraft to kill her husband's young girlfriend, a Tasmanian, for whom he is about to leave her. Marianne promises her that if this plan succeeds, she will give up her share of the house in return. Eleanor has inherited this power from their dead mother, who was a servant girl to their father's family. Their mother, who brought her dark skills with her from 'the wild west of Ireland', reminds us, perhaps, of Nora Barnacle, Joyce's wife and inspiration. Though Joyce lived most of his life in self-imposed-exile, Nora always seemed to cloak him in the very essence of Ireland. Through their mother's and Eleanor's witchcraft, the Henrysons seem to carry within them a kindred essence, which is still vividly alive. The witchcraft, which utilises voodoo-like chicken bones tied with coloured thread, successfully kills the Tasmanian, who happens to be reading Tolstoy's *Anna Karenina* on a train when she dies in an awful train accident. This is another of McGuinness's jokes, since Tolstoy's heroine herself dies in a train accident. Marianne assures Eleanor that the house will now be Eleanor's for life. This killing is depicted in a similar manner to Algernon's killing of Bumbury in *The Importance of Being Earnest*. No one questions the implausibility of plot in Wilde's play. The farcicality of a lost child in a handbag, for instance, is read as coherent within the play's own fictional terms, and *The Bird Sanctuary* should be read in just this manner.[9]

Having faced their confusion and dark past, the play ends in a kind of serene harmony. Eleanor tells Marianne, who is about to return to her husband in England, that the painting of the sanctuary is finished:

I have locked myself away to seek that sanctuary. And dear, sister, I wish to show you why. For once, keep your silence. This is, as I've said, proof I have existed, proof we have lived in Booterstown Avenue. You have travelled the earth, to Asia, to Australia. This night let your carriage drive down our avenue. You see this house, walk up the path and enter. A woman answers you, for she saw a shiver pass through your soul. And seeing this sorrow, the woman, dressed in black, opens the door, shows you her room, points to the walls and lets one melt, so that you may be granted your wish, you shall walk with me into eternity, into the bird sanctuary that is waiting outside. It is as simple as stepping outside, Marianne. Don't, until I tell you. (*Bird*, 87)

This is something of a reminiscence of the wandering of Mary and

Lizzie. The stage direction stipulates that now 'the back wall magically reveals the birds'[sic] sanctuary' (*Bird*, 87). This life-affirming homage is paid by McGuinness to his own 'new' Ireland and to Booterstown, where he lives.

Dolly West's Kitchen (1999)

This play, set in McGuinness's home town of Buncrana in Donegal, was produced at the Abbey Theatre as part of the 1999 Dublin Theatre Festival. It draws a picture of an isolationist Ireland between 1943 and 45, the last years of the Second World War, which became known in Ireland as 'the Emergency'. Its neutrality was announced by de Valera (who was in 1932 elected the Taoiseach, Prime Minister of the Irish Free State), on 3 September 1939 when Britain and France declared war on Germany. 'Neutrality in a war in which Britain was involved was the clearest possible statement of Irish independence,'[10] but some people objected that neutrality was an inadequate response to Nazism. Terence Brown, in his survey of the period, well captures the mixed feelings of the people:

Some Irishmen and women certainly favoured a German victory in the military struggle. Attitudes of respect for Hitler's reconstruction of the German nation combined with an old Irish nationalist conviction that England's difficulty might prove Ireland's opportunity were reflected in a limited sympathy for the German war-effort and in the IRA's clumsy efforts to establish contacts with the German intelligence service. The majority of the population, however, probably hoped for British survival and after America entered the war, for an Allied victory. De Valera himself certainly favoured the Allies' cause.[11]

Pro-allied government co-operation was secretly conducted:[12] Ireland supplied food and work force for Britain; allied planes flying Irish air-space were overlooked; allied sailors and airmen wrecked in Ireland were allowed to return to the North when Germans were interned. Despite this pro-allied policy, the government kept up the public image of strict neutrality. Early in December 1942 De Valera even protested to Roosevelt about the stationing of American troops in the North. Reflecting this situation, one of the characters in the play says: 'My mind's on this war. We're living in a port . . . Buncrana is a port. Our beloved leader, De Valera, has warned this part of the country they might invade us for our ports, coming at us from all sides, the English, The Germans and the Yanks' (*D*, 5).

De Valera also paid a visit to Dr Hempel, the German Minister to Ireland, to express his condolences on the death of Adolf Hitler, again to maintain the country's strict neutrality. At the end of the war, there was a public exchange on the radio between de Valera and Churchill. Churchill expressed his bitterness about the Irish government's policy of neutrality and reproached Ireland for not having helped the allies. De Valera replied four days later:

> Mr Churchill makes it clear that, in certain circumstances, he would have violated our neutrality and that he would justify his action by Britain's necessity. It seems strange to me that Mr Churchill does not see that this, if accepted, would mean that Britain's necessity would become a moral code and that when this necessity became sufficiently great, other people's rights were not to count . . . Mr Churchill is proud of Britain's stand alone, after France had fallen and before America entered the war. Could he not find in his heart the generosity to acknowledge that there is a small nation that stood alone, not for one year or two, but for several hundred years against aggression; a small nation that could never be got to accept defeat and has never surrendered her soul?[13]

This speech struck the right chord of the majority of the Irish people. At the same time most people in Ireland and abroad regarded the Taoiseach's visit to Hempel as a 'blunder'.[14] Robert Fisk points out that 'it was that small, critical, explosive gesture which has often defined Irish neutrality – indeed, the country in the 1940s – for later generations'.[15] The country was left in some disfavour with the allies and would pay a huge political cost in the immediate post-war years. Indeed, a sense of shame, which is crystallised in the image as a backer of Nazism, is never to be blotted out from the national memory. It is possible that this memory might have affected Irish reception of the play; most of the Dublin reviews were unfavourable and negative, whereas in London it received many positive reviews.

This is the material and background for McGuinness's *Dolly West's Kitchen*. Dolly has returned from Mussolini's Italy to the big house where her mother, Rima, Dolly's sister, Esther and her husband Ned, and Dolly and Esther's younger brother, Justin, live. (The West family has much in common with the Henrysons of *The Bird Sanctuary*: the dead father who was a doctor; a big house that implies wealth; two daughters and a son.) In addition to the family members, there is a servant girl, Anna, who was brought up in a near-by convent because she was born out of wedlock. Three foreign soldiers, one English and two American, stationed across the border in Derry/Londonderry, come to visit the Wests on a regular basis. They are English Alec, Dolly's old friend from Trinity College, Dublin; and Marco and Jamie, two GIs found by Rima at the local pub. Alec and the GIs actually bring change, or 'a bit of badness, which is good', to use Rima's phrase.

The tone of the play is not so light-hearted as that of 'The Bird Sanctuary', which obviously belongs to the genre of comedy. Nevertheless, one should still categorise it as comedy, in much the same manner as Chekhov did his own plays, *The Cherry Orchard* and *Three Sisters*. And Patrick Mason, the director of *The Dolly West's Kitchen*, 'freely acknowledges its debt'[16] to these plays of Chekhov.

As in 'The Bird Sanctuary', there are also Wildean moments in this play. Here, the dominant personality is the spirited, adventurous, warm-hearted Rima West, mother of the three West children. McGuinness, whose mother died four years before the London production, wanted 'some form of elegy for her' . . . 'Not in an autobiographical way, but to create a character where I could pour that grief and respect'.[17] She dominates the whole course of the play, as does Lady Bracknell in *The Importance*. Rima is always in the centre of the play even after her death in the middle of it. We might consider Rima as Lady Bracknell's avatar in present-day Donegal, albeit disguised as a character from the 1940s. Some critics are puzzled by this play's lack of verisimilitude, which includes such instances as Rima's approving of her son's homosexuality at that time.[18] But this is to miss the point, since McGuinness aimed not for some historical drama faithfully based on life in 1943–45. This is a play *of* history, made for the purpose of providing a contemporary audience with the means for 'disentangling the contradictions of the present by placing them at a distance',[19] to borrow Fintan O'Toole's phrase. Patrick Mason writes in the programme for the London production of the play that 'in both form and content it is quintessentially a contemporary "Abbey" play.'[20] Lady Bracknell's main concern is to find an eligible young man for her daughter, whereas Rima's, in this modern world refracted through an old one, is to liberate her children from their sexual impasse: Esther's marriage with Ned is in deadlock; Dolly is unable to decide her future with Alec, and Justin's suppressed sexuality has turned him into a fanatical Nationalist.

Rima leads us to hilarious moments: when Dolly asks Anna, the servant girl, if she has found her mother, Rima, who overhears this, says: 'What do you mean, did you find Mammy? Was I lost or what?' (*D*, 5). This remark reminds one of Jack Worthing's reply to Lady Bracknell, when he was asked about his parents: 'I said I lost my parents. It would be nearer the truth to say that my parents seem to have lost me.'[21] When she speaks, this Lady Bracknell of Donegal can sound like the women of *The Factory Girls*, with their vital, vulgar repartee. In this sense, too, the play is an Irish comedy of bad manners. When Rima complains about being fed too many eggs, Dolly asks her what she wants. Rima replies: 'A slice of the cat's arse, please'. To this Dolly retorts: 'You've cut that many slices off the cat, it has no arse left' (*D*, 6). The sharp exchanges go further. Rima: 'The eggs will be enough to poison me.' Dolly: 'Mother dear, I would not poison you. That would be too slow' (*D*, 7). Here, as in *The Factory Girls*, McGuinness's memory of the Donegal quickness of tongue is at work.

'What Rima West had set in motion' (*D*, 65) has considerable results: Justin gains Marco, one of the GIs, as a life-long partner; Esther falls in love with Jamie, another GI, who, it is hinted, is the father of the baby daughter Esther later gives birth to, though she chooses to stay with her husband, Ned; Dolly finally decides to live with Alec in England; and Anna takes Jamie, 'Esther's leavings' (*D*, 82), and goes to the States to marry him.

In the play hate is again the key emotion around which everything revolves. Marco, who, Rima says, is from Mars (a character somewhat reminiscent of Dido in *Carthaginians*), is the one who hates the most. For him, (as with Eleanor in 'The Bird Sanctuary'), hatred gives a kind of power, and provides an impetus to keep him going. Marco says to Justin: 'I like your hatred. Don't lose your hatred' (*D*, 38). This is repeated several times in the play. He recalls how, when he was seven years old, his mother reacted when she found some of his sketches of dresses: 'She poured ketchup on every page, salt and lots of pepper. She made me eat them one by one until I vomited. I thought it was blood, the red coming up my throat' (*D*, 60). Now, he has lost his mother, and perhaps his father, too, a rather careless thing to do, as Lady Bracknell would say. Marco says: 'I hate her. I hate him. My mother. My father. Don't lose your hatred? Remember. I am fighting this war because of hatred. . . . Don't lose your hatred. I told you. Hatred brought me to you' (*D*, 60). Hate is the dark side of love, and in Justin he sees a lonely man even lonelier than himself.

The Englishman, Alec, is also burdened by hatred. While studying at Trinity College in Dublin, he never went home. He never 'took a holiday back there. Even Christmas he spent wandering through blizzards in the west of Ireland' (*D*, 14). He felt driven from the family home, from England, by discord between his parents, who hated each other. His kind of Englishman, a Hibernophile, is something of an innovation in the Irish theatre: Broadbent, in Shaw's *John Bull's Other Island*, is another example. Like Broadbent, Alec eventually decides to marry an Irishwoman and to go back to England with her. When Alec says that she might love England, Dolly says:

No, Alec, I won't love it. They won't love me. I'll make sure of that. That is your country. Yes, it has suffered. Yes, it's on its knees. But I am not. All right, I'll stand by you. But I'll be standing on my own two feet. And I'll be doing it for you. Not for your country. (*D*, 84)

She anticipates the difficulty she will face in England, but she will never be another Marianne of 'The Bird Sanctuary', who suffers because she tries so hard to love her husband's country and to earn the love of its people. Instead, Dolly recites with Alec an English hymn, 'I Vow to Thee, My Country'.[22] Some of the Irish audience at the Abbey might have felt awkward when they heard this English hymn, which expresses avowed loyalty to Britain. However, Dolly accepts Alec's love of his country, as she does himself; she, in turn, relates that 'there is another country' (*D*, 85), implying the love of her own country.

The ending of *Dolly West's Kitchen* is somewhat similar to that of Friel's *Dancing at Lughnasa*, which McGuinness adapted for film in 1998. While McGuinness's play is certainly more positive, or upbeat in overall effect, nevertheless the quiet, serene tableau of the family at a dinner table, which is Chekhovian in tone, recalls the enigmatic peacefulness at the close of Friel's play.

CONCLUSION

I am very fond of a particular anecdote of Joseph Campbell's. It concerns my country, Japan, and its religion. At a conference in Japan on religion, Campbell overheard another American delegate, a social philosopher from New York, say to a Shinto priest: 'We've been now to a good many ceremonies and have seen quite a few of your shrines. But I don't get your ideology. I don't get your theology.' The priest paused as though in deep thought, then slowly shook his head. 'I think we don't have ideology', he said. 'We don't have theology. We dance.'[1]

In 1979, I came to Ireland for the first time, from such a culture, to read for a post-graduate diploma in Anglo-Irish literature at the University of Dublin. I found the people very kind, friendly, generous and hospitable. Nonetheless, I still felt an outsider, and I knew that sometimes I was considered 'a poor pagan Japanese'. In Japan, as Campbell's story suggests, people are not quite so imbued with religious doctrines or ideology and we take religious attitudes, both Buddhist and Shintoist, for granted. I had no words or training to explain this to Irish friends in 1979. Or maybe I was the one who wanted an explanation, to satisfy my own need for self-knowledge and integrity. At that time I knew some Japanese Catholics, one of whom, christened when she was ten, was educated at the Sacred Heart Convent school in Tokyo. To my mind, she had much in common with the people I encountered in Ireland. (Sacred Heart Convent schools had the same curriculum all over the world; my friend was even awarded the same medals as Irish pupils educated at the Sacred Heart Convent in Dublin.) Seeing that Japanese Catholics had little difficulty fitting into Catholic Ireland, I realised that there was no such thing as an objective map of the world. For me Ireland was a country light years from Japan, while for Japanese Catholics, Japan was already within Christendom and Ireland was only one step away from where they had been.

This was just before Dublin began burgeoning into a truly

cosmopolitan city, before Ireland began to change in so many ways. It was the year of the Pope's visit, which would have such an enormous impact on the island. Despite that hospitality, that warmth, the society I enountered in 1979 struck me as oppressive and melancholic. It was my understanding that religion had something to do with the salvation of people's souls. I was prepared to pay my respects to this other faith without interfering, but what I heard all around me was command and stricture from the Church. That, at least, was how I felt.

Marco Delavicario in *Dolly West's Kitchen* says: 'All I want from the Catholic church is an apology. A long apology. And I hope they will understand when I refuse to accept it' (*D*, 60). When McGuinness wrote this, and when this was spoken on stage in 1999, few could have guessed that on 7 March 2000 the Vatican and the Pope would request forgiveness for past wrongs done in the name of the Catholic Church. It was a long apology, as Marco wanted: a document of over seventy pages, issued as part of the Bull of Indiction of the Great Jubilee of the Year 2000. The Pope, John Paul II, said:

As the successor of Peter, I ask that in this year of mercy the Church, strong in the holiness which she receives from her Lord, should kneel before God and implore forgiveness for the past and present sins of her sons and daughters. In reiterating that Christians are invited to acknowledge, before God and before those offended by their actions, the faults which they have committed. Let them do so without seeking anything in return, but strengthened only by the love of God which has been poured into our hearts.[2]

Many people are still sceptical about this, and regard it as a merely diplomatic gesture, but I, unlike Marco, am able to accept it. After all, the Catholic Church did not actually do anything terribly wrong to me, apart from creating what impressed me as that air of depression. So I can, I am in a position to, appreciate that open acknowledgement by the Church that it might have made a mistake.

Well, I still enjoyed staying in Ireland. I loved the country, but at the same time hated it. It was a typical love-hate relationship. (You can love and hate a country even in the space of one year.) Despite this, or maybe because of it, I have been working on Irish literature, on Irish drama especially, and also teaching in this field ever since. It is true that I was influenced by the Nationalist perspective on Ireland. Reading about its unhappy history, it was, perhaps, natural for me to sympathise with 'the oppressed'. I did not realise how unbalanced this perspective could be, until I read Frank McGuinness's *Observe the Sons of Ulster Marching Towards the Somme*. The last word of the play, 'dance', which represents the possibility of transcending the boundaries of enmity and hatred, had a powerful impact on me. It was the beginning of a different kind of understanding of Ireland.

Still, when I embarked on this thesis in 1995, I did not really know why I had chosen Frank McGuinness and his work. I soon realised, however, that for me he had opened up many different ways of seeing the country where he was born. He presented me with several windows, differently-angled visions (or anamophoses, if you will), through which to understand Irish society. His work taught me to re-construct a history of Ireland and brought me to Northern Ireland to live for a year. His works, especially *Innocence*, helped me understand Irish Catholicism in its essence. And I had no difficulty understanding his way of explaining it, since we are both, in our own different ways, outsiders.

There is a phrase which is repeatedly used by McGuinness's characters, by Mary and Lizzie Burns, by Peer Gynt, by the wife of the Sinner, by Rosmersholm and Rebecca, by the Baglady: they all say, 'so be it', which is a translation of *amen* as used in the Bible and Christian liturgy. I read in this set phrase, again as an outsider to Jewish/Christian culture, a hint of apathetic defiance, not a religious meekness. But an acceptance of the world as it is in order, paradoxically, to survive. McGuinness's characters say this, after 'they work hard and fight with all their might for their own corner.' It has a resonance with that affirmative 'no' spoken by the singer in the prologue to *The Caucasian Chalk Circle*, when he is asked to shorten the story. McGuinness writes about this 'No' in the production programme for his version of the play:

I love the Prologue because of its last word, *No*. It is a roar of defiance, quietly articulated by the wisdom of the play's Singer. It is an assertion of human rights, a marvellous dissidence. Everything in the Prologue is leading to that *No*; everything in the rest of *The Caucasian Chalk Circle* is loaded by it.[3]

McGuinness commented on Brian Friel: 'It's very strange when you look at the body of the work, how one play does seem to lead to the next.'[4] He could as well be talking about his own work, in which his concerns are more clustered than sequential or linear. When he was asked about the future of the Abbey Theatre, he answered:

I wish it crisis. I wish it continued crisis, because crisis is the root of creativity and the Abbey thrives on crisis, on attack, on dispute. I hope the Abbey is always confused. I hope it doesn't know where it is going. I hope it will have confusion aplenty. I hope that mischief will abound. I hope it will stage big, dirty, sexy, wonderful plays.[5]

In speaking of the Abbey Theatre, McGuinness reveals what he has striven for in his own drama.

APPENDIX

A List of Plays McGuinness directed at the New University of
Ulster at Coleraine

1. 1978   February

   (Lecture Theatre No. 9)

   Federico Garcia Lorca, *The House of
   Bernarda Alba*
   (Student production)

2. 1978

   (Lecture Theatre No. 9)

   Oscar Wilde,*The Importance of Being
   Earnest*
   (Staff production)

3. 1978
   (Lecture Theatre No. 9)

   Moliere, *Misanthrope*
   (Staff production)

4. 1978   December
   (The Riverside Theatre)

   William Shakespeare, *Macbeth*
   (Student production)

5. 1983
   (The Riverside Theatre)

   Alan Ayckbourn, *Bedroom Farce*
   (Staff production)

6. 1983/4?
   (The Riverside Theatre)

   Noel Coward, *Hay Fever*
   (Staff production)

BIBLIOGRAPHY

Plays by Frank McGuinness:
The Factory Girls (Dublin: Monarch Line, 1982)
Observe the Sons of Ulster Marching Towards the Somme, (London: Faber and Faber, 1986)
Innocence (London: Faber and Faber, 1987)
Carthaginians and Baglady (London: Faber and Faber, 1988)
The Factory Girls (Dublin: Wolfhound Press, 1988)
Mary and Lizzie (London: Faber and Faber, 1989)
Someone Who'll Watch Over Me (London: Faber and Faber, 1992)
Frank McGuinness: Plays 1 (London: Faber and Faber, 1996). Contains *The Factory Girls; Observe the Sons of Ulster Marching Towards the Somme; Innocence; Carthaginians;* and *Baglady*
Mutabillitie (London: Faber and Faber, 1997)
Dolly West's Kitchen (London: Faber and Faber, 1999)

Published Collections of Poems:
Booterstown (Dublin: Gallery Books, 1994)
The Sea with No Ships (Dublin: Gallery Books, 1999)

Unpublished Plays:
Gatherers (TEAM Theatre Company, Dublin, 1985)
Ladybag (Peacock Theatre, Dublin, 1985)
Times in It (Peacock Theatre, Dublin, 1988)
Beautiful British Justice in *Fears and Miseries of the Third Reich* (Produced Liverpool and London, 1989)
The Bread Man (Gate Theatre, Dublin, 1990)
Bird Sancturary (Abbey Theatre, Dublin, 1994)

Published Film Script:
Dancing at Lughnasa by Brian Friel (London: Faber and Faber, 1998)

Translations by Frank McGuinness:
Peer Gynt by Henrik Ibsen (London: Faber and Faber, 1990)

Three Sisters by Anton Chekhov (London: Faber and Faber, 1990)
A Doll's House by Henrik Ibsen (London: Faber and Faber, 1996)
The Storm by Alexander Ostrovsky (London: Faber and Faber,
    1998)
Miss Julie by August Strindberg (London: Faber and Faber, 2000)

Unpublished Translations:
Yerma, by Federico Garcia Lorca (Peacock Theatre, Dublin)
Rosmersholm, by Henrik Ibsen (Royal National Theatre, London)
Dracula, based on a novel by Bram Stoker (Druid Theatre, Galway)
The House of Bernarda Alba, by Federico Garcia Lorca (Lyric
    Theatre, Belfast)
Threepenny Opera, by Bertolt Brecht (Gate Theatre, Dublin)
Hedda Gabler, by Henrick Ibsen (Roundabout Theatre, Broadway)
Uncle Vanya, by Anton Chekhov(Field Day Theatre Company,
    Derry)
The Caucasian Chalk Circle, by Bertolt Brecht (Royal National
    Theatre, London)
Barbaric Comedies, by Ramón María del Valle-Inclán (Abbey
    Theatre, Dublin)

Miscellaneous:
'Catherine and John', *Fifth Estate*, Fifth Estate Co-operative,
    History Department, New University of Ulster, Coleraine, vol.1,
    no.1, January, 1979, pp. 4–5
A poem by McGuinness, 'Hanover Place, July Eleventh', *Cyphers*,
    13, Summer 1980
'Fort of what Stranger?', *Northwards to Donegal*, Reprinted from
    Ireland of the Welcomes, 31.5. September/October, 1982, Bord
    Fáilte (Irish Tourist Board)
A poem by McGuinness, 'Man at Portumna', *Cyphers* 17, Summer
    1982
Programme note for *Bedroom Farce*, Riverside Theatre, Coleraine,
    1983
'Mothers and Fathers', McGuinness talks to Joe Dawling and
    Patrick Mason, *Theatre Ireland*, 4 (September/December 1983),
    pp. 14–16
Programme note for *Hay Fever*, 'Hay Fever: Is This a Game?',
    Riverside Theatre, Coleraine, 1983/4
F. K. Lyn Oslo, *Plankton*, no.1, 1985, Wolfhound Press, pp. 33–35
'Pity & Terror', Review of *The Kindness of Strangers: The Life of
    Tennessee Williams* by Donald Spoto, *Sunday Tribune*, 16 June
    1985

'The Artist as a Young Pup', Review of *Is That It?* by Bob Geldof, *Irish Literary Supplement*, (Fall 1986), p. 9

Programme note for *Innocence*, Gate Theatre, Dublin, 1986

'The Voice of the Somme', Review of *The Road to the Somme* by Philip Orr, Blackstaff Press, *Sunday Press*, 24 January 1988

'Ulster's marching season lauds men of peace, not war', *The Sunday Times*, 10 July 1988

'Carlow', in *32 Counties*, Photographs of Ireland by Donovan Wylie with new writing by thirty-two Irish writers, (London: Secker & Warburg, 1989), p. 95

'A Voice from the Trees: Thomas Kilroy's Version of Chekhov's *The Seagul"*, *Irish University Review*, 21. 1, (1991), pp. 3–14

'Unforgotten men in the oubliette', *Irish Times*, 26 September 1992

Three Poems by Frank McGuinness: 'The Palm of his Hand', 'The Baker Goes for a Walk', 'The Torn Sleeves', *Poetry Ireland Review*, 34, Dublin: Poetry Ireland (Colour Books) (1992), 25–27

'The Violent Kiss – Frank McGuinness, author of *Innocence*, about Caravaggio on the "deeply seductive" *Taking Christ'*, *Irish Times*, 6 November 1993

Programme note for *Peer Gynt*, RSC, London, 1994

'A Sense of Irish Identity – The Playwright Frank McGuinness explains why the Abbey in Dublin must survive to fulfil its role as Ireland's National Theatre', *Guardian*, 5 October 1994

'Forward Out of Her Shell', Preface to *Faithful* by Marianne Faithful, (London: Penguin, 1995

'Don't worry, be Abbey', *Fortnight*, February 1995, p. 35

'Masks', Introduction to *The Dazzling Dark; New Irish Plays*, selected and introduced by Frank McGuinness (London: Faber and Faber, 1996), pp. ix-xii

'Perhaps', Programme note for *The Caucasian Chalk Circle*, London: Royal National Theatre, 1997

Works by other dramatists:

Beckett, Samuel, *The Complete Dramatic Works* (London: Faber and Faber, 1986)

Friel, Brian, *Selected Plays* (London: Faber and Faber, 1984) Contains *Philadelphia, Here I Come!; The Freedom of the City; Living Quarters; Aristocrats; Faith Healer;* and *Translations*

— *Dancing at Lughnasa* (London: Faber and Faber, 1990)

— *The Communication Cord* (London: Faber and Faber, 1982)

Thomas Kilroy, *Double Cross* (London: Faber and Faber, 1986)

— *The Madam MacAdam's Travelling Theatre* (London: Methuen, 1991)

— *Double Cross,* (Dublin: Gallery Press, 1994)

Murphy, Tom, *Plays 1* (London: Methuen, 1993)

— *Plays 2* (London: Methuen, 1993)

— *Plays 3* (London: Methuen, 1993)

— *Plays 4* (London: Methuen, 1997)

Parker, Stewart, *Three Plays for Ireland: Northern Star, Heavenly Bodies,* and *Pentecost* (Birmingham: Oberon Books, 1989), with an Introduction by Stewart Parker.

Yeats, W.B., *Collected Plays* (London: Macmillan, 2nd rev.ed., 1952)

Secondary and related materials:

Abel, Lionel, *Metatheatre: A New View of Dramatic Form* (New York: Hill and Wang, 1969)

Achilles, Jochen, 'Religion in Modern Irish Drama: Social Criticsm and Spiritual Reorientation', *Anglistentag,* 15 (1993), pp. 459–470

— 'Religious Risk in the Drama of Contemporary Ireland', *Éire-Ireland,* 28.3 (1993), pp. 17–37

Allen, Paul, 'Kaleidoscope: Frank McGuinness Special', (BBC) 1 May 1987

Andrews, Elmer, *The Art of Brian Friel* (London: Macmillan, 1995)

Aston, Elaine, *An Introduction to Feminism & Theatre* (London: Routledge, 1995)

Baltrusaitis, Jurgis, *Anamorphic Art* (New York: Harry N. Abrams, 1969)

Binyon, Laurence, *Collected Poems of Laurence Binyon* (London: Macmillan, 1931)

Bonsanti, Giorgio, *Caravaggio,* translated by Paul Blanchard, (Milano: SCALA/Riverside, 1994)

Brown, Georgiana, 'Three hostages to fortune', *Independent,* 10 July 1992, p. 15

Brown, Terence, *Ireland: A Social and Cultural History 1922 – 1985,* (London: Fontana Press, 1981, 1985)

— *Ireland's Literature* (Mullingar: the Lilliput Press, 1988)

Burke, Patrick, 'Dance Unto Death', *Irish Literary Supplement,* 6. 2 (1987), p. 45

Burnett, Mark Thornton and Ramona Wray, *Shakespeare and Ireland: History, Politics, Culture* (London: Macmillan, 1997)

Cairns, David and Shaun Richards, *Writing Ireland: Colonialism, Nationalism and Culture* (Manchester: Manchester University Press, 1988)

Campbell, Joseph and Bill Moyers, *The Power of Myth* (New York: Doubleday, 1988)

Case, Sue-Ellen, *Feminism and Theatre* (London: Macmillan, 1988)

Cave, Richard Allan and Martin McLoone, 'J'Accuse', (Cave on *Mary and Lizzie*, and McLoone on 'The Hen House'), *Theatre Ireland*, 21 (1989), pp. 58–62

Charles, Louise Stafford, 'Someone Who'll Watch Over Me', *Theatre Ireland*, 28 (Summer, 1993), pp. 84–87

Childs, Peter and Patrick Williams, *An Introduction to Post Colonial Theory* (London: Prentice Hall, 1997)

Clarke, Jocelyn, 'Observe the Son of Ulster', *Sunday Tribune*, 11 April 1993: B1

Comiskey, Ray, 'Plots with Hard Political Edges', *Irish Times*, 11 March 1982

— 'Frank McGuinness: a new breed of Irish playwright', *Irish Times*, 2 May 1987

Cosgrove, Brian, 'Orpheus Descending: Frank McGuinness's *Someone Who'll Watch Over Me*', *Irish University Review*, 23. 2 (1993), pp. 197–201

Coughlan, Patricia, ed., *Spenser and Ireland: An Interdisciplinary Perspective* (Cork: Cork University Press, 1989)

Cullingford, Elizabeth Butler, 'British Romans and Irish Carthaginians: Anticolonial Metaphor in Heaney, Friel, and McGuinness, *PMLA*, (March, 1996), pp. 222–239

Curtis, Liz, *Nothing But the Same Old Story: The Roots of Anti-Irish Racism* (London: Information on Ireland, 1984)

Dante Alighieri, *The Divine Comedy*, translated by C. H. Sisson (Oxford: Oxford University Press, 1980)

Darnton, Robert, *The Kiss of Lamourette: Reflections in Cultural History* (New York: W.W.Norton & Company, 1990)

Dawe, Gerald, 'Review on Factory Girls', *Theatre Ireland*, 15 (May/August 1988), p. 52

de Breffny, Brian, *The Irish World: The History and Cultural Achievements of the Irish People* (London: Thames & Hudson, 1977)

de Jonge, Nicholas, *Not in Front of the Audience: Homosexuality on Stage* (London: Routledge, 1992)

de Vries, Ad, *Dictionary of Symbol and Imagery* (Amsterdam and London: North-Holland Publishing Company, 1974)

Dillon, Myles, *Early Irish Literature* (Chicago: University of Chicago Press, 1948)

Doherty, Richard, *The Sons of Ulster: Ulstermen at War from the Somme to Korea* (Belfast: Apple Tree Press, 1992)

Downing, Taylor, ed., *The Troubles: The Background to the Questions of Northern Ireland* (A Channel Four Book, Thames Macdonald, 1980)

Doyle, Bill, 'The Bill Doyle File', *The Bridge: An Droichead* (The Bilingual Journal from Ireland), (Irish version by Sean O Conaill) Fall/Fomhar (1987), pp. 4–5

Eagleton, Terry, Fredric Jameson & Edward W. Said, *Nationalism, Colonialism, and Literature*, Introduced by Seamus Deane, (Minneapolis: University of Minnesota Press, 1990)

Engels, Friedrich, *The Condition of the Working-Class in England: From Personal Observation and Authentic Sources* (Moscow: Progress Publishers, 1973)

Etherton, Michael, *Contemporary Irish Dramatists* (London: Macmillan Modern Dramatists, 1989).

Evans, E. Estyn, *Irish Folk Ways* (London: Routledge & Kegan Paul, 1957)

— *The Personality of Ireland: Habitat, Heritage and History* (London: Cambridge University Press, 1973)

— *Ireland and the Atlantic Heritage: Selected Writings* (Dublin: Lilliput Press, 1996)

Evans, Martin Marix, *The Battle of the Somme* (London: Orion, 1996)

Farnham, Willard, *The Medieval Heritage of Elizabethan Tragedy* (Berkeley: University of California Press, 1936)

Farren, Ronan, 'No category for Frank's new play', *Evening Herald*, 11 March 1982

Ferguson, George, *Signs & Symbols in Christian Art* (New York: Oxford University Press, 1954, 1977)

Foster, R. F., ed., *The Oxford Illustrated History of Ireland*, (Oxford: Oxford University Press, 1989)

Foucault, Michel, *Language, Counter-Memory, Practice: Selected Essays and Intervies*, ed. with an Introduction by Donald F. Bouchard, translated from the French by Donald F. Bouchard and Sherry Simon, (New York: Cornell University Press, 1977)

Gailey, Alan, *Irish Folk Drama* (Cork: Mercier Press, 1969)

Gilbert, Helen and Joanne Tompkins, *Post-Colonial Drama: Theory, Practice, Politics* (London: Routledge, 1996)

Glassie, Henry, *All Silver and No Brass: An Irish Christmas Mumming* (Dublin: Dolmen Press, 1976; repr. Dingle: Brandon Books, 1983)

Gleitman, Clare, *Theatrical Negotiations on a Modern Irish Terrain: A Study of Three Contemporary Irish Dramatists* (unpublished doctoral dissertation, New York University, 1994)

— '"Like Father, Like Son": *Someone Who'll Watch Over Me* and the Geopolitical Family Drama', *Éire-Ireland*, 31. 1&2 (1996), 78–88

Graves, Robert, *The White Goddess* (London: Faber and Faber, 1958)

Grene, Nicholas, *The Politics of Irish Drama: Plays in Context from Boucicault to Friel* (Cambridge: Cambridge University Press, 1999)

Hadfield, Andrew, *Spenser's Irish Experience: Wilde Fruit and Salvage Soyl* (Oxford: Clarendon Press, 1997)

Hamilton, A.C. ed., *The Spenser Encyclopedia* (Toronto: University of Toronto Press, 1990, reprinted in 1997)

Hammond, Paul , *Love between Men in English Literature* (London: Macmillan, 1996)

Hargaden, John, 'The Stage Irishman in Modern Irish Drama', *Studies*, 79. 313 (1990), pp. 45–54

Healy, Dermont, 'An Interview with Michael Longley', *Southern Review*, 31, 1 June, 1995

Heaney, Seamus, *Field Work* (London: Faber and Faber, 1979)

— *Sweeney Astray* (Derry: Field Day, 1983, London: Faber and Faber, 1984)

Henry, Jacobs, 'Shakespeare, Revenge Tragedy, and the Ideology of Memento Mori', *Shakespeare Studies*, 1993

Henderson, Lynda, 'Innocence and Experience', *Fortnight*, November 1986, p. 24

Hibbard, Howard, *Caravaggio* (London: Thames and Hudson, 1983)

Highley, Christopher, *Shakespeare, Spenser, and the Crisis in Ireland* (Cambridge: Cambridge University Press, 1997)

Hinks, Roger, *Michelangelo Merisi da Caravaggio: His Life, His Legend, His Works* (London: Faber and Faber, 1953)

Holland, Peter, 'The Play of Eros: Paradoxes of Gender in English Pantomine', *New Theatre Quarterly*, 13. 51 (1997), pp. 195–204

Holmes, Paul, 'Classical Psychodrama: An Overview', in *Psychodrama: Inspiration and Technique*, eds. Paul Holmes and Marcia Karp, (London: Routledge, 1991), pp. 7–13

Hosey, Seamus, 'Frank McGuinness', *Speaking Volumes* (RTE, Blackwater Press, 1995), pp. 28–34

Hunter, Charles, 'Starange Passion About the Somme', *Irish Times*, 15 February 1985

Humm, Maggie, *The Dictionary of Feminist Theory*, Second Edition (Harvester Wheatsheaf: Prentice Hall, 1995)

Hurtley, Jacqueline, and others, eds., *Ireland in Writing: Interviews with Writers and Academics* (Amsterdam-Atlanta: Rodopi, 1998)

Jackson, Joe, 'The Bread Man Cometh . . . ', *Hot Press*, 1 November 1990, pp. 44–45

Jackson, Kevin, 'Speaking for the Dead: Playwright Frank McGuinness talks to Kevin Jackson', *Independent*, 27 September 1989

Jeffery, Keith, 'Under the blood-red hand', *TLS*, 22 November 1985

Jordan, Eamon, *The Feast of Famine: The Plays of Frank McGuinness* (Berne: Peter Lang, 1997)

Keenan, Brian, *An Evil Cradling* (London: Vintage Edition, 1993)

Kennedy, Douglas, 'Poetic politics', *New Statesman & Society*, 6 October, pp. 50–52

Kenner, Hugh, *Samuel Beckett: A Critical Study* (Berkeley and Los Angeles: University of California Press, 1968)

Kermode, Frank, *The Sense of an Ending* (New York: Oxford University Press, 1966)

Kiberd, Declan, 'Irish Literature and Irish History', in *The Oxford Illustrated History of Ireland*, ed. by R. F. Foster, (Oxford: Oxford University Press, 1989), pp. 275–337

— *Inventing Ireland: The Literature of the Modern Nation* (London: Jonathan Cape, 1995)

Lapointe, Michael Patrick, 'A Place Elsewhere: 'Displacement in Frank McGuinness' and Michael Longley's Response to the Northern Irish "Troubles"' (unpublished master's thesis, McMaster University, August 1994)

Law, Gary, *The Cultural Traditions Dictionary* (Belfast: Blackstaff Press, 1998)

Lawley, Paul, 'Contemporary Dramatists: McGuinness', ed. K. A. Berney, *Contemporary Dramatists* (St. James Press, 1993), pp. 436–438

Lewis, C.S., *Allegory of Love: A Study of Medieval Tradition* (Oxford: Oxford University Press, 1958)

Liddy, James, 'Voices in the Irish Cities of the Dead: Melodrama and Dissent in Frank McGuinness's *Carthaginians*, *Irish University Review*, 25. 2, (1995), pp. 278–283

Lojek, Helen, 'Myth and Bonding in Frank McGuinness's *Observe the Sons of Ulster Marching Towards the Somme*', in *Canadian Journal of Irish Studies*, 14, 1(1988), pp. 45–53

— 'Differences Without Indifference: The Drama of Frank McGuinness and Anne Devlin', *Éire-Ireland*, 25, 2 (1990), pp. 56–68

— Watching Over Frank McGuinness' Stereotypes'. *Modern Drama*, 38 (1995), pp. 348–361

— 'Frank McGuinness', in *Irish Playwrights, 1880–1995*, eds. Bernice Schrank and William W. Demastes, (Westport: Greenwood Press, 1997)

Long, Joseph, 'Dancing in the Borderlands', *Theatre Ireland*, 7 (Autumn, 1984), pp. 46–7

Longley, Edna, *Living Stream* (Newcastle upon Tyne: Bloodaxe Books, 1994)

— 'Pamphlets and professors', *TLS*, 17 March 1995

Longley, Michael, *Poems 1963–1983* (Harmondsworth: Penguin, 1986)

Lucy, Gordon, ed., *The Ulster Covenant: A Pictorial History of the 1912 HOME RULE Crisis* (Belfast: New Ulster Publications Ltd., 1989), p. 44

MacCurtain, Margaret, 'Moving Statues and Irish Women', in *Irish Women's Studies Reader*, ed. by Ailbhe Smyth, (Dublin: Attic Press, 1993), pp. 203–213

Maley, Willy, *Salvaging Spenser: Colonialism, Culture and Identity* (London: Macmillan Press, 1997)

Malone, Andrew, *Irish Drama* (1929, reissued New York: Benjamin Blom, 1965)

Marcus, Steven, *Engels and Manchester and the Working Class* (London: Weidenfeld and Nicolson, 1974)

Matsutani, Kenji, *Karutago Kobo-shi (The Rise and Fall of Carthage)*, (Tokyo: Hakushui-sha, 1991)

McCann, Eamonn, *War and an Irish Town: New Edition* (London: Pluto Press, 1993)

McCormack, Jerusha, ed., *Wilde The Irishman* (New Haven and London: Yale University Press, 1998)

McGuinness, Shane, 'Breaking the barrier', *Sunday Tribune*, 10 May 1987

McLoone, Martin, 'On the Henhouse', *Theatre Ireland*, 21 (1989), pp. 61–2

McNamara, Gerald, 'The Out Interview', *Out*, November/December 1986, pp. 20–21.

Metzger, Bruce M. and Michael D. Coogan, eds., *The Oxford Companion to the Bible* (Oxford: Oxford University Press, 1993)

Moir, Alfred, *Caravaggio* (London: Thames and Hudson, 1989)

Morley, Henry, ed., *Ireland under Elizabeth and James I* (London: George Routledge and Sons, 1890)

Morrison, Kristin, *Canters and Chronicles: The Use of Narrative in the Plays of Samuel Beckett and Harold Pinter* (Chicago: University of Chicago Press, 1983)

Murray, Christopher, *Twentieth-Century Irish Drama: Mirror Up to Nation* (Manchester: Manchester University Press, 1997)

Nadel, George H. and Perry Curtis, *Imperialism and Colonialism* (New York: Macmillan, 1964)

Neumann, Erich, *The Great Mother*, translated by Ralph Manheim, (Princeton, NJ: Princeton University Press, 1963)

Ní Dhonnchadha, Máirín and Theo Dorgan, eds. *Revising the Rising* (Derry: Field Day, 1991)

O Connor, Fionnuala, *In Search of a State: Catholics in Northern Ireland* (Belfast: Blackstaff Press, 1993)

O'Dwyer, Riana, 'Dancing in the Borderlands: The Plays of Frank McGuinness', in *The Crows Behind the Plough*, ed. by Greet Lernout, (Amsterdam: Rodopi, 1991), pp. 99–116

Orr, John and Dragan Klaic, eds., *Terrorism and Modern Drama* (Edinburgh: Edinburgh University Press, 1990)

Orr, Philip, *The Road to the Somme* (Belfast: Blackstaff, 1987)

O'Toole, Fintan, 'The Factory Girls', *In Dublin*, 148, 5–18th March, 1982

— 'Over the top', *Sunday Tribune*, 17 February 1985

— 'Innocence Uprooted', Fintan O'Toole profiles playwright Frank McGuinness, *Magill*, November 1986, pp. 48–54

— 'You don't think I'm as stupid as Yeats, do you', *Irish Times*, 24 September, 1988: Weekend: 3

— 'Judged by its Peers', *Theatre Ireland*, 17 (December 1988/March 1989), pp. 28–29.

— 'Dissension in the fifth province', *Irish Times*, 8 March 1993

— *The Irish Times: Book of the Century* (Dublin: Gill & Macmillan, 1999)

Paglia, Camile, *Sexual Personae: Art and Decadence from Nefertiti to Emily Dickinson* (Harmondsworth: Penguin, 1992)

Parker, Michael and Roger Starkey, eds., *Postcolonial Literatures: Achebe, Ngugi, Desai, Walcott* (London: Macmillan, 1995)

Pearse, Pádraic H., *Collected Works of Pádraic H. Pearse: Political Writings and Speeches* (Phoenix Publishing, Dublin, 1924)

Penny, Liz, 'In the Forbidden City', *Theatre Ireland*, 12 (1987), p. 62

Pine, Richard, 'Frank McGuinness: A Profile', *Irish Literary Supplement*, 10.1 (1991), pp. 29–30

— *The Diviner: the Art of Brian Friel* (Dublin: University College Dublin Press, 1999)

Pollard, Carolyne, 'An Ulster Son Observed: Interview with Frank McGuinness, *Quarto*, Winter 1987/88 (Literary Society of the University of Ulster), pp. 12–13

Purcell, Deirdre, 'On Fire', *Sunday Tribune*, 15 May 1988, p. 17

Redmond, Lucile, 'Sharp, strong shirt saga', *Sunday Triibune*, 14 March 1982

Roche, Anthony, *Contemporary Irish Drama: From Beckett to McGuinness* (Dublin: Gill & Macmillan, 1994)

— 'Recent Trends in Contemporary Irish Drama', *Ireland: Literature, Culture, Politics*, Heidelberg: Universitätsverlag C. Winter, 1994, pp. 71–88

Roche, William, 'The Tale of the Shirt Girls!', *Sunday Press*, 7 March 1982

Russell, Richard Rankin, 'Ulster Unionism's Mythic and Religious Culture in *Observe the Sons of Ulster*', Working Papers in Irish Studies, Department of Liberal Arts, Nova Southeastern University, 1998

Said, Edward W., *Orientalism* (London: Routledge, 1978)

— *Culture & Imperialism* (London: Chatto & Windus, 1993)

Schneider, Ulrich, 'Staging History in Contemporary Anglo-Irish Drama: Brian Friel and Frank McGuinness', in *The Crows Behind the Plough*, ed. by Greet Lernout, (Amsterdam: Rodopi, 1991), pp. 79–98

Smyth, Ailbhe, ed., *Irish Woman's Studies Reader* (Dublin: Attic Press, 1993)

Sheehan, Helen, *Irish Television Drama: A Society and its Stories* (Dublin: Radio Telefís Éireann, 1987)

Spenser, Edmund, *A View of the State of Ireland*, ed. by W.L.Renwick, (Oxford: Clarendon Press, 1970)

— *A View of the State of Ireland*, eds. by Andrew Hadfield and Willy Maley, (Oxford: Blackwell, 1997)

— *The Mutabilitie Cantos*, ed. by S. P. Zitner (London: Thomas Nelson and Sons, 1968)

Sweeney, Paul, *The Celtic Tiger: Ireland's Economic Miracle Explained* (Dublin: Oak Tree Press, 1998)

Tóibín, Colm, ed., *Seeing is Believing: Moving Statues in Ireland*, (The Lodge, Mountrath, Co. Laois: Pilgrim Press, 1985)

Tierney, Mark, *Modern Ireland* (Dublin: Gill & Macmillan, rev. ed., 1978)

Vanek, Joe, 'Designing for the Gate', Production Programme, The Gate Theatre: Dublin, October, 1986

Walker, Barbara G., *The Woman's Encyclopedia of Myths and Secrets* (San Francisco: Harper, 1983)

Waters, John, 'Alone Again, Naturally', *In Dublin*, 14 May 1987, pp. 15–18

Welch, Robert, *The Kilcolman Notebook* (Dingle, Co. Kerry: Brandon Press, 1994)

— ed., *The Oxford Companion to Irish Literature* (Oxford: Oxford University Press, 1996)

— *The Abbey Theatre 1899–1999: Form & Pressure* (Oxford: Oxford University Press, 1999)

White, Victoria, 'Someone to Watch Over Him?', *Theatre Ireland*, 31(1993), pp. 22–24

— , 'Towards Post-Feminism?', *Theatre Ireland*, 18 (1989), pp. 33–35

Wilcox, Angela, 'The Temple of the Lord is ransacked', *Theatre Ireland*, 8 (1984), pp. 87–89

— 'The Memory of Wounds', *Theatre Ireland*, 16 (1988), pp. 6–8

William, Patrick and Laura Chrisman, eds., *Colonial Discourse and Post-Colonial Theory: A Reader* (New York: Columbia University Press, 1994)

Wilson, Edmund, *To the Finland Station: A Study in the Writing and Acting of History*, Collins, the Fontana Library, 1960 (originally published by W. H. Allen in 1940)

Woodworth, Paddy, 'My Goodness, McGuinness', *Image*, April 1985, pp. 100–101

Worth, Katharine, *The Irish Drama of Europe from Yeats to Beckett* (London: The Athlone Press, 1978)

— 'Book Review on *Someone Who'll Watch Over Me*', *Irish University Review*, 23. 2 (1993), pp. 324–326.

THE TILLING ARCHIVE

The Archive List
(Updated on 5 April 2001)

This Archive is privately owned by Mr Philip Tilling, English Department, University of Ulster at Coleraine. All the materials are in a chronological order.
The Archive list was made and is copyright © 2002 by Hiroko Mikami.

The material in the Archive is categorised as follows:

1. Books & Manuscripts
    Published (Original) Plays, shown as PP82–1
    Unpublished (Original) Plays, shown as UP85–1
    Unpublished and Unstaged Playscript, shown as UPUS-1
    Published Translations, shown as PT90–1
    Unpublished Translations, shown as UT87–1
    Published Film Script, shown as PF98–1
    Published Collections of Poems, shown as PPm94–1
    Published Foreign Translations of his work, shown as FTr96–1

2. (Writings/Articles by McGuinness)
    Poems published in *Irish Press*, undated, shown as (a)
    Writings/Articles by McGuinness, shown as (74–1)
    Unpublished and undated manuscript, shown as (U-M-1)
    Unpublished and undated typescript, shown as (U-T-1)

3. <Interviews>
    Interviews, shown as <80–1>

4. [Articles on McGuinness]
    Articles/Essays on McGuinness, shown as [83–1]

5. Production History and Review
    (a) Original Plays
    (b) Television Drama
    (c) Plays directed by McGuinness
    (d) Translations

1. Books & Manuscripts:

Published (Original) Plays:
PP82–1   *The Factory Girls* (Dublin: Monarch Line, 1982)
PP86–1   *Observe the Sons of Ulster Marching Towards the Somme* (London: Faber and Faber, 1986)
PP87–1   *Innocence* (London: Faber and Faber, 1987)
PP88–1   *Borderlands* in *Three TEAM Plays*, ed. Martin Druty (Dublin: Wolfhound Press, 1988)
PP88–2   *The Factory Girls* (Dublin: Wolfhound Press, 1988)
PP88–3   *Carthaginians* and *Baglady* (London: Faber and Faber, 1988)
PP89–1   *Mary and Lizzie* (London: Faber and Faber, 1989)
PP92–1   *Someone Who'll Watch Over Me* (London: Faber and Faber, 1992)
PP92–2   *Someone Who'll Watch Over Me* (New York: Samuel French, 1992)
PP96–1   *Frank McGuinness: Plays 1* (London: Faber and Faber, 1996). Contains *The Factory Girls; Observe the Sons of Ulster Marching Towards the Somme; Innocence; Carthaginians* and *Baglady*
PP97–1   *Mutabillitie* (London: Faber and Faber, 1997)
PP99–1   *Dolly West's Kitchen* (London: Faber and Faber, 1999)

Unpublished (Original) Plays: in order of the date of production
UP85–1   *Gatherers* (Produced in Dublin, 1985)
UP85–1   *Ladybag* (Peacock Theatre, Dublin, 1985)
UP88–1   *Times in It* (Produced in Dublin, 1988)
UP89–1   *Beautiful British Justice* in *Fears and Miseries of the Third Reich* (Produced in Liverpool and London, 1989)
UP90–1   *The Bread Man* (Gate Theatre, Dublin, 1990)
UP94–1   *The Bird Sanctuary* (Abbey Theatre, Dublin, 1994)

Unstaged (Original) Playscript:
US-1   *Bigword* for TEAM Educational Theatre Company.
US-2   *The Gospel According to Judas*

Published Translations : in order of the date of publication
PT90–1 *Peer Gynt* by Henrik Ibsen (London: Faber and Faber, 1990)
PT90–2 *Three Sisters* by Anton Chekhov (London: Faber and Faber, 1990)
PT96–1 *A Doll's House* by Henrik Ibsen (London: Faber and Faber, 1996)
PT97–1 *A Doll's House* by Henrik Ibsen (New York: Dramatists Play Service, 1997)
PT97–2 *Electra* by Sophocles (London: Faber and Faber, 1997)
PT98–1 *The Storm* by Alexander Ostrovsky (London: Faber and Faber, 1998)
PT00–1 *Miss Julie & The Stronger* by August Strindberg (London: Faber and Faber, 2000)

Unpublished Translations: in order of the date of production
UT87–1 *Yerma* by Federico Garcia Lorca (Peacock Theatre, Dublin)
UT87–2 *Rosmersholm* by Henrik Ibsen (Royal National Theatre, London)
UT87–1 *Dracula* (Druid Theatre, Galway) (unobtained)
UT91–1 *Threepenny Opera* by Bertolt Brecht (Gate Theatre, Dublin)
UT91–2 *The House of Bernarda Alba* by Federico Garcia Lorca (Lyric Theatre, Belfast)
UT94–1 *Hedda Gabler* by Henrick Ibsen (Roundabout Theatre, Broadway)
UT95–1 *Uncle Vanya* by Anton Chekhov (Field Day Theatre Company, Derry)
UT97–1 *The Caucasian Chalk Circle* by Bertolt Brecht (Royal National Theatre, London)
UT00–1 *Barbaric Comedies* by Ramón María del Valle-Inclán (Abbey Theatre, Dublin)
(UT87–1, UT91–1, and UT91–2 are unobtained for the archive.)

Unstaged Translation:
UST–1 *Ghost* by Henrik Ibsen

Published Film Script
PF98–1 Friel, Brian, *Dancing at Lughnasa* (London: Faber and Faber, 1998)

Published Collections of Poems:
PPm94–1 *Booterstown* (Dublin: Gallery Books, 1994)

PPm99–1 *The Sea with No Ships* (Dublin: Gallery Books, 1999)

Published Foreign Translations of his Work: in order of the date of publication
FTr96–1 *Regarde les fils de l'Ulster marchant vers la Somme*, translated by Joseph Long and Alexadra Poulain, (Paris:Actualité Théâtrle, 1996)
FTr96–2 *Quelqu'un pour veiller sur moi*, translated by Isabelle Famchon, (Paris: THEATRALES, 1996)
FTr99–1 *Les ruines du temps*, translated by Isabelle Famchon, (Paris: Circé, 1999)

2.   (Writings/Articles by McGuinness):

Published dates are unspecified for the following (a)~(f).

(a)   'The Field of Time'

(b)   'King Bolingbroke'

(c)   'Prelocked'

(d)   'The Statue of David'

(e)   'Thanksgiving'

(f)   'The Visit'

(74–1)   'The Anniversary' (1. Grandfather, 2. The Widow, 3. Ghost At The Wake), *Irish Press*, date unspecified, March 1974.

(75–1)   'The Death of W.H.Auden', *Irish Press*, date unspecified, March 1975.

(76–1)   'Matt Talbot', *Irish Press*, date unspecified, April 1976.

(76–2)   'Gnomic Verses', 'Beardless', 'Miscarriage', *Irish Press*, date unspecified, September, 1976.

(76–3)   'Home', *Irish Press*, date unspecified, December, 1976.

(77–1)   'End', *Irish Press*, date unspecified, February, 1977.

(78–1)   'Baked Apples', 'The Mummers of Inch Island', 'Spare Room', *Irish Press*, date unspecified, April, 1978.

(78–2)   'Advertizing and Ritual',*Quarto,* April, 1978, pp. 12–15.

(78–3)   'Oisin i ndiaidh Na Feinne',*Quarto,* April, 1978, pp. 24–25.

(78–4)   'The Statue of David', *Quarto,* May, 1978, p. 21.

(79–1)   'Catherine and John', *Fifth Estate,* Fifth Estate Co-operative, History Department, New University of Ulster, Coleraine, vol.1, no.1, January 1979, 4–5.

(79–2)   'Hearing English Spoken', *Irish Press,* 2 June 1979. (with type-script)

(80–1)   A poem by McGuinness, 'Hanover Place, July Eleventh', *Cyphers* 13, Summer 1980. (with manuscript)

(80–2)   'New Year in Kinsale', 'Laurel and Hardy', *Irish Press,* 1 March 1980.

(80–3)   'Thy Neighbour', *Irish Press,* 18 October 1980.

(81–1)   'The Linen Library in Belfast', *Irish Press,* 14 March 1981.

(81–2)   'Thanksgivings', *Irish Press,* 20 June 1981.

(81–3)   'The Dunmore Caves', *New Leaf* 5 (Poetry & Prose), Humanities Department, Chelsea College (University of London), Autumn 1981, p. 23.

(81–4)   'Man Shot One West Seventy Second', *Outposts,* 129, Summer 1981, pp. 8–9.

(82–1)   'Fort of what Stranger?', *Northwards to Donegal,* Reprinted from Ireland of the Welcomes, 31.5. September/October, 1982, Bord Failte(Irish Tourist Board).

(82–2)   'Man at Portumna', *Cyphers* 17, Summer 1982.

(82–3)   'Rusticaat', *Irish Press*, 4 September 1982.

(83–1)   Programme note for *Bedroom Farce*, Riverside Theatre, Coleraine, 1983.

(83–2)   'Mothers and Fathers', McGuinness talks to Joe Dowling and Patrick Mason. *Theatre Ireland* 4 September/December 1983: 14–16.

(83–3)   'Passivity', *identity: A Quarterly Review* 7, October-December 1983, 22.

(84–1)   Programme note for *Hay Fever*, 'Hay Fever: Is This a Game?', Riverside Theatre, Coleraine, 1984.

(84–2)   'Beyond O'Casey: Working Class Dramatists: Dramatists from the North', *Irish Literary Supplement*, Spring 1984: 35

(84–3)   'A Popular Theatre', Patrick Mason and Frank McGuinness, *The Crane Bag*, 8.2. 1984, pp. 109–110.

(84–4)   'F. K. Lyn Oslo', *Quarto*, (the Literary Society of the New University of Ulster), vol. 9. 1983–84: 2–5, (with typescript).

(84–5)   Three Poems: 'Something Nasty', 'Echo and Narcissus', 'David Hockney', *Identity: A Quarterly Review Issue*, no. 8, January–March, 1984, pp. 18–19.

(84–6)   'A Rough House', Programme note for Sean O'Casey's *The Plough and the Stars*, (Abbey Theatre, Dublin, 1984).

(85–1)   'F. K. Lyn Oslo', *Plankton*, no.1, 1985, (Dublin: Wolfhound Press), 33–35.

(85–2)   'Pity & terror', Review of *The Kindness of Strangers: The Life of Tennessee Williams* by Donald Spoto, *Sunday Tribune*, 16 June 1985.

(85–3)   'The Arts and Ideology', Jennifer Fitzgerald, Seamus Deane, Joan Fowler, Frank McGuinness, *The Crane Bag*, vol. 9. no.2, 1985 (Final Issue).

(85–4) 'The Recruiting Officer', Programme note for George Farquhar's *The Recruiting Officer*, (Gate Theatre, Dublin, 1985).

(86–1) 'In the Forefront of Irish Writing: Michael Longley's Poems', *Irish Literary Supplement*, (Spring 1986), 23.

(86–2) 'The Artist as a Young Pup', Review of *Is That It?* by Bob Geldof, *Irish Literary Supplement*, (Fall 1986), 9.

(86–3) Programme note for *Innocence*, (Dublin Gate Theatre, 1986).

(86–4) Three Poems: 'Lullaby', 'Anne', 'Prisoner of War', *Krino: Theatre and Ireland*, no. 13, 1986, pp. 93–95.

(86–5) 'The Mythic Dracula', programme note for *Dracula*, (Galway Druid Theatre, 1986)

(88–1) 'The Voice of the Somme', Review of *The Road to the Somme* by Philip Orr, *Sunday Press*, 24 January 1988.

(88–2) 'Ulster's marching season lauds men of peace, not war', *Sunday Times*, 10 July 1988.

(88–3) 'Preface', *Borderlines: A Collection of New Writing from the North West*, ed. Sam Burnside, (Londonderry: Holiday Project West, 1988) (with a poster).

(89–1) 'Carlow', *32 Counties*, Photographs of Ireland by Donovan Wylie with new writing by thirty-two Irish writers, (London: Secker & Warburg, 1989), p. 95.

(89–2) 'Something Natural, Something Wonderful', *Irish Literary Supplement*, (Spring 1989), p. 24.

(90–1) Programme note for *Shaughraun* by Dion Boucicault, (Dublin: Abbey, 5 July 1990).

(91–1) 'A Voice from the Trees: Thomas Kilroy's Version of Chekhov's *The Seagull*', *Irish University Review*, 21.1(1991), pp. 4–15.

(91–2) 'A Dream World', programme note for *The Threepenny Opera*, (Dublin: Gate Theatre, 1991).

(92–1) 'Unforgotten men in the oubliette', *Irish Times, 26* September 1992.

(92–2) Three Poems by Frank McGuinness: 'The Palm of his Hand', 'The Baker Goes for a Walk', 'The Torn Sleeves', *Poetry Ireland Review* 34 (1992), 25–27.

(92–3) 'Truth is more trouble than fiction', *Guardian*, 1 October 1992.

(92–4) 'Traveller (In memory of Barbara Hayley)': 'Japan', 'Caen', 'Maynooth', *Poetry Ireland Review* 37 (1992), 83–87.

(93–1) 'The Violent Kiss – Frank McGuinness, author of *Innocence*, about Caravaggio on the "deeply seductive" *Taking Christ*, *Irish Times*, 6 November 1993.

(93–2) 'Paint, print and the Nazi genocide', *Sunday Tribune*, 17 September 1993.

(93–3) 'Extract from The Birds' Sanctuary', *Soho Square*, ed. by Colm Tóibín, (London: Bloomsbury Publishing, 1993), 164–5.

(93–4) 'Introduction' to *The Saving Life: An Anthology of Poetry by Irish People with Special Needs*, collected by Stuart Milson (Tipperary: Grangemocker Camphill, 1993) p. i.

(93–5) 'Theatre: Critics Darling' (Review of *Arcadia* & *The Real Inspector Hound* by Tom Stoppard), *London Magazine*, 33. 7–8 (1993), pp. 88–95.
This article is NOT by Frank McGuinness, the playwright, but by another Frank McGuinness. It caused great embarrassment when published, since the *Independent* repeated that Frank had written unfavourably of Stoppard's play (which he, in fact, admires). A correction was later made in the *Independent*.

(93–6) 'For Potra Kelly' in *A Page Falls Open: Stories and Poems by Irish Writers* (Ennis, Co. Clare: Co. Clare Reading and Writing Scheme, 1993), p. 95.

(94–1)   Programme note for *Peer Gynt*, (London: RSC, 1994).

(94–2)   'A Sense of Irish Identity – The Playwright Frank McGuinness explains why the Abbey in Dublin must survive to fulfil its role as Ireland's National Theatre', *Guardian*, 5 October 1994.

(94–3)   'Forward Out of Her Shell', Preface to *Faithful* by Marianne Faithful, (London: Michael Joseph, 1994, rep. Penguin, 1995).

(94–4)   'The Plays of Brian Friel', *London Magazine*, 34.1–2(1994), 85–92.
          This article is NOT by Frank McGuinness, the playwright, but by another Frank McGuinness.

(95–1)   'Don't worry, be Abbey', *Fortnight*, February 1995, p. 35.

(95–2)   'A good guy wins', *Irish Independent*, 6 October 1995.

(95–3)   'Learning in Russian: For Stephen', programme note for *Uncle Vanya*, (Derry: Field Day, 1995).

(95–4)   *A Woman Untouched: An Elegy for Anne O'Callaghan*, privately published in June 1995 in a limited edition of three hundred copies.

(95–5)   'The Spirit of Play in Oscar Wilde's *De Profundis*, in *Creativity and its Contexts*, ed. by Chris Morash, (Dublin: Lilliput Press, 1995), pp. 49–59.

(96–1)   'Masks', Introduction to *The Dazzling Dark; New Irish Plays*, selected and introduced by Frank McGuinness, (London: Faber and Faber, 1996), pp. ix-xii.

(97–1)   'Perhaps' programme note for *The Caucasian Chalk Circle*, (London: Royal National Theatre, 1997).

(97–2)   'Trees in Spain for Brian', *Printings by Brian Bourke*, (Dublin: Taylor Galleries, 1997).

(97–3)   'Foreword', *Shakespeare and Ireland: History, Politics, Culture*, eds. by Mark Thornton Burnett and Ramona

Wray, (London: Macmillan, 1997), pp. xi-xii.

(98–1)   'The Spirit of Play in *De Profundis*', in *Wilde the Irishman*, ed. by Jerusha McCormack, (New Haven and London: Yale University Press, 1998), pp. 140–145.

(98–2)   'Catacombs', in *Or Volge L'Anno at the Year's Turning: An Anthology of Irish Poets Responding to Leopardi*, ed. by Marco Sonzogni, (Dublin: Dedalus Press, 1998), pp. 176–7.

(98–3)   'An Extract from *The Wild Duck*', *The Irish Review*, Frank McGuinness as the Guest Editor, Summer, 1998, pp. 16–22.

(98–4)   'Writing in Greek', programme note for *By the Bog of Cats* by Marina Carr, (Dublin: Abbey Theatre, 7 October, 1998)

(98–5)   'A Hard Year', programme note for *Juno and the Paycock* by Sean O'Casey, (Edinburgh: Royal Lyceum Theatre, 13 February 1998)

(98–6)   'Van Gogh in Donegal' (by a name of T.P.O'Donnell), in *The Ring of Words: Poems from the Daily Telegraph*, Arvon International Poetry Competition 1998, ed. by Andrew Motion, (Thrupp, Stroud, Gloucestershire: Sutton Publishing Limited), 1998, pp. 215–219.

(99–1)   '*Faith Healer*: All the Dead Voices', *Irish University Review*, 29.1(1999), pp. 60–63.

(99–2)   'The Woman Herself: A Tribute to Dusty Springfield, for Lar Cassidy', *Graph: Irish Cultural Review*, 3.2, Autumn/Winter 1998, pp. 25–6.

(99–3)   'Did she know how great she was?', *Irish Times*, March 6, 1999, reprinted version of (99–2).

(99–4)   'The music and the fury' (on Salman Rushdie's fictional world), *Irish Times*, 3 April, 1999.

(99–5)   'The reason why I hate cricket', *Yearbook of the Theatrical Cavaliers Cricket Club*, 1999 with his original typescript.

(00–1) 'Damaged man, seductive monster', book review on Rimbaud by Graham Robb, *Irish Times*, 14 October 2000.

(00–2) 'John Millington Synge and the King of Norway', in *Interpreting Synge: Essays from the Synge Summer School 1991–2000*, ed. by Nicholas Grene (Dublin: Lilliput Press, 2000), pp. 57–66.

Unpublished and undated manuscript:
(MS-1) 'Mabel Tilling: For The Tiger', a poem.
(MS-2) 'A poem on the paper'

Unpublished and undated typescript:
(TS-1) 'Paradiso'(First version), 8 pages.
(TS-2) 'Paradiso'(Second version), 16 pages including the title cover.
(TS-3) 'Keen', 4 pages including the title cover.

3. <Interviews>:

<82–1> Fintan O'Toole, 'The Factory Girls', *In Dublin*, no. 148, 5–18 March 1982.

<82–2> William Roche, 'The Tale of the Shirt Girls!', *Sunday Press*, 7 March 1982.

<82–3> Ronan Farren, 'No category for Frank's new play', *Evening Herald*, 11 March, 1982.

<82–4> Ray Comiskey, 'Plots with Hard Political Edges', *Irish Times*, 11 March 1982.

<82–5> Lucile Redmond, 'Sharp, strong shirt saga', *Sunday Triibune*, 14 March 1982.

<83–1> 'An Interview with Frank McGuinness', *Inis Duinn: Magazine of Carndonagh Community School*, 1983.

<85–1> Charles Hunter, 'Strange Passion About the Somme', *Irish Times*, 15 February 1985.

<85–2> Fintan O'Toole, 'Over the top', *Sunday Tribune*, 17 February 1985.

<85–3> Paddy Woodworth, 'My Goodness, McGuinness', *Image*, April 1985, pp. 100–101.

<85–4> 'The Arts and Ideology', Jennifer Fitzgerald, Seamus Deane, Joan Fowler, Frank McGuinness, *The Crane Bag*, vol. 9. no. 2, 1985 (Final Issue).

<86–1> Gerald McNamara, 'The Out Interview', *Out*, November/ December 1986, pp. 20–21.

<87–1> John Waters, 'Alone Again, Naturally', *In Dublin*, 14 May 1987, pp. 15–18.

<87–2> Paul Allen, 'Kaleidoscope: Frank McGuinness Special', (BBC) 1 May 1987.

<87–3> Carolyne Pollard, 'An Ulster Son Observed: Interview with Frank McGuinness, *Quarto*, Winter 1987/88 (Literary Society of the University of Ulster), pp. 12–13.

<87–4> Lyn Gardner, 'Irish Double First', *City Limits*, 7–14 May 1987, pp. 21–23.

<88–1> Deirdre Purcell, 'On Fire',*The Sunday Tribune*, 15 May 1988, p. 17.

<88–2> Fintan O'Toole, 'You don't think I'm not as stupid as Yeats, do you', *Irish Times*, Saturday, 24 September 1988, Weekend: p. 3.

<88–3> Nell Stewart-Liberty, 'Times In It', *Dublin Event Guide*, 12–25 May 1988, p. 11, (from the Abbey Archive).

<89–1> Kevin Jackson, 'Speaking for the Dead: Playwright Frank McGuinness talks to Kevin Jackson', *Independent*, 27 September 1989.

<89–2> Douglas Kennedy talks to Playwright Frank McGuinness, 'Poetic politics', *New Statesman & Society*, 6 October, pp. 50–52.

<90–1> Joe Jackson, 'The Bread Man Cometh . . .', *Hot Press*, 1 November 1990, pp. 44–45.

<92–1> Georgiana Brown, 'Three hostages to fortune', *Independent*, 10 July 1992.

<92–2> Peter Lewis, 'Making drama out of a crisis', *Sunday Times*, 12 July 1992.

<92–3> Mic Moroney, 'Trying to celebrate the dead', *Irish Times*, 29 January 1992.

<93–1> Jocelyn Clarke, 'Observe the Son of Ulster', *Sunday Tribune*, 11 April 1993: B1.

<93–2> Lorcan Roche, 'Time for Frank speaking', *Irish Independent Weekender*, 10 April 1993: 11, (from the Abbey Archive).

<93–3> Mary Carr, 'The play that finally meant writer Frank could buy a suit', *Evening Herald*, 13 April 1993, (from the Abbey Archive).

<94–1> Jocelyn Clarke, 'Painting, watching, witching', *Sunday Tribune*, 6 February 1994, (from the Abbey Archive).

<94–2> Carmel Monahan, 'Frank's felicitous felines', *Sunday Independent*, 20 February 1994, (from the Abbey Archive).

<94–3> 'Take 10 Ten', *RTE Guide*, 7 October 1994, (from the Abbey Archive).

<94–4> Trish Murphy, 'Bird Sanctuary', *Dublin Event Guide*, 16 February–1 March 1994, (from the Abbey Archive).

<95–1> Seamus Hosey, 'Frank McGuinness', *Speaking Volumes*, RTE, Blackwater Press, 1995, pp. 28–34.

<97–1> Mary Holland, 'Mini-Interview: So Shakespeare's the only one who can solve the Irish problem . . .', *Observer*, 16 November 1997.

<97–2> John Whitley, 'The Troubles with Shakespeare', *Daily*

Telegraph, 20 November 1997.

<97–3>   Jane Edwardes, 'Frank's Spenser: McGuinness returns to Irish history with his new play, *Mutabilitie*', *Time Out*, 19–26 November 1997, p. 158.

<97–4>   Mic Moroney, 'Coming home', *Irish Times*, Sunday 29 November 1997:1.

<98–1>   'Dialogue: Frank McGuinness with John Whitley on *Mutabilitie*', 9 January 1998, at Cottesloe at Royal National Theatre.

<98–2>   An Interview with Jacqueline Hurtley in *Ireland in Writing: Interviews with Writers and Academics*, Rodopi, Amsterdam-Atlanta, GA 1998, pp. 51–70 (The interview was carried out on 12 February 1996).

<98–3>   Catherine Lee, 'McGuinness's Middle Ages', *RTE Guide*, July 24, 1998.

<98–4>   'Interview with Frank McGuinness', *Studies*, 87: 347, pp. 269–273.

<99–1>   'The tomes of Donegal', *Irish Times*, 30 September 1999: p. 13.

<99–2>   'Frank's Wild Years', *RTE Guide*, 1 October 1999.

<00–1>   Deborah Ballard, 'Forces of Change: Frank McGuinness talks to Deborah Ballard about his play *Mutabilitie*, which premiers in Ireland on September 6', *GCN*, September 2000, issue 132.

<00–2>   Diarmuid Doyle, 'From Buncrana to barbaric', *Sunday Tribune*, 27 August 2000.

<01–1>   Joseph Long, 'The Sophoclean Killing Fields' (forthcoming).

<01–2>   Sheila O'Hagan, 'The Horse was a Protestant' (forthcoming).

4. [Articles on McGuinness]:

[83–1]   Paul Hadfield, 'Writers on the Rampage', *Fortnight*, March 1983, p. 28.

[84–1]   Joseph Long, 'Dancing in the Borderlands', *Theatre Ireland* 7 (Autumn, 1984) pp. 46–7.

[84–2]   Angela Wilcox, 'The Temple of the Lord is ransacked', *Theatre Ireland* 8 (Winter, 1984) pp. 87–89.

[85–1]   Keith Jeffery, 'Under the blood-red hand', *TLS*, November 22, 1985.

[85–2]   'Exciting Times Ahead for Derry Drama', *Derry Journal*, 10 December 1985.

[86–1]   Fintan O'Toole, 'A State: Innocence', *Sunday Tribune*, 12 October 1986, p. 19.

[86–2]   Fintan O'Toole, 'Innocence Uprooted', Fintan O'Toole profiles playwirght Frank McGuinness, *Magill*, Novmber 1986, pp. 48–54.

[86–3]   Lynda Henderson, 'Innocence and Experience', *Fortnight*, November 1986, p. 24.

[86–4]   Emilie Fitzgibbon, 'All Change: Contemporary Fashions in the Irish Theatre', in *Irish Writers and the Theatre*, ed. Masaru Sekine, Gerrards Cross, Bucks: Colin Smythe, 1986, pp. 33–46.

[86–5]   James Simmons, 'The Humour of Deprivation', in *Irish Writers and the Theatre*, ed. Masaru Sekine, Gerrards Cross, Bucks: Colin Smythe, 1986, pp. 167–178.

[87–1]   Ray Comiskey, 'Frank McGuinness: a new breed of Irish playwright', *Irish Times*, 2 May 1987, Weekend, p. 9.

[87–2]   Paul Allen, 'McGuinness is good for you', *Radio Times*, 2–8 May 1987.

[87–3] Shane McGuinness, 'Breaking the barrier', *Sunday Tribune*, 10 May 1987.

[87–4] Liz Penny, 'In the Forbidden City', *Theatre Ireland* 12, 1987, p. 62.

[87–5] Patrick Burke, 'Dance Unto Death', *Irish Literary Supplement*, 6.2.(1987), p. 45.

[87–6] Bill Doyle, 'The Bill Doyle File', *The Bridge: An Droichead* (The Bilingual Journal from Ireland), (Irish version by Sean O Conaill) Fall/Fomhar 1987, pp. 4–5.

[87–7] 'Q & A: Nuala Ní Dhomhnaill', *Irish Literary Supplement*, 6.2. (1987), p. 42.

[87–8] John Peter, 'The pitfalls of the creative translator', *Sunday Times*, 7 June 1987.

[87–9] Michael Etherton, 'The Field Day Theatre Company and the New Irish Drama', *New Theatre Quarterly*, 3.2.(1987), pp. 64–70.

[88–1] Angela Wilcox, 'The Memory of Wounds', *Theatre Ireland* 16, 1988, pp. 6–8.

[88–2] Gerald Dawe, Review of *Factory Girls*, *Theatre Ireland* 15 (May/August 1988) p. 52.

[88–3] Helen Lojek, 'Myth and Bonding in Frank McGuinness's *Observe the Sons of Ulster Marching Towards the Somme*', in *Canadian Journal of Irish Studies*, Vol. 14, No.1 (1988) pp. 45–53.

[88–4] Fintan O'Toole, 'Judged by its Peers', *Theatre Ireland* 17 (December 1988/March 1989), pp. 28–29.

[88–5] Fintan O'Toole, 'A leap beyond the dark', *Irish Times*, 1 October 1988: Weekend: p. 11.

[88–6] John Keyes, 'Gender-bender inherits the earth', *Fortnight*, November 1988 (267), p. 25.

[89–1]   J'Accuse – McGuinness: Stage and Screen, *Theatre Ireland* 21 (December, 1989) pp. 58–62.

[89–2]   Michael Etherton, *Contemporary Irish Dramatists*, Macmillan, 1989, pp. 47–51.

[89–3]   Marie Kai, 'Airurando kara no Kaze' ('A Wind from Ireland'), *Higeki-Kigeki*, (November 1989), pp. 39–43. (In Japanese)

[89–4]   'Marathon Effort', *Act One*, Spring 1989, no. 3.

[89–5]   Emelie Fitzgibbon, 'Three TEAM Plays', *Irish Literary Supplement*, Spring 1989: p. 13.

[89–6]   Ger Fitzgibbon, 'Sex, Politics and Religion', *Irish Literary Supplement*, Spring 1989: p. 15.

[90–1]   John Hargaden, 'The Stage Irishman in Modern Irish Drama', *Studies*, Spring 1990 (vol.79, no. 313).

[90–2]   Helen Lojek, 'Differences Without Indifference: The Drama of Frank McGuinness and Anne Devlin', *Eire-Ireland*, V.25, no.2 (1990), pp. 56–68.

[91–1]   Ulrich Schneider, 'Staging History in Contemporary Anglo-Irish Drama: Brian Friel and Frank McGuinness', in *The Crows Behind the Plough*, ed. Greet Lernout, Amsterdam, 1991, pp. 79–98.

[91–2]   Riana O'Dwyer, 'Dancing in the Borderlands: The Plays of Frank McGuinness', in *The Crows Behind the Plough*, ed. Greet Lernout, Amsterdam, 1991, pp. 99–115.

[91–3]   Richard Pine, 'Frank McGuinness: A Profile', *Irish Literary Supplement*, 10.1. (1991), pp. 29–30.

[91–4]   Victoria White, 'Irish dramatists: in fear of the female?', *Irish Times*, 18 June 1991, p. 8.

[92–1]   Matt Wolf, 'Two Vehicles Carry an Irish Actor to America', *New York Times*, 22 November 1992, p. 21.

[92-2]   Bernice Schrank, 'World War I in the Plays of Shaw, O'Casey and McGuinness', *Études Irlandaises*, 17.2. 1992, pp. 29–36.

[92-3]   Imelda Foley, 'History's moral guardians alerted', *Fortnight*, April 1992, pp. 36–37.

[92-4]   Claire Armitstead, 'The vocabulary of racial tension', *The Guide*, July 1992.

[92-5]   Roy Foster, 'Appreciations: Baroness Ewart-Biggs', *The Times*, 15 October 1992.

[93-1]   Louise Stafford Charles, 'Someone Who'll Watch Over Me', *Theatre Ireland* 28 (Summer, 1993), pp. 84–87.

[93-2]   Brian Cosgrove, 'Orpheus Descending: Frank McGuinness's *Someone Who'll Watch Over Me*', *Irish University Review*, Vol. 23, No. 2 (1993), pp. 197–201.

[93-3]   Katharine Worth, 'Book Review on *Someone Who'll Watch Over Me*', *Irish University Review*, Vol. 23, No. 2 (1993), pp. 324–326.

[93-4]   Victoria White, 'Someone to Watch Over Him?', *Theatre Ireland* 31 (Summer, 1993), pp. 22–24.

[93-5]   Paul Lawley, 'Contemporary Dramatists: McGuinness', ed. K.A. Berney, *Contemporary Dramatists*, St. James Press, 1993, pp. 436–438.

[93-6]   Achilles, Jochen, 'Religion in Modern Irish Drama: Social Criticsm and Spiritual Reorientation', *Anglistentag*, 15 (1993), pp. 459–470.

[93-7]   — 'Religious Risk in the Drama of Contemporary Ireland', *Eire-Ireland*, 28.3 (1993), pp. 17–37.

[93-8]   Barry Sloan, 'Sectarianism and the Protestant Mind: Some Approaches to a Recurrent Theme in Irish Drama', *Études Irlandaises*, 18.2. (1993), pp. 33–43.

[93-9]   Helen Meany, 'A Love Story in Hell', *Irish Times*, 13 April 1993, p. 8.

[94–1] Anthony Roche, *Contemporary Irish Drama: From Beckett to McGuinness*, Gill & Macmillan, 1994, pp. 265–78.

[94–2] 'Playwright of passionate variety', *Irish Times*, 9 February 1994.

[94–3] Michael Patrick Lapointe, *A Place Elsewhere: Displacement in Frank McGuinness' and Michael Longley's Response to the Northern Irish 'Troubles'*, Unpublished MA Thesis, McMaster University, August 1994.

[94–4] Claire Gleitman, *Theatrical negotiations on a modern Irish terrain: A study of three contemporary Irish dramatists*, Unpublished Ph.D Thesis, New York University, 1994.

[94–5] Anthony Roche, 'Recent Trends in Contemporary Irish Drama', *Ireland: Literature, Culture, Politics*, Heidelberg: Universitätsverlag C. Winter, 1994, pp. 71–88.

[94–6] Claire Gleitman, '"Isn't it just like real life?": Frank McGuinness and the (Re)writing of Stage Space', in *Canadian Journal of Irish Studies*, Vol. 20, No.1 (1994) pp. 60–73.

[94–7] Margot Gayle Backus, 'Homophobia and the Imperial Demon Lover: Gothic Narrativity in Irish Representations of the Great War', in *Canadian Review of Comparative Literature*, Vol. 21, No.1–2 (1994) pp. 45–63.

[95–1] Edna Longley,'Pamphlets and professors', *TLS*, 17 March 1995, (on *Uncle Vanya*).

[95–2] James Liddy, 'Voices in the Irish Cities of the Dead: Melodrama and Dissent in Frank McGuinness's *Carthaginians*, *Irish University Review*, Vol. 25, No. 2, 1995.

[95–3] Helen Lojek, 'Watching Over Frank McGuinness' Stereotypes', *Modern Drama*, 38 (1995), pp. 348–361.

[95–4] Kenji Kono, *Gendai-Airurando Bungaku Josetu* (Modern Irish Literature: An Introduction), Tokyo: Kindai-Bungeisha (1995), pp. 34–58 (in Japanese).

[96–1] Elizabeth Butler Cullingford, 'British Romans and Irish Carthaginians: Anticolonial Metaphor in Heaney, Friel, and McGuinness', *PMLA*, March 1996, pp. 222–239.

[96–2] Claire Gleitman, '"Like Father, Like Son": *Someone Who'll Watch Over Me* and the Geopolitical Family Drama', *Eire-Ireland*, 31. 1&2 (1996), pp. 78–88.

[96–3] Catherine Bedarida, 'Les plaies de la guerre au coeur du theatre de Frank McGuinness', *Le Monde*, 24 May 1996, p. 27.

[96–4] Olivier Shmitt, 'A la recherche de la paix sur les rives de la Somme', *Le Monde*, 24 May 1996, p. 27.

[96–5] Hiroko Mikami, 'On Frank McGuinness's *Someone Who'll Watch Over Me*', *Kyoyoshogaku Kenkyuu*, 100 (1996), pp. 315–334.

[97–1] Eamon Jordan, *The Feast of Famine: The Plays of Frank McGuinness*, Bern: Peter Lang, 1997.

[97–2] Helen Lojek, 'Frank McGuinness', in *Irish Playwrights 1880–1995*, eds. by Bernice Schrank and William W. Demastes, Westport: Greenwood Press, 1997, pp. 78–88.

[97–3] Hiroko Mikami, 'On Psychodrama and Storytelling in *Carthaginians*', *Kyoyoshogaku Kenkyuu*, 102 (1997), pp. 235–253.

[97–4] Cullingford, Elizabeth Bulter, 'Gender, Sexuality, and Englishness in Modern Irish Drama and Film', in *Gender and Sexuality in Modern Ireland*, eds. by Anthony Bradley and Maryann Gialanella Valiulis, Amherst: University of Massachusetts Press, 1997, pp. 159–186.

[97–5] Remy Charest, 'L'Irlande de toutes pieces: Le rapport a l'identite se lit de pulusieurs manieres dans l'oeuvre du dramaturge irlandais', *Le Devoir*, 22 December 1997.

[98–1] Enda McDonagh, 'Inhabited by the Others: After the Plays of Frank McGuinness', *Ceide*, March/April, 1998, pp. 12–14.

[98–2]   Richard Rankin Russell, 'Ulster Unionism's Mythic and Religious Culture in *Observe the Sons of Ulster*', Working Papers in Irish Studies, Department of Liberal Arts, Nova Southeastern University, 1998.

[98–3]   Colomba Damiani, 'The Queening of Dido: Gender and Sexuality in Virgil's *Aeneid*, Christopher Marlowe's *The Tragedy of Dido Queen of Carthage*, and Frank McGuinness's *Carthaginians*', unpublished dissertation submitted to University of Ulster, Coleraine.

5.   Production History and Reviews

(a) Original Plays:
The Factory Girls (1982)
I   Peacock Theatre, 11 March 1982.(leaflet)
       (Directed by Patrick Mason)

1. David Nowlan, '"The Factory Girls" at the Peacock', *Irish Times*, 11 March 1982.
2. Emmanuel Kehoe, 'Trouble At All', *Sunday Press*, 14 March 1982.
3. Treasa Brogan, 'More than just factory girls . . .', *Evening Press*, 13 March 1982.
4. Fintan O'Toole, 'Sweet Shirts', *In Dublin*, 19 March – 1 April 1982.
5. Colm Cronin, 'Factory girls' not all fun, *Sunday Tribune*, 14 March 1982.
6. Kevin Faller, 'Collapse of "The Factory Girls"', *Irish Independent*, 12 March 1982.
7. Michael Sheridan, 'Cliches in "Factory Girls"', *Irish Press*, 12 March 1982.
8. 'Play by former N.U.U. lecturer', *Coleraine Chronicle*, 13 March 1982.
9. (photo), *Irish Press*, 12 March 1982.
10. (photo), *In Dublin*, 5–18 March 1982.
11. (photo), *Irish Times*, 6 March 1982.
12. 'Sweat Shirts', *In Dublin*, 18–31 March 1982.
13. Ronan Farren, 'No category for Frank's new play', *Evening Herald*, 11 March 1982.
14. Sarah O'Hara, 'Productive lives', *Irish Press*, 17 March 1982.
15. Maureen Fox, 'Applause for *Factory Girls*', *Cork Examiner*, 2

November 1982.
16. Fionnuala O Connor, *Irish Times*, 22 November 1982.
17. Bronagh Taggart, 'Flashpoint: factory floor', *Metro*, January 1983, p. 15.
18. Charles Fitzgerald, 'Play a hit not to be missed', *Newsletter*, 10 November 1982.

II-a Druid Theatre, 16 March 1988.
      (Directed by Garry Hynes)

II-b Druid Theatre, Riverside Studio 2, 12–21 May 1988.

Theatre Record:
1. Jane Edwardes, *Time Out*, 18 May 1988.
2. Victoria Radin, *New Statesman*, 20 May 1988.
3. Michael Coveney, *Financial Times*, 13 May 1988.
4. Hugh Barnes, *Glasgow Herald*, 4 May 1988.
5. Sarah Hemming, *Independent*, 5 May 1988.
6. Michael Billington, *Guardian*, 14 May 1988.
7. David Browne, *What's On*, 18 May 1988.
8. John Connor, *City Limits*, 19 May 1988.
9. Annalena AcAfee, *Evening Standard*, 12 May 1988.
10. Allen Wright, *Scotsman*, 7 May 1988.
11. Maureen McAlpine, *Tribune*, 13 May 1988.
Others:
12. Jeremy Kingston, 'McGuinness on draught', *The Times*, 9 May 1988.
13. Patricia Craig, *TLS*, 27 May–2 June 1988: 585

III The Tricycle, London, 18 January 1991.
     (Directed by Nicolas Kent)

Theatre Record:
1. Antonia Denford, *City Limits*, 18 October 1990.
2. Milton Shulman, *Evening Standard*, 9 October 1990.
3. Kenneth Hurren, *Mail on Sunday*, 14 October 1990.
4. Charles Spencer, *Daily Telegraph*, 10 October 1990.
5. Paul Taylor, 'Getting shirty', *Independent*, 10 October 1990.
6. Irving Wardle, *Independent on Sunday*, 14 October 1990.
7. Clare Bayley, *What's On*, 17 October 1990.
8. Hugo Williams, *Sunday Independent*, 14 October 1990.
9. Benedict Nightingale, *The Times*, 9 October 1990.

10. Jane Edwardes, *Time Out*, 17 October 1990.
11. John Gross, *Sunday Telegraph*, 14 October 1990.

IV   The Bay Street Theatre, New York, 14 July 1999
     (Directed by Nye Heron, produced in association with
     Williamstwon Theatre Festival)
Amateur performances:
AI   Gerry Colgan, '"The Factory Girls" at UCD', *Irish Times*, 27
     January 1989.
     (by Dramasoc at UCD)
AII 'Finals begin with a winner', *Newsletter*, 31 May 1989.
     (by Armagh Theatre Group)

Borderlands (1984)
I   TEAM Theatre on tour
     8 February 1984
     (Directed by Martin Drury)

  1. Charles Hunter, 'TEAM Theatre's "Borderlands" on tour of
     schools', *Irish Times*, 27 March 1984.
  2. Fintan O'Toole, 'Pictures of dying societies', *Sunday Tribune*, 1
     April 1984.

Observe the Sons of Ulster Marching Towards the Somme (1985)
I-a Peacock, 18 February, 1985.
     (Directed by Patrick Mason)

  1. (Notice with a picture), *Irish Times*, 16 February 1985.
  2. David Nowlan, '*Observe the Sons of Ulster Marching Towards
     the Somme* at the Peacock', *Irish Times*, 19 February 1985.
  3. Michael Sheridan, 'Somme march, alive in style and
     conviction', *Irish Press*, 19 February 1985.
  4. Treasa Brogan, 'Sons of Ulster march to battle', *Evening Press*,
     19 February 1985.
  5. Desmond Rushe, 'Splendid acting in drama of Somme', *Irish
     Independent*, 19 February 1985.
  6. 'Beating the Orange drum', *Irish Times*, 23 February 1985.
  7. Jennifer Johnston, *Irish Times* (Letters to the Editor), 23
     February 1985.
  8. Kevin Barry, *Irish Times* (Letters to the Editor), 23 February
     1985.
  9. Tim Harding, 'When Ulster marched on the Somme', *Sunday*

Press, 24 February 1985.

10. Fintan O'Toole, 'Life on the brink', *Sunday Tribune,* 24 February 1985.
11. David Nowlan, 'Prompts: A Lively Fortnight', *Irish Times,* 28 February 1985.
12. Michael Longley, *Irish Times* (Letters to the Editor), 2 March 1985.
13. Fergus Linehan, 'Backdrop', *Irish Times,* 2 March 1985.
14. John Devitt, *Irish Times* (Letters to the Editor), 8 March 1985.
15. Nick Carter, *In Dublin,* 7–20th March (no. 224) 1985.
16. Terrence Brown, 'From the Somme to Armageddon', *Fortnight,* 18–31 March 1985.
17. Colm Cronin, 'Theatre', *Hibernia,* March 1985, vol.2, no.3.
18. P. P. Murray, 'Theatre Review: *Observe the Sons of Ulster Marching Towards the Somme'*, *Out,* April/May 1985.
19. 'Festival Wins the race', *Newsletter,* 26 June 1985.
20. The Spectator, 'Auspicious and happy events at the Riverside', *Coleraine Chronicle,* 16 May 1985.
21. Graham Sennett, 'Over the top at the Somme', *Evening Press,* 16 Februaary 1985.
22. Terry McGeehan, 'When Ulster marched on the Somme', *Sunday Press,* 24 February 1985.
23. Joseph O'Connor, 'Theatre', *Mcgill,* 7 March 1985.
24. Charles Fitzgerald, 'Face to face with Ulster', *Newsletter,* date unspecified, March 1985.

I-b Abbey Theatre on tour leaflet, (Cork, Belfast, Coleraine, Sligo, Limerick, Dublin) 28 October–14 December 1985.

1. Michael Coveney, 'Sons of Ulster/Belfast Festival', 7 November 1985.
2. Michael Billington, 'The Orange march to destruction', 8 November 1985.
3. 'Abbey Theatre back in Coleraine', *Coleraine Chronicle,* 9 November 1985.
4. Mary Campbell, '"Brighter" Belfast packs 'em in', *Sunday Tribune,* 10 November 1985.
5. David Nowlan, McGuinness play at the Abbey Theatre', *Irish Times,* 4 December 1985.
6. *Sunday Press,* 1 December 1985.
7. Eugene Moloney, 'Breaking the closing time barrier for post-festival thirsts', *Irish News,* 7 November 1985.
8. Charles Fitzgerald, 'Actor shines as star of war play',

Newsletter, 7 November 1985.
9. (photo), *Coleraine Chronicle,* 9 November 1985.
10. (photo), *Irish Times,* 3 December 1985.
11. Clare Cronin, 'Abbey cast excels in powerful drama', *Cork Examiner,* 29 October 1985.
12. 'Sons in Ulster triumph', *Newsletter,* 6 November 1985.
13. John Boland, 'Dubliner's Diary: Church and State at the Abbey', 3 December 1985.
14. David Simpson, 'A perceptive look at Ulster', *Belfast Telegraph,* 6 November 1985.
15. Desmond Rushe, 'Going over the top', *Irish Independent,* 3 December 1985.
16. Seamus O Cinneide, 'Superbly delivered play at Belltable', *Limerick Leader,* 27 November 1985.
17. S. O C., 'Abbey's compelling Anti-war production', *Limerick Chronicle,* 26 November 1985.
18. The Spectator, 'Auspicious and happy events at the Riverside', (source and date unspecified).

II   Hampstead Theatre, 24 July 1986
     (Directed Michael Attenborough)

Theatre Record:
1. Sheridan Morley, *Punch,* 6 August 1986.
2. Kenneth Hurren, *Mail on Sunday,* 27 July 1986.
3. Steve Grant, *Time Out,* 30 July 1986.
4. Michael Billington, *Guardian,* 26 July 1986.
5. David Nathan, *Jewish Chronicle,* 1 August 1986.
6. Milton Shulman, *London Standard,* 25 July 1986.
7. Jim Hiley, *Listener,* 7 August 1986.
8. Michael Ratcliffe, *Observer,* 27 July 1986.
9. Eric Shorter, *Daily Telegraph,* 28 July 1986.
10. Michael Coveney, *Financial Times,* 25 July 1986.
11. Francis King, *Sunday Telegraph,* 3 August 1986.
12. Christopher Edwards, *Spectator,* 2 August 1986.
13. Lyn Gardner, *City Limits,* 31 July 1986.
14. Robert Gore Langton, *Plays & Players,* September 1986.

III Centaur theatre company, 8 March-3 April 1988.
     (Directed by Joe Dowling)

IV   Lyric Players Theatre, 29 March-5 May 1989?
     (Directed by Noel McGee)

V-a The Abbey Theatre(13 October 1994)
(Directed by Patrick Mason)

1. 'Abbey revival', *Irish Times,* 15 September 1994.
2. '"Somme" play for revival at Abbey', 14 September 1994.
3. Patsy McGarry, 'Observe the sons of Ulster marching to the Abbey!', *Irish Press,* 19 October 1994.
4. Victoria White, 'Mining a rich heritage, or digging trenches?', *Irish Times,* 19 October 1994.
5. Aoife MacEoin, 'Unionist "Observe" no lessons', *Irish Press,* 20 October 1994.
6. Robert O'Byrne, 'Warm smiles all round as Ulster takes centre stage', *Irish Times,* 20 October 1994.
7. Kim Bielengerg, 'Dubliner's Diary: Ulster's Sons at Abbey', *Evening Press,* 20 October 1994.
8. Gerry Colgan, 'Rhetoric, imagery in significant stage event', *Irish Times,* 20 October 1994.
9. 'Archetypal men in theatre of battlefield', *Irish Press,* 20 October 1994.
10. 'Review of Observe the Sons of Ulster Marching Towards the Somme', RTE Radio 1: The Art Show, 20 October 1994.
11. Ronan McGeevy, 'No surrender in the trenches', *Evening Press,* 20 October 1994.
12. 'Observe the Abbey at its best', *Irish Independent,* 20 October 1994.
13. Gerald Morgan, 'Sons of Ulster', *Irish Times,* 22 October 1994.
14. Christopher Fitz-Simon, 'Winkling On', *Irish Times,* 22 October 1994.
15. Kevin Myers, 'An Irishman's Diary', *Irish Times,* 22 October 1994.
16. Tim Harding, 'Into the minds of Ulster's sons', *Sunday Press,* 23 October 1994.
17. Emer O'Kelly, 'Sacred heroes', *Sunday Independent,* 23 October 1994.
18. 'Culture Ireland: Theatre', *Sunday Times,* 23 October 1994.
19. Ann Marie Hourihane, 'Upfront', *Tribune Magazine,* 23 October 1994.
20. Liam O Murchu, 'Sons of Ulster in the U.S.', *Irish Echo,* 23 October 1994.
21. J. C., 'Critics' Choice', *Tribune Magazine,* 23 October 1994.
22. Eddie Doyle, 'The sons of Ulster come to observe', *Sunday Business Post,* 23 October 1994.
23. 'Observe the Sons of Ulster Marching Towards the Somme',

(source unspecified), 24 October 1994.
24. Kay Hingerty, 'Assumptions about the North are challenged', *Cork Examiner*, 25 October 1994.
25. 'Observe the Sons of Ulster', RTE Radio 1, Gay Byrne Show, 28 October 1994.
26. William Rocke, 'Curtain to rise on 90 years of the Abbey', *Sunday Press*, 13 November 1994.
27. Conor Kostick, 'Horror in the Somme', *Socialist Worker*, November 1994.
28. Mary Hyland, 'Observe the Sons of Ulster Marching Towards the Somme', *In Dublin*, 23 November 1994, (with photo).
29. *Sunday Times*, 16 July 1995.

V-b King's Theatre (Edinburgh International Festival)
18–23 August 1995.

Theatre Record:
1. Clare Bayley, 'All's unfair in war and love', *Independent on Sunday*, 27 August 1995.
2. Paul Taylor, *Independent*, 22 August 1995.
3. Simon Reade. *Guardian*, 21 August 1995.
4. Catherine Lockerbie, *Scotsman*, 21 August 1995.
5. John Gross, 'Never forget the ghosts in bonnets', *Sunday Telegraph*, 27 August 1995.
6. Charles Spencer, *Daily Telegraph*, 22 August 1995.
7. Alastair Macaulay, *Financial Times*, 22 August 1995.
8. Bill Hagerty, *Today*, 25 August 1995.
9. Michael Coveney, *Observer*, 27 August 1995.
10. Bemedoct Nightingale, *The Times*, 22 August 1995.
11. Mark Fisher, *Herald*, 21 August 1995.
12 Nicholas de Jongh, *Evening Standard*, 21 August 1995.
Others:
13. Catherine Lockerbie, 'Men of Ulster march in unity', *Scotsman*, 18 August 1995.
14. John Peter, 'Out with the truth', *Sunday Times*, 27 August 1995.
15. Mary Kenny, 'Letters to the editor', *Daily Telegraph*, 24 August 1995.

V-c RSC by arrangement with Thelma Holt presents the Abbey Theatre
Barbican, 6–16 March 1996.

Theatre Record:
1. *Daily Express*, 8 March 1996.
2. Sheridan Morley, *Spectator*, 16 March 1996.
3. Robert Butler, *Independent on Sunday*, 10 March 1996.
4. Clive Hirschhorn, *Sunday Express*, 10 March 1996.
5. Nicholas de Jongh, *Evening Standrd*, 7 March 1996.
6. Benedict Nightingale, *The Times*, 8 March 1996.
7. Jane Edwards, *Time Out*, 13 March 1996.
8. Ian Shuttleworth, *Financial Times*, 12 March 1996.
9. Robert Gore-Langton, *Daily Telegraph*, 12 March 1996.
10. John Gross, *Sunday Telegraph*, 10 March 1996.
11. Neil Smith, *What's On*, 13 March 1996.
12. Jack Tinker, *Daily Mail*, 15 March 1996.

V-d Presented by the Northern Ireland Group in Belgium
Koninklijke Vlaamse Schouwburg(6–8 June 1996)

V-e The Abbey Theatre
(*Observe the Sons of Ulster Marching Towards the Somme, The Well of the Saints*)
Odeon Theatre de L'Europe (28 May-1 June 1996)

VI Dundee Rep Theatre, 4–21 November 1998.
(Directed by Michael Duke)

1. John di Folco, 'Observe the Sons of Ulster Marching Towards the Somme', *The Stage*, 19 November 1998.

Amateur Performances:
AI 'Amateur Play Final', *Irish Times*, 24 April 1988.
(by the Newpoint Players, Newry at the 36th All Ireland Amateur Drama Festival)

AII 'Observing the Sons', *Irish News*, 2 June 1988.
'Derry Drama Festival', *Derry Journal*, 11 March 1988.
(by the Bangor Drama Club)

AIII Albert Hunt, 'Over the top for peace', *Guardian*, 17 March 1992.
(by Freelance, Derry, at Realto Theatre)

AIV Patrick Ryan, 'Abbey's adaptation proves a hit on all fronts', *Newry Democrat*, 22 November 2000.

(by Abbey Grammar School, Newry)

Baglady **(1985)**
I-a   Peacock lunchtime, 5–8 March 1985.
      (Directed by Patrick Mason)

1. Desmond Rushe, 'Rhythm, tax and topical junkets', *Irish Independent*, 6 March 1985.
2. Kevin Myers, 'An Irishman's Diary', *Irish Times*, 6 March 1985.
3. David Nowlan, '"Baglady" at the Peacock', *Irish Times*, 7 March 1985.
4. (photo), *Irish Times*, 2 March 1985.
5. (photo), *In Dublin*, 7–20 March (no. 224) 1985.
6. 'Somme and Baglady offer Abbey hope', *Irish Press*, 9 March 1985.
7. Peter Thompson, 'Baglady the perfect package', *Irish Press*, 6 March 1985.
8. Peter Thompson, 'Baglady the perfect package', *Irish Press*, 6 March 1985.

I-b   (Riverside Studio 2, 14 Sep–1 October 1988)
Theatre Record:
1. Michael Coveney, *Financial Times*, 14 September 1988.
2. Lyn Gardner, *City Limits*, 8 September 1988.
3. Patrick Marmion, *What's On*, 21 September 1988.
4. Charles Spencer, *Daily Telegraph*, 16 September 1988.
5. Michael Goldfarb, *Guardian*, 16 September 1988.
6. Annalena AcAfee, *Evening Standard*, 15 September 1988.

II   Bristol Old Vic, 12–22 October 1988
     (Sorcha Cusack as Baglady)
     (at Traverse Theatre, Edinburgh, as part of the Edinburgh Festival, prior to its New Vic opening)

Gatherers **(1985)**
I   TEAM Theatre Company. (Autumn Tour 1985)
    (Directed by Joe Dowling)

1. 'The man from TEAM', *Irish Times*, 28 September 1985.
2. Mary MacGoris, 'The Papal Mass . . . five pilgrims' tales', *Irish Independent*, 30 September 1985.
3. 'Gatherers', *In Dublin*, 19 September 1985.

Baglady/Ladybag (1985)

I Abbey Theatre on tour in association with Dublin Theatre Festival, October 1985.
(Directed by Patrick Mason)
(Programme at Riverside Theatre, Coleraine)

1. 'Contrast of two dramas', *Irish Press*, 25 September 1985.
2. Stephen Walsh, 'Monologue that leaves audience charmed', *Irish Independent*, 25 September 1985.
3. Martin Cropper, 'Baglady/Ladybag: Dublin Theatre Festival', *The Times*, 27 September 1985.
4. Colm Toibin, 'Toal scores on double', *Sunday Independent*, 29 September 1985.
5. Fintan O'Toole, 'Irreverent, indulgent . . . and fun', *Sunday Tribune*, 29 September 1985.
6. Nick Carter, 'Theatre Festival Midterm Report', *In Dublin*, 3 October 1985, p. 12.
7. Gerald Colgan at the Dublin Theatre Festival, *Plays International*, vol.1, no.4., November 1985.
8. Leslie Taylor, 'Bags of talent', *Evening Herald*, 24 September 1985.
9. Kay Hingerty, 'Maureen takes fall in fuchsia in her stride', *Cork Examiner*, 20 January 1986.
10. Crichton Healy, 'Abbey tour starts tonight', *Cork Examiner*, 20 January 1986.
11. Clare Cronin, 'Toal brilliant in McGuinness duet', *Cork Examiner*, 21 January 1986.

Innocence: the Life of Caravaggio (1986)

I Gate, 7 October 1986.
(Directed by Patrick Mason)

1. Michael Ratcliffe, 'Irish rides to the abyss: Irish plays in London and Dublin', *Observer*, 19 October 1986.
2. *In Dublin*, 16 October 1986, p. 46.
3. Lynda Henderson, 'Innocence and Experience', *Fortnight*, November 1986, p. 26.
4. Fintan O'Toole, 'A State of Mind: Innocence', *Sunday Tribune*, 12 October 1986, p. 19.

Amateur Performances:
AI Student production at University of Ulster at Coleraine.
   The date of the production unspecified.

Carthaginians (1988)

I-a Abbey, 26 September, 1988.
  (Directed by Sarah Pia Anderson)
  Programme, leaflet.

1. Fintan O'Toole, 'Vincent Dowling's Second Coming: Blessing or Damnation?', *Sunday Tribune*, 24 January 1988.
2. Seamus Hosey, *Carthaginians*, *Sunday Tribune*, 2 October, 1988.
3. Kevin Myers, ' An Irishman's Diary', *Irish Times*, 18 October, 1988.
4. John Peter, 'How farce can transcend the gags', *Sunday Times*, 2 October 1988.
5. Brian Brennan, 'Tending to the living', *Sunday Independent*, 2 October 1988.
6. Wendy Shea, Theatre Festival Sketchbook, *Irish Times*, 3 October 1988.
7. Patricia Sharkey, 'An Emotional Minefield: Derry-born critic attacks McGuinness play', *Derry Journal*, 21 October 1988.
8. John Keyes, 'Gender-bender inherits the earth', *Fortnight*, no. 267, November, 1988.
9. David Nowlan, 'Is Abbey biting off more than it can chew?', *Irish Times*, 21 January 1988.
10. 'Carthaginians', *Sunday Press*, 2 October 1988.
11. 'Bid to bridge North South divide', *Irish Independent*, 27 September 1988.
12. Hugh McFadden, 'Visions in a Derry graveyard', *Irish Press*, 27 September 1988.
13. Colm Cronin, 'Prey to its pretensions', *Evening Press*, 27 September 1988.
14. Desmond Rushe, 'Black fun in tangles', *Irish Independent*, 27 September 1988.
15. David Nowlan, '"Carthaginians" at the Peacock', *Irish Times*, 27 September 1988.
16. John Finegan, 'Derry Air waiting for a miracle', *Evening Herald*, 27 September 1988.
17. David Grant, 'Salt in the ashes', *Independent*, 28 September 1988.
18. Kay Hingerty, 'New McGuinness play blends fun and death', *Cork Examiner*, 28 September 1988.

I-b Hampstead, 13 July 1989.
  Programme, leaflet.

Theatre Record:
1. Michael Billington, 'Memories of wounds', *Guardian*, 14 July 1989.
2. Rhoda Koenig, *Punch*, 28 July 1989.
3. Christopher Edwards, *Spectator*, 22 July 1989.
4. Martin Hoyle, *'Carthaginians '*,*Financial Times*, 14 July 1989.
5. Charles Spencer, 'A blast of baloney', *Daily Telegraph*, 19 July 1989.
6. Sheridan Morley, *Herald Tribune*, 19 July 1989.
7. Graham Hassell, *What's On*, 19 July 1989.
8. Maureen Paton, *Daily Express*, 17 July 1989.
9. Kenneth Hurren, *Mail on Sunday*, 16 July 1989.
10. Jane Edwardes, *Time Out*, 19 July 1989.
11. Carole Woddis, *City Limits*, 20 July 1989.
12. Clive Hirschhorn, *Sunday Express*, 16 July 1989.
13. Milton Shulman, 'Slice of strife', *Evening Standard*, 14 July 1989.
14. Gavin Millar, *Listner*, 27 July 1989.
15. Michael Ratcliffe, 'Bringers of light', *Observer*, 16 July 1989.
16. Georgina Brown, 'Over the tumbled graves', *Independent*, 14 July 1989.

Others:
17. Graham Hassell, *Plays & Players*, September 1989.
18. Irving Wardle, 'A memory confronted', *Times*, 15 July 1989.
19. Patricia Craig, 'A graveside manner', *TLS*, 28 July 1989:824.

II   Druid, 5 February 1992.
     (Directed by Frank McGuinness)

1. Imelda Foley, 'History's moral guardians alerted', *Fortnight*, no. 305, April 1992.
2. Jim Tierney, 'Carthaginians', 16 March 1992, source unspecified.
3. Gerry Colgan, '"Carthaginians" in Galway', *Irish Times*, 7 February 1992.

III   Greenwich Studio, 13 April–2 May 1993.
      (Directed by Danny Carrick)

Theatre Record:
1. Suzi Feay, *Time Out*, 21 April 1993.
2. Jane Devane, *What's On*, 21 April 1993.
3. Sarah Hemming, *Independent*, 21 April 1993.

IV   Lyric Theatre, Belfast, 24 August–18 September
     (Directed by Simon Magill)

1. Grania McFadden, 'The Derry accent on a new beginning',
   Belfast Telegraph, 25 August 1999.
2. Ian Hill, 'Play portrays 30 years of pain', *Newsletter* (Belfast),
   26 August 1999.
3. Jane Coyle, 'Reviews: *Carthaginians*', *Irish Times*, 26 August
   1999.
4. Mary Preston Silver, 'Comedy and tragedy from a timely
   play', *Irish News*, 26 August 1999.
5. Jocelyn Clarke, 'The Queen of Bloody Sunday', *Sunday
   Tribune*, 29 August 1999.
6. Jane Coyle, 'Lyric theatre proves that Carthage is still
   standing', *Sunday Life*, 29 August 1999.
7. Gerry Colgan, 'Theatre(entertainment for the week ahead)',
   Irish Times, 21 August 1999, (prior to the opening).

Amateur Performances:
AI   St. Anthony's Little Theatre, Dublin, 9–10 May 1994.
     by La Touche Players (Bank of Ireland), 1994 All-Ireland
     Finalists

AII Grand Opera House, Ulster Drama Festival, 4 June 1994
     (by Donegal Drama Circle)

AIII Ngaio Marsh Theatre, 22 September 1999.
     (by University of Canterbury Drama Society)

1. Anna Dunbar, 'Bloody Sunday enacted', (source unspecified),
   22 September 1999.
2. Michele Burstein, 'The Carthaginians at Ngaio March',
   (source unspecified), 25 September 1999.
3. Olivia Mathias, 'Irish Drama at Ngaio Marsh: Bloody
   Sunday', CANTA, 22 September 1999.

Times In It (1988)
I   Peacock, 12 May 1988
     (Directed by Caroline FitzGerald)

1. Fintan O'Toole, 'Terrific trilogy', *Sunday Tribune*, 15 May 1988.
2. Kathy Sheridan, 'Acid test for a new director', *Irish Times*, 12

May 1988.
3. 'Joyous view of life', *Irish Press*, 13 May 1988.
4. David Nowlan, '"Times In It" at the Peacock', *Irish Times*, 13 May 1988.
5. John Finegan, 'Trilogy at the Peacock', *Evening Herald*, 13 May 1988.
6. Tim Harding, 'Frank's Madcap Menagerie', *Sunday Press*, 15 May 1988.
7. *Sunday Independent*, 15 May 1988.
8. Lorcan Roche, 'Simple perfect trilogy', *Irish Independent*, 15 May 1988.
9. 'Arts & Books', *Dublin Opinion*, Summer 1988, p. 53.
10. Tom Mathews, 'Reviews', (source unspecified), 3 June 1988.
11. Michael Coveney, 'Times In It/Abbey, Dublin', *Financial Times*, 6 June 1988.

Mary and Lizzie (1989)
I   RSC(The Pit), 20 September 1989.(signed by McG)
(Directed by Sarah Pia Anderson)

Theatre Record:
1. Michael Coveney, *Financial Times*, 28 September 1989.
2. Milton Shulman, *Evening Standard*, 29 September 1989.
3. Georgina Brown, *Independent*, 29 September 1989.
4. Michael Billington, *Guardian*, 29 September 1989.
5. Kenneth Hurren, *Mail on Sunday*, 1 October 1989.
6. James Christopher, *Time Out*, 4 October 1989. (photo)
7. Carl Miller, *City Limits*, 5 October 1989.
8. David Nathan, *Jewish Chronicle*, 6 October 1989.
9. Rhoda Koenig, *Punch*, 13 October 1989.
10. Roger Gillett, *What's On*, 4 October 1989.
11. Hugo Williams, *Sunday Correspondent*, 8 October 1989.
12. Michael Ratcliffe, *Observer*, 1 October 1989.
13. Charles Spencer, *Daily Telegraph*, 4 October 1989.
Other source
14. Neil Taylor, 'Wandering lives', *TLS*, 13 October 1989: 1124.

II   Dublin Castle Crypt, October 1994.
(Part of Dublin Theatre Festival)
(Directed by Jo Mangan)

1. David Nowlan, 'Curious trip through history' *Irish Times*, 8 October 1994.

Beautiful British Justice (1989)
in *Fear and Misery of the Third Reich* (Young Vic 6–22 July 1989)
A series of short plays by Kay Adshead, Pat Anderson, Anne Caulfield, Nick Darke, Noel Greig, Catherine Hayes, Terry Heaton, Debbie Horsfield, Charlotte Keatley, and **Frank McGuinness.**

1. Paul Arnott, *Independent*, 12 July.
2. Suzi Feay, *Time Out*, 12 July.
3. Patrick Marmion, *What's On*, 12 July.
4. Charles Spencer, *Daily Telegraph*, 8 July.

The Bread Man (1990)
I   Gate Theatre, 2 October 1990.
     (Directed by Andy Hinds)

1. David Nowlan, 'Turmoil without resolution in a Donegal town', *Irish Times*, 4 October 1990.
2. Mary O'Donnell, "Verdict on 'The Bread Man', 'Hamlet', and 'Good-night Siobhan'", *Sunday Tribune*, 7 October 1990.
3. Tim Harding, 'Bread man's towering performance', *Sunday Press*, 7 October 1990.
4. 'World Premiere: The Bread Man by Frank McGuinness', Dublin Theatre Festival 1990: Official Festival Programme.
5. 'The Bread Man', Jennifer Johnston, Paul Arthur and Linda Henderson on Frank McGuinness's new play for the Gate Theatre, *Theatre Ireland*, 24, Winter 90/91, 35–39.

Someone Who'll Watch Over Me (1992)
I-a   Hampstead Theatre, 4 July 1992.
      (Directed by Robin Lefevre)

Theatre Record:
1. Robert Hewison, 'Spirits rise above less than zero', *Sunday Times*, 19 July 1992.
2. Benedict Nightingale, 'Held hostage to old misfortunes', *Times*, 13 July 1992.
3. Irving Wardle, *Independent on Sunday*, 19 July 1992.
4. Kenneth Hurren, *Mail on Sunday*, 19 July 1992.
5. Nicholas de Jongh, 'Winning Wimbledon from a cell in Beirut', *Evening Standard*, 13 July 1992.
6. Clive Hirschhorn, *Sunday Express*, 19 July 1992.

7. Paul Taylor, *Independent*, 15 July 1992.
8. Charles Spencer, 'Laughter in the dark', *Daily Telegraph*, 14 July 1992.
9. Sheridan Morley, *Herald Tribune*, 15 July 1992.
10. Kirsty Milne, *Sunday Telegraph*, 19 July 1992.
11. David Murray, 'Someone Who'll Watch Over Me', *Financial Times*, 13 July 1992.
12. Ian Shuttleworth, *City Limits*, 16 July 1992.
13. Claire Harris, *What's On*, 15 July 1992.
14. Michael Wright, *Time Out*, 15 July 1992.
15. Michael Coveney, *Observer*, 19 July 1992.
16. Maureen Paton, 'Hostage hell breaches old national divisions', *Daily Express*, 13 July 1992.
17. David Nathan, *Jewish Chronicle*, 24 July 1992.
18. Ian Dodd, *Tribune*, 24 July 1992.
Others:
19. Michael Billingron, *Guardian*, 13 Jully 1992.
20. Megan Rutherford, 'No Joke', *Time*, 3 August 1992.
21. 'Hostage play: Just imagine', *Economist*, 25 July 1992.
22. Matt Wolf, 'Trying to please himself more', *The Times*, 4 July 1992.
23. Kate Bassett, 'Someone Who'll Watch Over Me', *Plays & Players*, August 1992.

I-b   Vaudeville Theatre, London, 8 September 1992

Theatre Record:
1. Jack Tinker, 'Triumph of the hostages who make a glory of hell', *Daily Mail*, 10 Sep.
2. Thomas Sutcliffe, *Independent*, 12 September 1992.
3. Jeremy Kingston, *The Times*, 12 September 1992.
4. Vincent Mahon, *What's On*, 16 September 1992.
5. Keith Stanfield, *City Limits*, 17 September 1992.
6. Rick Jones, *Time Out*, 16 September 1992.
Others:
7. Imelda Foley, 'Observe the watched', *Fortnight*, September 1992.

I-c   Booth Theatre, NW, 23 November 1992.

1. Frank Rich, 'Coping With Incarceration, Or, the Lighter Side of Beirut', *New York Times*, 24 November 1992: C13.
2. Matt Wolf, 'The buzz moves from Broadway', *The Times*, 4 January 1993.

II   Abbey, 13 April, 1993.
      (Directed by Robin Lefevre)

1. David Nowlan, 'An Elegant work of art', *Irish Times*, 14 March 1993.
2. 'Drama at Abbey stays on stage', 14 March 1993.
3. Mary Carr, 'Tears and laughter in a Beirut cell', *Evening Herald*, 14 April 1993.
4. John Boland, 'Hostages to credibility', *Evening Press*, 14 April 1993.
5. Brian Keenan, 'Out of the Shadows', *Irish Times*, 8 May 1993.
6. Philip Nolan, 'Taking no prisoners', *Evening Press*, 14 April 1993.
7. John Pankow, 'It was never like this on Broadway', *Evening Herald*, 16 April 1993.
8. Mary Carr, 'Mary Carr's critical guide to the theatre', *Evening Herald*, 1 April 1993.
9. Desmond Rushe, 'An unmoving triumph of human spirit', *Irish Independent*, 14 April 1993.
10. Emer O'Kelly, 'Hostage drama lacks tension', *Sunday Independent*, 18 April 1993.
11. Tim Harding, 'Hostage play is moving, powerful and funny', *Sunday Press*, 18 April 1993.
12. Kay Hingerty, 'A great McGuinness play', *Cork Examiner*, 21 April 1993.
13. 'Theatre', *Phoenix*, 23 April 1993.
14. 'Stage: People's choice', *Hot Press*, (date unspecified), p. 33.

III   Gateway Theatre, Chester, 3 September, 1993.
       (Directed by Les Waters)

IV   Citadel Theatre, 1993/94 Season
      (Directed by Robin Phillips)

V   Old Globe Theatre, (Place), 13 July, 1994.
      (Directed by Sheldon Epps)

VI   'Not the National Theatre' on tour

VII   Alguen Olhara' For Mim, Teatro Aberto, Portugal, Agost 1994.
      (Directed by Joao Lourenco)

VIII Tinderbox on tour
　　18 September ~ 28 October, 1995
　　(directed by Stephen Wright)

IX　Theatr Clwyd, Mold, March 1997.
　　(Directed by Greg Doran)

　1. Pauline McLean, 'Hostage play performance to help relatives',
　　Western Mail, 21 March 1997.

X　Vienna's English Theatre, 4 September – 11 October 2000.
　　(Directed by Terence Lamude)

Amateur Performances:
AI　(by Thurles Drama Group, at the Athlone All Ireland
　　Amateur Drama Festival)

The Bird Sanctuary (1994)
I　Abbey, 15 February 1994. (2 copies, one signed by McG)
　(Directed by Robin Lefevre)

　1. Ian Hill, *The Bird Sancturary*, *Guardian*, 9 March 94.
　2. Grainne Farren, 'Bird mouths', *Fortnight*, April 1994, p. 43.
　3. Lise Hand, 'Actress takes sanctuary in her new role', *Sunday Independent*, 6 February 1994.
　4. 'McEwan treads Abbey's boards', *Irish Press*, 10 February 1994.
　5. Lorcan Roche, 'Just the part', *Irish Independent*, 15 February 1994.
　6. David Nowlan, 'Masterly tapestry of characterisation', *Irish Times*, 16 February 1994.
　7. Patsy McGarry, '"Bird sanctuary" a very safe bet', *Irish Press*, 16 February 1994.
　8. Mary Carr, 'Ramshackle house party fails to please', *Evening Herald*, 16 February 1994.
　9. David Lawlor, 'Family in limbo', *Evening Press*, 16 February 1994.
　10. Lorcan Roche, '"Bird" is a lame duck', *Irish Independent*, 16 February 1994.
　11. 'Review of "Bird Sanctuary" at the Abbey Theatre', RTE Radio 1, Gay Byrne Show, 17 February 1994.
　12. 'Culture Ireland: Theatre', *Sunday Times*, 20 February 1994.

13. 'The goodness in McGuinness', *Sunday Press*, 20 February 1994.
14. 'Addams family, McGuinness-style', *Sunday Tribune*, 20 February 1994.
15. Emer O'Kelly, 'Family striptease', *Sunday Independent*, 20 February 1994.
16. 'The Bird Sanctuary', *Sunday Times*, 27 February 1994.
17. Polly Devlin, 'No sanctuary at the Abbey', *Irish Times*, 8 March 1994.
18. Sebastian Barry, 'A letter to the editor', *Irish Times*, 11 March 1994.
19. Peter Denman, 'A letter to the editor', *Irish Times*, 11 March 1994.
20. Patrick Mason, 'A letter to the editor', *Irish Times*, 12 March 1994.
21. Elizabeth & Paul Moore, 'A letter to the editor', *Irish Times*, 16 March 1994.
22. Denise Meagher, 'A letter to the editor', *Irish Times*, 19 March 1994.
23. Michael J. Cassidy, 'A letter to the editor', *Irish Times*, 21 March 1994.
24. John Grady, 'A letter to the editor', *Irish Times*, 26 March 1994.
25. Mary Donohoe, 'A letter to the editor', *Irish Times*, 26 March 1994.
26. John Gaffney, 'A letter to the editor', *Irish Times*, 29 March 1994.
27. Emer O'Kelly, 'What did you *really* think of the play?', *Sunday Independent*, 3 April 1994.
28. P. J. Tynan, 'A letter to the editor', *Irish Times*, 12 April 1994.
29. 'New McGuinness play on cruelty of family relations', *Woman's Way*, February 18, 1994, p. 9.
30. John O'Riordan, 'The Bird Sanctuary', (source, date unspecified).

Mutabilitie (1997)
I   Royal National Theatre, 20 November 1997.
    (Directed by Trevor Nunn)

1. Nicholas de Jongh, *Evening Standard*, 21 November.
2. Sheridan Morley, *Spectator*, 29 November.
3. Robert Gore-Langton, *Express*, 25 November.
4. Bill Hagerty, *News of the World*, 30 November.
5. Michael Billington, *Guardian*, 24 November.

6. Robert Butler, *Independent on Sunday*, 23 November.
7. David Nathan, *Jewish Chronicle*, 28 November.
8. Susannah Clapp, *Observer*, 23 November.
9. Michael Coveney, *Daily Mail*, 21 November.
10. John Gross, *Sunday Telegraph*, 23 November.
11. Carole Woddis, *Herald*, 25 November.
12. Charles Spencer, *Daily Telegraph*, 24 November.
13. Benedict Nightingale, 'Elizabethan adventurers are brought to book in Irish fable',*TheTimes*, 22 November.
14. Roger Foss, *What's On*, 26 November.
15. Paul Taylor, 'All for love, and nothing for reward', *Independent*, 22 November.
16. Kate Stratton, *Time Out*, 26 November.
17. Georgina Brown, *Mail on Sunday*, 30 November.
18. Alastair Macaulay, *Financial Times*, 24 November.
19. John Peter, *Sunday Times*, 30 November.
Others:
20. Daniel Rosenthal, 'Next stage for a class act', *The Times*, 11 November 1997.
21. Rolf C. Hemke, 'Images of three English productions', *Ubu: Scenes d'Europe: Revue Theatrale Europeenne* (European Stages: European Theatre Review), no.9, April 1998.
22. Kate Kellaway, 'Shapespeare meets an Irish question', *New Statesman*, 28 November 1997.

II The Samuel Beckett Theatre, Trinity College, Dublin, 4 September 2000.
    (Directed by Michael Caven)

1. David Nowlan, 'Mutabilitie: Samuel Beckett Theatre', *Irish Times*, 8 September 2000.
2. John Waters, 'Where society fears to tread', *Irish Times*, 8 September 2000.
3. Michael Cavan, 'Mistaken Identity: Is Mutabilitie the greatest of all Irish plays? Michael Caven, the director of a new production running in Trinity College thinks so', *Hot Press*, 27 September 2000.
4. Emer O'Kelly, 'Spellbound by this Faerie epic', *Sunday Independent*, 10 September 2000.

Dolly West's Kitchen **(1999)**
I-a Abbey Theatre, 6 October 1999.
     (Directed by Patrick Mason)

1. David Nowlan, 'Ambitious play with a logical fallacy: Dolly West's Kitchen', *Irish Times*, 8 October 1999.
2. Bruce Arnold, 'War drama had "no real theme"', *Irish Independent*, 8 October 1999.
3. Emer O'Kelly, 'History, geography and lots of class', *Sunday Independent*, 10 October 1999.
4. Mary Holland, 'Uneasy peace pact with past', *Observer*, 10 October 1999.
5. Jocelyn Clarke, 'Playing with fire', *Sunday Tribune*, 10 October 1999.
6. Luke Clancy, 'Irish Theatre: Dublin Theatre Festival', *The Times*, 8 October 1999.
7. Ian Hill, 'All arts and parts: an arts diary by Ian Hill', *Newletter* (Belfast), 18 October 1999.
8. 'Dolly West Kitchen: Abbey Theatre', *In Dublin*, 21 Oct.–3 Nov (vol. 24–no. 20), 1999.
9. 'Dolly West Kitchen', *Phoenix*, 22 October 1999.
10. Michael Billington, 'You couldn't make it up', *Guardian*, 24 October 1999.
11. 'Festival Reviews', *Dublin Event Guide*, 20 Oct.–2 Nov. 1999.
12. Jocelyn Clarke, 'Creating a scene', *Sunday Tribune*, 24 October 1999.

I-b   Old Vic Theatre, London, 17 May 2000.
(Directed by Patrick Mason)

(b) Plays directed by McGuinness:

The Gentle Island (by Brian Friel)
I   Peacock, 12 December, 1988.
(Directed by Frank McGuinness)

1. 'The Gentle Island by Frank McGuinness', *Sunday Tribune*, 11 December 1988.
2. Tim Harding, 'Island is not perfect', *Irish Press*, 18 December 1988.

Carthaginians **(1992)**
II   Druid, 5 February 1992.
(Directed by Frank McGuinness)

1. Imelda Foley, 'History's moral guardians alerted', *Fortnight*, no. 305, April 1992.

2. Jim Tierney, 'Carthaginians', 16 March 1992, source unspecified.

(c) Original Television Drama by McGuinness:

Scout **(1987)** BBC2

1. John Keys, 'Bleak visions of the adult world', *Fortnight*, October 1987.
2. Gethyn Stoodley Thomas, 'Friendlier face of Ulster', *Western Mail*, 12 September 1987.
3. David Nokes, 'Dreaming dreams without drama', *TLS*, 18–24 September 1987, p. 1018.
4. Helena Sheehan, *Irish Television Drama: A Society and its Stories*, Dublin: Radio Telefís Éireann, 1987.

The Hen House **(1989)** BBC2

1. Patricia Craig, 'A backward boy', *TLS*, 15–21 September 1989, pp. 1005.
2. Martin McLoone, 'On The Hen House' in 'J'Accuse — McGuinness: Stage and Screen', *Theatre Ireland* 21 (December, 1989), pp. 58–62.

(d) Adaptations by McGuinness:

Dracula based on a novel by Bram Stoker **(1986)**
I   Druid, 10 April 1986.

Yerma **(1987)** by Federico García Lorca (leaflet)
I   Peacock Theatre, 5 May 1987.
     (Directed by Michael Attenborough)

1. Michael Sheridan, 'Lorca's poetic tragedy', *Irish Press*, 6 May 1987.
2. Desmond Rushe, 'Lorca's brooding passion', *Irish Independent*, 6 May 1987.
3. Davic Nowlan, '"Yerma" at the Peacock', 7 May 1987.
4. Fintan O'Toole, 'Paring language to the bone', *Sunday Tribune*, 10 May 1987.
5. Tim Harding, 'Love and marriage are not enough', *Sunday Press*, 10 May 1987.
6. Colm Toibin, 'The troubles of Juan and Yerma', *Sunday*

Independent, 10 May 1987.
7. Claire Armitstead, 'Sex and moral hypocrisy', *Financial Times*, 9 May 1987.
8. Robert Gore Langton, 'Lorca in Dublin', *Plalys & Players*, May 1987.
9. Fintan O'Toole, *Yerma/Pygmalion*, *Plalys & Players*, August 1987.
10. Colin Dean, 'A Lonely Kind of Love', *Dublin Opinion*, May 1987, 45.
11. (photo), *Sunday Tribune*, 3 May 1987.
12. (photo), *Sunday Tribune*, 10 May 1987.
13. (photo), *Sunday Tribune*, 2 June 1987.
14. (photo), *Irish Times*, 6 May 1987.
15. (photo), *Irish Times*, 18 May 1987.
16. Treasa Brogan, 'Beautiful evening with Yerma', *Evening Press*, 6 May 1987.
17. Jane Coyle, 'Yerma', *Guardian*, 9 May 1987.
18. Colm Cronin, 'From Peace to Passion', *New Hibernia*, June 1987, p. 36.
19. Martin Madden, 'Yerma and infertility', *Irish Press*, 19 May 1987.

Rosmersholm by Henrik Ibsen (1987)
I-a National Theatre, London(the Cottesloe), 6 May 1987.
(Directed by Sarah Pia Anderson)

Theatre Record:
1. David Nathan, *Jewish Chronicle*, 15 May 1987.
2. Clive Hirschhorn, *Sunday Express*, 10 May 1987.
3. Robin Ray, *Punch*, 20 May 1987.
4. Kenneth Hurren, *Mail on Sunday*, 10 May 1987.
5. Helen Rose, *Time Out*, 13 May 1987.
6. Peter Kemp, *Independent*, 8 May 1987.
7. Charles Osborne, *Daily Telegraph*, 8 May 1987.
8. Michael Billington, *Guardian*, 8 May 1987.
9. Sue Jameson, *London broadcasting*, 7 May 1987.
10. Michael Coveney, *Financial Times*, 7 May 1987.
11. Della Couling, *Tablet*, 16 May 1987.
12. Milton Shulman, *London Evening Standard*, 7 May 1987.
13. D. A. N. Jones, *Sunday Telegraph*, 10 May 1987.
14. Mary Harron, 'Incest-free',*Observer*, 10 May 1987.
15. Jim Hiley, *Listener*, 14 May 1987.
16. Lyn Gardner, *City Limits*, 14 May 1987.

17. Giles Gordon, *London Daily News*, 8 May 1987.
Others:
18. Michael Meyer, 'The weight of tradition', *TLS*, 15 May 1987: 518.
19. Irving Wardle, *The Times*, 7 May 1987.
20. John Peter, 'Passion without flames in the ice kingdom of Ibsen', *Sunday Times*, 10 May 1987.
21. Della Couling, *The Tablet*, 16 May 1987, 526.
22. Paul Taylor, 'Good sense of direction', *Independent*, 8 May 1987.
23. Peter Lewis, 'Wrestling with Ibsen', 9 May 1987.

I-b   La Mama E.T.C. Annex Theatre, NW., December 1988.

1. Mel Gussow, 'An Enemy of the People, With Personal Problems', *New York Times*, 14 December 1988: C21.

***Peer Gynt* by Henrik Ibsen (1988)**
I   Gate, 4 October 1988.
(Directed by Patrick Mason)

1. David Nowlan, '"Peer Gynt" at the Gate', *Irish Times*, 6 October 1988.
2. Keving Myers, 'An Irishman's Diary', *Irish Times*, 18 October 1988.
3. (photo), *Sunday Press*, 2 October 1988.
4. (photo), *Irish Times*, 5 October 1988.
5. Michael Coveney, 'Peer Gynt: Gate Theatre, Dublin', *Financial Times*, 10 October 1988.

II-a   RSC, 3 March, 1994.
(Directed by Yukio Ninagawa)

Theatre Record:
1. Alastair Macaulay, 'A flawed but fabulous Peer', *Financial Times*, 5 March 1994.
2. Paul Taylor, 'Virtual reality', *Independent*, 5 March 1994.
3. Sheridan Morley, *Spectator*, 12 March 1994.
4. Clive Hirschhorn, *Sunday Express*, 6 March 1994.
5. Kate Kellaway, 'Looking through a glass onion', *Observer*, 6 March 1994.
6. David Nathan, *Jewish Chronicle*, 11 March 1994.

7. Benedict Nightingale, 'Ibsen lands in video age', *The Times*, 5 March 1994.
8. Jack Tinker, *Daily Mail*, 4 March 1994.
9. John Gross, *Sunday Telegraph*, 6 March 1994.
10. Charles Spencer, 'Big name, big gimmick', *Daily Telegraph*, 7 March 1994.
11. John Peter, *Sunday Times*, 13 March 1994.
12. James Christopher, *Time Out*, 9 March 1994.
13. Michael Billington, 'Peer pressure', *Guardian*, 5 March 1994.
14. Irving Wardle, *Independent on Sunday*, 6 March 1994.
15. Neil Smith, *What's On*, 9 March 1994.
16. Nicholas de Jongh, *Evening Standard*, 4 March 1994.
Others:
17. Michael Arditti, 'Ageing will not weary him', *Times*, 2 March 1994.
18. Michael Coveney, 'Peer of the realm', *Observer*, 6 March 1994.
19. Paul Hadfield, '"Peer Gynt" Palace Theatre, Manchester', *Irish Times*, 5 April 1994.
20. Herb Geer, 'A world-class Peer Gynt', *World & I*, 1 July 1994, p. 104.

II-b Season Theatre, Tokyo, 20 April, 1994.

III Royal National Theatre, London, 13 November 2000.
(Directed by Trevor Nann)

Pre-production press release:
1. 'One-man band at the National', *Evening Standard* (Editorial Comment), 9 October 2000.
2. Alexa Baracaia, 'Supple stalled', *Stage*, 28 September 2000.
3. Heather Neill, 'Romeo not built in a day' (features Chiwetel Ejiofor, who plays Peer Gynt), *the Times*, 29 September 2000.
4. Richard Brooke, 'Drama "but no crisis" at the National', *Sunday Times*, 8 October 2000.
5. Kate Bassett, 'The National Theatre: Mounting debts, cancelled productions, charges of artistic incompetence – what is going on at the nation's leading repertory company?', *Independent on Sunday*, 8 October 2000.
6. 'Conflict over real cause of NT delays', *Stage*, 12 October 2000.
7. Flyman, 'If truth be told', *Stage*, 12 October 2000.
8. Doyla Alberge, 'Nunn steps in after director leaves theatre', *The Times*, 28 October 2000.

9. Severin Carrell, 'New crisis strikes at National Theatre as director leaves production in ill health', *Independent*, 28 October 2000.
10. Patrick Sawer, 'Director frogmarched out of National preview', source unspecified.
11. Nigel Reynolds, 'Noises off at the National: Is the mounting criticism of the National Theatre justified, asks Nigel Reynolds', *Daily Telegraph*, 14 November 2000.

Theatre Record:
1. Sheridan Morley, *Spectator*, 25 November 2000.
2. Robert Gore-Langton, *Express*, 11 November 2000.
3. Nicholas de Jongh, *Evening Standard*, 14 November 2000.
4. John Nathan, 'Peerless and pleasurable', *Jewish Chronicle*, 17 November 2000.
5. Alastair Macaulay, 'Tired at the end of the Peer show', *Financial Times*, 15 November 2000.
6. Dominic Cavendish, 'If this is a company in trauma, it certainly doesn't look it', *Daily Telegraph*, 15 November 2000.
7. Georgina Brown, *Mail on Sunday*, 18 November 2000.
8. Susannah Clapp, *Observer*, 19 November 2000.
9. Paul Taylor, *Independent*, 21 November 2000.
10. Kate Bassett, *Independent on Sunday*, 19 November 2000.
11. Michael Billington, *Guardian*, 14 November 2000.
12. Michael Coveney, 'The end of the Peer show', *Daily Mail*, 14 November 2000.
13. Ian Johns, 'Unbowed by Peer pressure', *The Times*, 15 November 2000.
14. Brian Logan, *Time Out*, 22 November 2000.
15. John Gross, *Sunday Telegraph*, 19 November 2000.
16. John Peter, *Sunday Times*, 19 November 2000.
17. Roger Foss, *What's On*, 22 November 2000.
Others:
18. Peter Roberts at Peer Gynt, *Plays International*, vol. 16, no. 3, December/January 2000/2001, p. 18.
19. Ben Dowell, 'Pared down but peerless', *Stage*, 16 November 2000.
20. Roddy Lumsden, 'True to itself', *TLS*, 1 December 2000.

Three Sisters by Anton Chekhov (1990)
I-a Gate Theatre, 28 March, 1990. (2 copies)
    (Directed by Adrian Noble with the Cusack family)

I-b   Royal Court, 24 July–29 September 1990.

Theatre Record:
1. Michael Coveney, *Observer*, 1 April 1990.
2. Irving Wardle, *Independent on Sunday*, 1 April 1990.
3. Alasdair Cameron, *Times*, 4 April 1990.
4. Michael billington, *Guardian*, 2 April 1990.
5. Charles Osborne, *Daily Telegraph*, 26 July 1990.
6. Martin Hoyle, *Financial Times*, 26 July 1990.
7. Milton Shulman, *Evening Standard*, 25 July 1990.
8. Paul Taylor, *Independent*, 26 July 1990.
9. Clare Bayley, *What's On*, 1 August 1990.
10. Benedict Nightingale, *The Times*, 25 July 1990.
11. John Gross, *Sunday Telegraph*, 29 July 1990.
12. Sheridan Morley, *Herald Tribune*, 12 August 1990.
13. Robert Gore-Langton, *Sunday Correspondent*, 29 July 1990.
14. Michael Billington, *Guardian*, 26 July 1990.
15. Jack Tinker, *Daily Mail*, 25 July 1990.
16   Jim Hiley, *Listner*, 2 August 1990.
17. Irving Wardle, *Independent on Sunday*, 29 July 1990.
18. Christopher Edwards, *Spectator*, 11 August 1990.
19. Clive Hirschhorn, *Sunday Express*, 29 July 1990.
20. Kenneth Hurren, *Mail on Sunday*, 29 July 1990.
21. Lyn Gardner, *City Limits*, 2 August 1990.
22. Jane Edwardes, *Time Out*, 1 August 1990.
23. David Nathan, *Jewish Chronicle*, 27 July 1990.
24. Rhoda Koenig, *Punch*, 3 August 1990.
Other source:
25. T.J.Binyon, 'The cry from the provinces', *TLS*, 3 August 1990: 825.

The House of Bernarda Alba by Federico Garcia Lorca **(1991)**
I   Lyric Players Theatre, Belfast, 7 March 1991.
    (Directed by Elena Kaut-Howson)

The Threepenny Opera by Bertolt Brecht **(1991)**
I   Gate Theatre, 9 July 1991.
    (Directed by Patrick Mason)

1. Ciaran Carty, 'Catching Brecht's humour in Dublinese', *Sunday Times*, 7 July 1991.
2. Helen Lucy Burke, 'How to make deviants feel at home', *Sunday Tribune*, 14 July 1991.

3. Ian Fox, 'Maarianne's whore stays Faithfull to Brecht', *Sunday Tribune*, 14 July 1991.
4. Fergus Linehan, 'Life is a cabaret', *Irish Times*, ? July 1991.
5. 'Weill Bodies', *Sunday Press*, 14 July 1991.

Hedda Gabler by Henrik Ibsen**(1994)**

I   Roundabout Theatre, Broadway, 29 June 1994.
(Directed by Sarah Pia Anderson)

1. Aileen Jacobson, 'Taking Ibsen's "Hedda" Lightly', *Newsday*, 11 July 1994.

Uncle Vanya by Anton Chekhov **(1995)**

I-a   Field Day Theatre Company, on tour, 20 February 1995 (Derry)–1 April (Coleraine)
(Directed by Peter Gill)

1. Gerry Colgan, 'Not a field day for Chekhov's Vanya', *Irish Times*, 22 February 1995.
2. Jeremy Kingston, 'Looking a bit pale, Uncle', *The Times*, 22 February 1995.
3. Jocelyn Clarke, 'Playing the field', *The Tribune Magazine*, 19 February 1995, 7–8.
4. Harry MaGee, 'Stephen Rea — Unplugged', *Sunday Press*, 19 February 1995.
5. Many Holland, 'The trouble with peace: Times have changed for Derry's "cultural provos"', *Observer*, 26 February 1995.

I-b   Tricycle theatre, London, 10–29 April, 1995
Theatre Record:
1. Alastair Macaulay, *Financial Times*, 24 February 1995.
2. Michael Billington, *Guardian*, 22 February 1995.
3. Irving Wardle, *Independent on Sunday*, 26 February 1995.
4. Jeremy Kingston, *Times*, 22 February 1995.
5. Charles Spencer, *Daily Telegraph*, 22 February 1995.
6. Nicholas de Jongh, *Evening Standard*, 11 April 1995.
7. Clive Hirschhorn, *Sunday Express*, 16 April 1995.
8. Bennedict Nightingale, *Times*, 12 April 1995.
9. Michael Coveney, *Observer*, 23 April 1995.
10. David Nathan, *Jewish Chronicle*, 21 April 1995.
11. Sheridan Morley, *Spectator*, 22 April 1995.
12. Jack Tinker, *Daily Mail*, 11 April 1995.
13. Bill Hagerty, *Today*, 14 April 1995.

14. John Gross, *Sunday Telegraph*, 16 April 1995.
15. James Christopher, *Time Out*, 19 April 1995.
16. Clare Bayley, *Independent*, 14 April 1995.
17. Neil Smith, *What's On*, 19 April 1995.
Others:
18. Aline Waites, *Plays & Players*, May 1995.
19. John Peter, 'Real life drama', *Sunday Times*, 16 April 1995.

A Doll's House by Henrik Ibsen **(1996)**
I-a The Playhouse, London, 24 October 1996.
(Directed by Anthony Page)

Theatre Record:
1. John Peter, *Sunday Times*, 3 November 1997.
2. Joseph Farrell, *Scotsman*, 17 October 1997.
3. Mark Fisher, *Herald*, 17 October 1997.
4. John Gross, 'Independence day',*Sunday Telegraph*, 27 October 1997.
5. Nicholas de Jongh, *Evening Standard*, 29 October 1997.
6. Jeremy Kingston, *The Times*, 26 October 1997.
7. Paul Taylor, 'The definition of catharsis', *Independent*, 26 October 1997.
8. Jane Edwardes, *Time Out*, 30 October 1997.
9. Shaun Usher, 'Ibsen's House is put in order', *Daily Mail*, 25 October 1997.
10. Alastair Macaulay, 29 October 1997.
11. John Peter, *Sunday Times*, 22 September 1997 (actually 3 November)
12. Robert Bulter, *Independent on Sunday*, 27 October 1997.
13. James Christopher, 'On dangerous ground', *Sunday Express*, 27 October 1997.
14. Tom Lubbock, *Observer*, 27 October 1997.
15. Georgina Brown, *Mail on Sunday*, 3 November 1996.
16. Bill Hagerty, *News of the World*, 3 November 1996.
17. Michael Billington, *Guardian*, 26 October 1997.
18. David Nathan, *Jewish Chronicle*, 1 November 1996.
19. Roger Foss, *What's On*, 30 November 1996.
20. Sheridan Morley, *Spectator*, 2 November 1996.
Others:
21. Charles Spencer, 'McTeer's star quality brings the house down', *Daily Telegraph*, 26 October 1997.
22. A A Gill, 'Hello dollies, everywhere', *Sunday Times*, 27 October 1996.

23. Michael Billington, source and date unspecified.
24. Nicholas de Jongh, 'Londoner's Diary', 25 October, source unspecified.

I-b   Belasco Theatre, NY, 2 April, 1997.

1. Ben Brantley, 'A Nora Who Makes Ibsen's Rebellious Housewife New', *New York Times*, 3 April 1997.
2. Clive Barnes, 'Wow! What a living "Doll"', *New York Post*, 3 April 1997.
3. Liz Smith, *New York Post*, 3 April 1997.
4. David Patrick Stearns, 'Like "A Doll's House" on fire: Sexually charged staging gives Ibsen classic new sizzle', *USA Today*, 3 April 1997.
5. David Lyons, *Wall Street Journal*, 4 April 1997.
6. Clive Barnes, 'The best of plays brush us with reality', *New York Post*, 6 April 1997.
7. Richard Zoglin, 'Thunderclap', *Time Magazine*, 14 April 1997.
8. John Lahr, 'Husbands and Wives', *New Yorker*, 14 April 1997.
9. Greg Evans, *Variety*, 7–13 April 1997.
10. Michael Sommers, 'A luminous Nora shines in "Doll's House"', 3 April 1997.
11. Allan Wallach, 'All Dolled Up: The Olivier Award-winning Janet McTeer gives Ibsen's Nora a make-over', *Newsday*, 30 March 1997.
12. Linda Winer, 'An Unbuttoned Nora: A new, freer staging of Ibsen's "A Doll's House"', *Newsday*, 3 April 1997.
13. Patrick Pacheco, *Newsday*, 3 April 1997.
14. 'Channel Two News at Eleven' (transcript), 2 April 1997.
15. 'AP Entertainment Review', 2 April 1997.

II   The Fairfax Victorian Arts Centre, Melbourne, 23 April 1998. (Directed by Roger Hodgman, Melbourne Thetre Company)

1. Helen Thomson, 'New Woman updated', *Age*, 30 April 1998.
2. Christine Davey, 'Stage: A Doll's House', *MSO*, 1 May 1998.
3. Lee Christofis, 'On the verge of a verbal breakdown', *Austrian*, 1 May 1998.
4. Zelda Cawthorne, 'Exposing the marital arts', *Herald Sun*, 1 May 1998.
5. Veronica Matheson, 'Doll's House Not A Home', *Sunday Herald Sun*, 3 May 1998.
6. Steven Carroll, 'A Doll's House', *Sunday Age*, 3 May 1998.

The Caucasian Chalk Circle by Bertolt Brecht **(1997)**
I The Olivier Theatre, Royal National Theatre, 21 April 1997.
(Directed by Simon McBurney)

Theatre Record:
  1. Paul Taylor, *Independent*, 23 April 1997.
  2. Benedict Nightingale, 'Morality played for our times', *The Times*, 23 April 1997.
  3. John Peter, 'Portrait of undying love', *Sunday Times*, 27 April 1997.
  4. Bill Hagerty, *News of the World*, 27 April 1997.
  5. Robert Gore-Langton, *Express*, 25 April 1997.
  6. Alastair Macaulay, *Financial Times*, 22 April 1997.
  7. Michael Billington, *Guardian*, 23 April 1997.
  8. Irving Wardle, 'Round in concentric circles',*Sunday Telegraph*, 27 April 1997.
  9. Nicholas de Jongh, *Evening Standard*, 22 April 1997.
  10. Michael Coveney, 'Ready Brecht', *Observer*, 27 April 1997.
  11. Robert Bulter, *Independent on Sunday*, 27 April 1997.
  12. Charles Spencer, *Dailey Telegraph*, 23 April 1997.
  13. Kate Stratton, *Time Out*, 30 April 1997.
  14. Neil Smith, *What's On*, 30 April 1997.
  15. Georgina Brown, *Mail on Sunday*, 27 April 1997.

II Ulster Youth Theatre, Ardhowen Theatre, Enniskillen (25–26 August, 1998), Lyric Theatre, Belfast (28–30 August, 1998).
(Directed by David Grant)

Electra by Sophocles **(1997)**
I-a Minerva studio Theatre (Chichester), 22 September 1997.
(Directed by David Leveaux)

Theatre Record:
  1. Susannah Clapp, 'The chorus speaks as one (well, one of them), *Observer*, 28 September 1997.
  2. Benedict Nightingale, 'Classic move from rags to riches',*The Times*, 24 September 1997.
  3. Michael Billington, *Guardian*, 23 September 1997.
  4. John Peter, *Sunday Times*, 28 September 1997.
  5. Michael Coveney, *Daily Mail*, 26 September 1997.
  6. Paul Taylor, *Independent*, 24 September 1997.
  7. Sam Ablasini, *Financial Times*, 24 September 1997.

8. Charles Spencer, 'Wanamaker unmasked as a classic actress', *Daily Telegraph*, 24 September 1997.
9. Nick Curtis, *Evening Standard*, 23 September 1997.
10. Bill Hagerty, *News of the World*, 28 September 1997.
11. David Nathan, *Jewish Chronicle*, 26 September 1997.

I-b   Donmar Warehouse, 23 October 1997.

Theatre Record:
1. Dominic Cavendish, *Time Out*, 29 October 1997.
2. John Gross, *Sunday Telegraph*, 26 October 1997.
3. Georgina Brown, *Mail on Sunday*, 2 November 1997.
4. Robert Bulter, *Independent on Sunday*, 26 October 1997.
5. Peter Stothard, *The Times*, 7 November 1997.
6. Neil Smith, *What's On*, 29 October 1997.

I-c   Ethel Barrymore Theatre, New York, 19 November 1998.

1. Toby Zinman, 'Ancient Passions That Illuminate Today's Tragedies', *New York Times*, 29 November 1998, pp. 7, 9.
2. Matt Wolf, 'A Director Who Sees Ancients As Realists', *New York Times*, 10 January 1999, pp. 7–8.

The Storm by Alexander Ostrovsky **(1998)**
I-a   Almeida Theatre (London), 12 November 1998.
      (Directed by Hettie Macdonald)

Miss Julie by August Strindberg **(1998)**
I-a   Theatre Royal Windsor (London), 8 February 2000.
      (Directed by Michael Boyd)

I-b   Theatre Royal Haymarket (London), 23 February 2000.

1. Paul Taylor, 'Miss Julie', *Independent*, 2 February 2000.
2. Benedict Nightingale, 'Miss Julie', *The Times*, 2 February 2000.
3. Lyn Gardner, 'Inferno of lust in need of a match', *Independent*, 2 March 2000.
4. Michael Coveney, 'at last night's first night', *Daily Mail*, 1 March 2000.
5. Charles Spencer, 'Turn up the heat', *Daily Telegraph*, 2 March 2000.

6. 'Monster ego goes eyes blazing', *Financial Times*, 2 March 2000.
7. John Gross, 'Marital breakdown — big band style', *Sunday Telegraph*, 5 March 2000.
8. Robert Bulter, 'Cracking with lust and power', *Independent on Sunday*, 5 March 2000.
9. Susannah Clapp, 'From snow job to toe job', *Observer*, 5 March 2000.
10. Georgina Brown, 'Drink, rage . . . but none of that jazz', *Mail on Sunday*, 5 March 2000.
11. Sheridan Morley, 'Lament for a lost world', *Spectator*, 11 March 2000.
12. 'Our friend in the north goes up west', Imogen Edwards-Jones's interview with Christopher Eccleston (who plays Jean), *The Times*, 22 February 2000.

Barbaric Comedies by Ramón del Valle-Inclán (2000)
Abbey Theatre, Dublin
Director: Calixto Bieito

I-a Edinburgh International Festival, Kings Theatre, 14–20, 23–28 August 2000.

Pre-production press release:
1. 'Edinburgh spectacular', *Stage*, 30 March 2000.
2. Antony Thorncroft, 'Popular touch, plenty of backbone', *Financial Times*, 20 May 2000.
3. Catherine Cooper, 'The world at your feet', *Stage*, 3 August 2000.
4. Jackie McGlone, 'Those magic moments (in full)' (interview with the director), *Scotland on Sunday*, 13 August 2000.

Edinburgh 2000 (Supplement to *Theatre Record*, issues 16–17, 2000):
1. Robert Thomson, *Herald*, 15 August 2000.
2 Michael Coveney, *Daily Mail*, 18 August 2000.
3. Nicholas de Jongh, *Evening Standard*, 15 August 2000.
4. Barry Didcock, *Sunday Herald*, 20 August 2000.
5. Steve Cramer, *List*, 17 August 2000.
6. Robert Gore-Langton, *Express*, 18 August 2000.
7. Michael Billington, *Guardian*, 17 August 2000.
8. John Peter, 'Shock full of surprises?', *Sunday Times*, 20 August 2000.
9. Susannah Clapp, *Observer*, 20 August 2000.

10. Paul Taylor, 'The pervert's progress', *Independent*, 16 August 2000.
11. Kate Bassett, 'Grand Guignol for ghastly Galicians', *Independent on Sunday*, 20 August 2000.
12. Alastair Macaulay, 'Sex, violence and ranting', *Financial Times*, 17 August 2000.
13. John Gross, *Sunday Telegraph*, 28 August 2000.
14. Benedict Nightingale, 'The best possible bad taste', *The Times*, 16 August 2000.
15. Charles Spencer, 'Nasty, brutish — but not short', *Daily Telegraph*, 17 August 2000.
16. Camilla Rockwood, *Three Weeks*, 21 August 2000.
17. Mark Brown, *Scotland on Sunday*, 20 August 2000.
Others:
18. Andrew Aldridge, 'About as epic as theatre gets', *The Stage*, 17 August 2000.
19. Eamonn Rodgers, 'Irony in a pagan mood', *TLS*, 25 August 2000.
20. Hayden Murphy, 'Barbaric handling of civil war's incivility', *Sunday Tribune*, 20 August 2000.
21. Jojo Moyes, 'Epic tale of perverted priests has the critics in a frenzy', *Independent*, 17 August 2000.
22. Victoria White, 'Bleak vision comes thrillingly to life', *Irish Times*, 16 August 2000.
23. Michael Billington, 'One for the barbarians', *Guardian*, 16 August 2000.

Controversies over the play:
1. 'A frayed Fringe', *Independent*, 17 August 2000.
2. Oliver Burkeman, 'Fringe benefits', *Guardian*, 17 August 2000.
3. Victoria White, 'Prompters leap to defence of Abbey after reports of walkouts', *Irish Times*, 17 August 2000.
4. Vanessa Thorpe, 'Welcome to the new brutalism', *Observer Review*, 20 August 2000.
5. Thomas Sutcliffe, 'Why Edinburgh needs failures', *Independent*, 17 August 2000.
6. Gwynne Edwards, 'Barbaric reviews show only ignorance', *Stage*, 31 August 2000.
7. Anthony Garvey, 'Controversy follows Barbaric Comedies', *Stage*, 31 August 2000.
8. Sean Alta, 'Festival should be taking risks' (a letter to the editor), *Stage*, 14 September 2000.

I-b   Dublin Theatre Festival, Abbey Theatre, 2–14 October 2000.

Pre-production press release:
1. Victoria White, 'Cooking up a controversy', A supplement with *the Irish Times*, 23 September 2000.
2. Victoria White, 'Holy show?', *Irish Times*, 28 September 2000.
3. Anthony Garvey, 'More Barbaric complaints', *Stage*, 12 October 2000.
4. Frank McNally, 'Play absorbed by audience impervious to shock', *Irish Times*, 2 October 2000.

Reviews:
1. David Nowlan, 'Significant, serious and rare', *Irish Times*, 3 October 2000.
2. Luke Clancy, 'Dublin Theatre Festival 2000', *The Times*, 23 October 2000.
3. Gerry McCarthy, 'Failed shock tactics produce a barbaric bore', *Sunday Times*, 8 October 2000.
4. Emer O'Kelly, 'A barbaric edge to comedy', *Sunday Independent*, 8 October 2000.
5. Jocelyn Clarke, 'It Ain't Half Barbaric', *Sunday Tribune*, 8 October 2000.
6. Rosy Barnes, 'Barbaric Melodrama', *irish theatre magazine*, vo.12 no.7, pp.26–30.

Controversies over the play (Letters to the editor):
1. Gerry Condon, 'Abbey's decline', *Sunday Independent* (Dublin), 17 September 2000.
2. Aisling Murray, 'Barbaric Comedies', *Irish Times*, 20 October 2000.
3. Mairead Anderson, 'Barbaric Comedies', *Irish Times*, 23 October 2000.
4. Philip Crosby, 'Barbaric Comedies', *Irish Times*, 27 October 2000.
5. Tara Lovett, 'Barbaric Comedies', *Irish Times*, 28 October 2000.
6. Aisling Murray, 'Barbaric Comedies', *Irish Times*, 3 November 2000.

(e) Screenplays:

Dancing at Lughnasa by Brian Friel (1998)
Director: Pat O'Connor
Producer: Noel Pearson

Irish Reviews:
1. Michael Dwyer, 'Spellbinding Summer', *Irish Times*, 25 September 1998.
2. *Sunday Times*, 26 September 1998.
3. Ciaran Carty, 'Faithful to Friel', *Sunday Tribune*, 26 September 1998.
4. Ronan Farrren, 'Lughnasa is a triumph', *Sunday Independent*, 27 September 1998.
5. Donald Clarke, 'Reviews: Dancing at Lughnasa', *Film Ireland*, August/September, pp. 32–33.
6. Interview with Noel Pearson, *Film Ireland*, August/September, 1998, pp. 18–19.
7. muiris macconghail, 'Dancing at Lughnasa', *film west: Ireland's Film Quarterly*, issue 34, October 1998, pp. 16–17.

UK Reviews:
1. Meave Walsh, 'Come dancing, but leave the sequins behind', *Independent on Sunday*, 22 November 1998.
2. Geoff Brown, ''New Movies', *Times*, 3 December 1998.
3. Anthony Quinn, 'Film: It's a web of intrigue out there', *Independent*, 3 December 1998.
4. Quentin Curtis, 'New Releases', *Daily Telegraph*, 4 December 1998.
5. Xan Brooks, 'Screen Reviews', *Gurardian*, 4 December 1998.
6. 'Film: Current Releases', *Daily Mirror*, 3 December 1998.
7. Allan Hunter, 'Down and out in LA', *Scotland on Sunday*, 6 December 1998.
8. Mike Higgins, 'Cinema', *Independent on Sunday*, 3 December 1998.
9. Philip French, 'Other film releases', *Observer*, 6 December 1998.
10. Mark Steyn, 'Cinema: Nothing doing', *Spectator*, 5 December 1998.
11. Anne Billson, 'Cinema', *Sunday Telegraph*, 6 December 1998.
12. Grath Pearce, 'Interview: Catherine McCormack', (source & date unspecified)

US Reviews:
1. Jay Carr, '"Dancing at Lughnasa" finds heart of play', *Boston Globe*, 15 September 1998.
2. 'New life in Lughnasa', *Ferndale Films*, 16 September 1998.
3. 'Dancing at Lughnasa', *New Yorker*, 28.12.98/4.1.99.
4. 'Dancing at Lughnasa', *Time Out New York*, January 7–14, 1999.

NOTES

INTRODUCTION

Frank McGuinness and Ireland in the 1980s and After

1 Barbara Walker, *The Woman's Encyclopedia of Myths and Secrets* (New York: Harper Collins, 1983), p. 675.
2 McGuinness's use of this cauldron of regeneration in *Mary and Lizzie* is one of the very few examples. See Chapter Three.
3 Walker, p. 151.
4 The Northern assembly was suspended over the issue of decommissioning on 11 February, 2000. Direct rule by Westminster was re-imposed. At midnight on 29 May 2000, power was restored to the Stormont executive. It was suspended for one day on 11 August 2001 as a tactical move to encourage implementation of Belfast Agreement.
5 *Landmarks of Irish Drama*, introduced by Brendan Kennelly, (London: Methuen, 1988), p. vii.
6 Tony Gary, *Ireland: This Century* (London: Warner Books, 1995), p. 292.
7 For the biographical background of McGuinness, see Fintan O'Toole's 'Innocence Uprooted', *Magill*, Nov. 1986, or Richard Pine, 'Frank McGuinness: A Profile', *Irish Literary Supplement* 10.1.(1991), pp. 29–30.
8 The city's original name was *Daire*, meaning 'an oak grove' and later renamed *Doire Colmcille*, 'the oak grove of St. Columcill' after the 6th-century saint who had established a monastery there. In 1609 the new king, James I, decided on the 'Plantation of Ulster' and this colonisation was organised by the Trades Guilds of London. The city was renamed 'Londonderry' to commemorate this association. When the Troubles started in 1969, the name by which people called the city had become a kind of shibboleth revealing which side the speaker belonged to: Derry for Catholic and Republican, Londonderry for Protestant and Unionist. The official name of the city is 'Londonderry', though the city council was renamed the Derry City Council in 1984. In the Eighties, Gerry Anderson, a DJ for Radio Ulster, coined a new phrase 'Derry/ Londonderry' (Derry-stroke-Londonderry) so as to be neutral and

politically correct for both sides of the listeners to his programme in Ulster. Since 'Derry-stroke-Londonderry' was rather too long for radio broadcasting and cumbersome, he then began to use 'stroke city' whenever he needed to refer to the city. Apart from quotations, I use 'Derry/Londonderry' in this book, following Anderson's example for the sake of neutrality. McGuinness himself always calls it 'Derry'.

9 Charles Hunter, 'Strange Passion About the Somme', *The Irish Times*, 15 Feb. 1985.
10 Carolyne Pollard, 'An Ulster Son Observed: Interview with Frank McGuinness', *Quarto*, Winter 1987/88 (Literary Society of the University of Ulster).
11 After its performance of Thomas Kilroy's *Madam MacAdam's Travelling Theatre* in 1991, Field Day was to cease activity for a while. In the next year, the revival of Friel's *The Freedom of the City*, commemorating the twentieth anniversary of Bloody Sunday in Derry/Londonderry, was cancelled. After McGuinness's adaptation of Chekhov's *Uncle Vanya* was produced in 1995, its activity came to a halt. Field Day still retain its office in Derry/Londonderry with a part-time secretary.
12 Friel, Deane, and Heaney are Catholics, and Rea, Paulin, and Hammond are Protestants.
13 When the three volumes of this anthology were first published in 1990, active feminists pointed out the lack of women editors involved in the anthology and the relatively sparse attention paid to women writers. In order to answer these criticisms, a fourth volume, focusing on women's writing by women editors, is under way.
14 Those who wrote the pamphlets were: Seamus Deane, Seamus Heaney, Tom Paulin, Richard Kearney, Declan Kiberd, Terence Brown, Marianne Elliott, R.L.McCartmey, Eanna Mulloy, Michael Farrell, Patrick J. McGrory, Terry Eagleton, Fredric Jameson, and Edward Said.
15 Seamus Deane, *Heroic Styles: The Tradition of an Idea* (1984), in *Ireland's Field Day* (London: Hutchinson, 1985), 43–58, p. 58.
16 Fergus Finlay, *Mary Robinson: A President with a Purpose* (Dublin: O'Brien Press, 1990), p. 156.
17 Thomas Kilroy, *Double Cross* (London: Faber & Faber, 1986), p. 7.
18 Thomas Kilroy, *Double Cross* (Dublin: Gallery Press, 1994), p. 13.
19 Edna Longley, *Living Stream* (Newcastle upon Tyne: Bloodaxe Books, 1994), p. 10. In an Irish context, 'revisionism' is often used in the context of anti-nationalist revisionism.
20 Anthony Roche, *Contemporary Irish Drama: From Beckett to McGuinness* (Dublin: Gill & Macmillan, 1994), p. 266.
21 McGuinness had an interesting relationship with the Field Day Theatre Company: the company turned down his *Observe the Sons of Ulster Marching Towards the Somme*, 'which was', said Fintan

O'Toole, 'both a very fine play and an opportunity to incorporate a serious attempt to understand loyalism into the Field Day canon'. The playwright withdrew *Carthaginians,* a play about Bloody Sunday, commissioned by Field Day for the 1987 season. The reasons for the rejection and the withdrawal are generally not known, but if Field Day had put these plays on stage, then the whole course of its activity, and consequent criticism towards it, would have been different. After the success of *Someone Who'll Watch Over Me* in 1992 in both London and Broadway, with Stephen Rea as Edward, he renewed the liaison with Field Day, and his version of Chekhov's *Uncle Vanya,* with Rea in the title role, was produced in 1994.

22 Robert Darnton, *The Kiss of Lamourette: Reflections in Cultural History* (New York: W. W. Norton & Company, 1990), p. 257.

23 Darnton, p. 261.

24 Although *Innocence* is set in 17th century Italy, the play also deals with contemporary Ireland.

25 Fintan O'Toole, *Tom Murphy: The Politics of Magic* (Dublin: Gill & Macmillan, 1994),p. 113.

26 Paul Sweeney, *The Celtic Tiger: Ireland's Economic Miracle Explained* (Dublin: Oak Tree Press, 1998), p. 9.

27 E. Estyn Evans, 'Introduction' to *The Irish World,* edited by Brian de Breffny ed., (London: Thames and Hudson, 1977), p. 18.

28 Richard Pine, 'Frank McGuinness: A Profile', *Irish Literary Supplement* 10.1 (1991), pp. 29–30, p. 29.

29 Georgiana Brown, 'Three hostages to fortune', *The Independent,* 10 July, 1992.

30 Frank McGuinness, 'The Artist as a Young Pup', Review of *Is That It?* by Bob Geldof, *Irish Literary Supplement,* Fall 1986, p. 9.

31 Pine, p. 29.

32 Kevin Jackson, 'Speaking for the Dead: Playwright Frank McGuinness talks to Kevin Jackson', *The Independent,* 10 July, 1989.

33 This is what Friel did when he wrote *The Communication Cord* (1982), being a bit perplexed after the enthusiastic reception of *Translations* (1980). These plays are meant to be read and considered 'in tandem' according to the playwright, but this intention of Friel's is quite often neglected by critics and *The Communication Cord* is not referred to as much as *Translations* is.

34 According to Paul Allen, who interviewed McGuinness on a BBC programme on 1 May 1987, 'there were ominous taking of notes in the theatre, then orchestrated disruptive walkouts.'

35 Douglas Kennedy, 'Poetic politics', *New Statesman & Society,* 6 October 1989: 50–51, p. 50.

36 Kennedy, p. 50.

37 Pine, p. 29.

38 McGuinness, '*Oisín i ndiaidh Na Feínne*'[sic], in *Quarto: the Literary Magazine,* New University of Ulster, vol. 4, no. 2, April 1978, p. 25.

CHAPTER 1

'Folk Memory as Lethal Cultural Weapon': Protestant Ireland vs.
Catholic Ireland

1 There are two texts of *Observe the Sons of Ulster Marching Towards the Somme*, a separate edition published by Faber and Faber in 1986 and another in *Frank McGuinness: Plays 1*, published again by Faber and Faber in 1996. Slight differences are to be found between them. Further references are to the 1996 edition, unless otherwise stated, and will be incorporated into the text.
2 The IRA exploded a bomb in London in 1996 and this temporarily ended the ceasefire, which was resumed in 1997. See Introduction.
3 *Irish Times*, 14 September, 1994.
4 Broadcasted by RTE Radio 1, 'The Arts Show', 20 October, 1994.
5 John Waters, 'Alone Again Naturally', *In Dublin*, 14 May, 1987, pp. 15–18, p. 16.
6 Charles Hunter, 'Strange Passion About the Somme', *Irish Times*, 15 Februrary, 1985.
7 *Collected Works of Pádraic H. Pearse: Political Writings and Speeches* (Dublin: Phoenix Publishing, 1924), p. 99.
8 Máirín Ní Dhonnchadha and Theo Dorgan, eds., *Revising the Rising* (Derry: Field Day, 1991).
9 Declan Kiberd quotes an interesting survey by *the Irish Independent* in 'The Elephant of Revolutionary Forgetfulness': '65 per cent of respondents said that they looked on the Rising with pride, as opposed to a mere 14 per cent who said they regretted it. Fifty-eight per cent thought that the rebels were right to take up arms, as opposed to 24 per cent who would have preferred them to try political means. And 66 per cent thought that 'the men of 1916' [sic] would oppose today's IRA violence, as opposed to just 16 per cent who considered that they would endorse it'. See *Revising the Rising*, p. 3.
10 Dermont Healy, 'An Interview with Michael Longley', *Southern Review*, 31, 1 June, 1995, p. 557.
11 McGuinness got a teaching job at the New University of Ulster at Coleraine from 1977–79. He came back to Dublin and then got a grant from the Irish Arts Council in 1983 to go back to Coleraine to live in order to research and write *Sons of Ulster*.
12 Jennifer Johnston was one of the first who wrote to *The Irish Times* in defence of *Sons of Ulster*, when it was criticised as 'one of the most comprehensive attacks ever made on Ulster Protestantism' by David Nowlan, an *Irish Times* drama critic. She wrote that '[t]o call the play an "attack" reduces to the levels of polemics a piece of work of true creativity in which the sons of Ulster are observed with wit and compassion rather than attacked.' (*Irish Times*, 23

February, 1985) Michael Longley immediately supported her in his letter regarding the review of *Sons of Ulster* to the *Irish Times* (2 March, 1985). He wrote: 'My father survived the Trenches, and over the years I tried to come to terms imaginatively with his memories and with accounts I have picked up elsewhere of the Ulster Division at the Somme. In light of this preoccupation I feel honour-bound to praise Frank McGuinness's abundant, profound and humane study of cultural confusion and military heroism. This play moved me to tears.' He has also written poems on the Somme. (cf: "Wounds" *Poems 1963–1983*, p. 86.)

13 *Revising the Rising*, pp. 4–5.

14 See Carolyne Pollard, 'An Ulster Son Observed: Interview with Frank McGuinness', *Quarto*, Winter 1987/88 (Literary Society of the University of Ulster):12–13. Also in an interview with Joe Jackson, McGuinness said 'when [he] visited Enniskillen and stood there something clicked which later became the story [he] addressed in *Sons of Ulster*. See Jackson, 'The Bread Man Cometh', *Hot Press*, 1 November 1990, p. 45.

15 BBC Interview by Paul Allen, 'Kaleidoscope: Frank McGuinness Special', 1 May, 1987.

16 Gary Law, *The Cultural Traditions Dictionary* (Belfast: Blackstaff Press, 1998), p. 110.

17 Kevin Jackson, 'Speaking for the dead: Interview/Playwright Frank McGuinness talks to Kevin Jackson', *The Independent*, 27 Sep. 1989.

18 Laurence Binyon, *Collected Poems of Laurence Binyon* (London: Macmillan, 1931), p. 210.

19 Frank McGuinness, 'The Voice of the Somme', review on *The Road to the Somme*, by Philip Orr, *Sunday Press*, 24 January 1988.

20 Richard Pine, 'Frank McGuinness: A Profile', *Irish Literary Supplement* 10.1.(1991), pp. 29–30.

21 This reflects the recent 'adoption of the hero as a role-model by the Protestant paramilitary grouping known as the Ulster Defence Association'. See Declan Kiberd, 'Irish Literature and Irish History', in *The Oxford Illustrated History of Ireland*, ed. by R.F. Foster (Oxford: Oxford University Press, 1989), pp. 275–337, p. 278.

22 Elmer Andrews, *The Art of Brian Friel* (London: Macmillan, 1995), p. 84.

23 Anthony Roche says that 'Frank McGuinness is the true son of Sam', and sees the affinity between the situation Elder Pyper confronts in this play and the void, in which Hamm in *Endgame* is entrapped. *Contemporary Irish Drama*, p. 278.

24 Hugh Kenner, *Samuel Beckett: A Critical Study* (Berkeley and Los Angeles: University of California Press, 1968), p. 155.

25 The title of critical work by Louis de Paor on Máirtín ÓCadhain, Irish language writer, was *Faoin mBlaoisc Bheag Sin* (1992) ('Under this little Skull').

26 Frank McGuinness, 'The Voice of the Somme', *Sunday Press*, 24 January 1988.
27 Gladstone's first Home Rule Bill was introduced in 1886 and was eventually defeated in the House of Commons. His second Home Rule Bill, which got through the Commons, was defeated by the House of Lords in 1893.
28 Although he was remembered as 'the uncrowned king of Ulster', Carson believed that the Union must be maintained for Ireland as a whole though his view, essentially a southern one, was not shared by his followers in the north. According to Mark Tierney, 'he regarded the opposition which he led in the North simply as a means for blocking Home Rule, believing that if Ulster stood firm against the scheme, it would have to be abandoned in the rest of the country . . . However, Carson was wise enough not to draw attention to differing viewpoints and concentrated instead on rallying resistance. His powerful and incisive speeches were carefully contrived pieces of acting which electrified his vast audiences, boosting their morale and fortifying their determination to persevere in their dangerous enterprise.' See *Modern Ireland* (Dublin: Gill & Macmillan, 1978), p. 81.
29 Gordon Lucy, ed., *The Ulster Covenant: A Pictorial History of the 1912 HOME RULE Crisis* (Belfast: New Ulster Publications Ltd., 1989), p. 44.
30 Philip Orr, *The Road to the Somme: Men of the Ulster Division Tell Their Story* (Belfast: Blackstaff Press, 1987), p. 45.
31 The armies of William of Orange and James II met along the River Boyne, about three miles west of Drogheda, on 1 July, 1690. William, whose victory ushered in the Protestant ascendancy, became a folk-hero to the Irish Protestants. July 12 , the date of the Battle under the new calendar, has become 'Orange Day' in Northern Ireland, and every year Orangemen parade to honour the 'glorious and immortal memory' of William III. (*The Troubles*, 17)
32 Martin Marix Evans, *The Battle of the Somme* (London: Orion, 1996), p. 26.
33 *Irish Times*, 19 October 1994.
34 McGuinness, 'The Voice of the Somme', 1988.
35 E. Estyn Evans, *Ireland and the Atlantic Heritage: Selected Writings* (Dublin: Lilliput Press, 1996), p. 164.
36 *Irish Times*, 19 October 1994.
37 Richard Rankin Russell reads Pyper's hand here as a symbol of the red hand of Ulster. See 'Ulster Unionism's Mythic and Religious Culture in *Observe the Sons of Ulster*', Working Papers in Irish Studies, Department of Liberal Arts, Nova Southeastern University, 1998.
38 Helen Lojek says that 'Carson's dance' implies 'the intense opposition to homosexuality revealed in the notorious trial of

Oscar Wilde', in addition to his Army and its militant resistance. See Helen Lojek, 'Myth and Bonding in Frank McGuinness's *Observe the Sons of Ulster Marching Towards the Somme'*, in *Canadian Journal of Irish Studies*, Vol. 14, No.1(1988) 45–53, p. 48.

39 Lucy, p. 90.
40 "Religious Doctrines and Dogmas: MAJOR THEMES AND MOTIFS: Covenant." *Encyclopædia Britannica Online.* <http://members.eb.com/bol/topic?eu=119719&sctn=1>.
41 Yoko Sato, 'On *Observe the Sons of Ulster Marching towards the Somme*' in *The Harp* (IASAIL-Japan Bulletin), XI , 1996: 80–87, p. 82.
42 "blood brotherhood" *Encyclopædia Britannica Online.* <http://members.eb.com/bol/topic?eu=15909&sctn=1>.
43 Waters, p. 18.
44 Waters, p. 18.
45 This legend became famous through Robert Browning's poem of the same title, which starts with the rich imagery of the river Weser, which, 'deep and wide,/ washes its wall on the southern side'.
46 "Hameln" Encyclopædia Britannica Online. <http://members.eb.com/bol/topic?eu=39817&sctn=1>.
47 Seamus Heaney wrote a poem on this carving:

> On Boa the god-eyed, sex-mouthed stone
> Socked between graves, two faced, trepanned,
> Answered my silence with silence.
> 'Triptych': III. *At the Water's Edge*, in *Field Work*, (5–7).

48 The same patterns, 'becoming clean again by water', are seen in McGuinness's other plays: Sarah in *Carthaginians*, Caravaggio in *Innocence*, and Hugh in *Mutabilitie*.
49 Yoko Sato points out that in medieval morality plays the David-Goliath story was part of the repertoire of the guild of blacksmiths, Craig's occupation before he enlisted. See 'On *Observe the Sons of Ulster Marching Towards the Somme*' in *The Harp* (IASAIL-Japan Bulletin), XI (1996), pp. 80–87, p. 82.
50 McGuinness said: 'I'd loved Caravaggio's paintings since I set eyes on them in Florence in 1977.' (*Frank McGuinness: Plays 1*, introduction, xi.)
51 Paul Hammond, *Love between Men in English Literature* (London: Macmillan, 1996), p. xii.
52 It is interesting to note that this metaphor of Pyper's, which seems to be dealing with a very contemporary and modern theme, in fact reflects some other interpretation of the painting. Giorgio Bonsanti writes that '[t]he youth's head is also a kind of idealized self-portrait that gazes with sadness at the giant's severed head.' (*Caravaggio*, SCALA/Riverside,1984, 1991, 73) Alfred Moir adds a decisive interpretation of the painting: '[s]ome letters partly legible on the blade of the sword have been read as H or M AC O and

interpreted as meaning "Michael Angelo Caravaggio Opus," as if in self-accusation.' See *Caravaggio* (London: Thames and Hudson, 1989), p. 116.

53 Helen Lojek briefly mentions the affinity between Pyper and the old man in Yeats's *Purgatory*. See Lojek, 1988.

54 'Interview with Frank McGuinness', *Studies*, 87: 347, 1998, pp. 269–273, p. 272.

55 'Interview with Frank McGuinness', p. 271.

56 Angela Bourke pointed out that Belfast artists, Paul Henry (1877–1958) and James Humbert Craig (1878–1944) were liberated from sectarian Protestant identity through art. (Personal interview)

57 The same technique is used in the later plays, such as 'The Bread Man' and *Mutabilitie*.

58 See Appendix: A List of Plays McGuinness Directed at the New University of Ulster.

59 Jacqueline Hurtley's interview with McGuinness in *Ireland in Writing: Interviews with Writers and Academics* (Amsterdam-Atlanta: Rodopi, 1998), p. 55.

60 This is one of the alterations McGuinness made in the 1996 edition, from which these parts are excepted. References to the 1986 edition are shown in parentheses as (*O*, 46).

61 It is true, of course, that the audience in the theatre cannot tell the difference between 'Word' and 'word', when they are spoken on stage.

62 Law, p. 140. He also points out the fact that the *Titanic* sank on 14 April 1912 and it was 'only two days after the third Home Rule Bill was read in the House of Commons'. It seemed, Law continues, 'an ill omen for those who supported the union'.

63 This mock battle is also called the 'Sham Fight': Scarva was the location of the headquarters of William III's army as it mustered for the advance towards the Boyne in 1690 after having been dispersed in winter quarters throughout Ulster. The Battle of the Boyne has been refought (with always the same outcome) at Scarva every year since at least 1835. In the early years of the re-enactment, Newry canal stood in for the Boyne and occasionally participants would get so carried away by events that serious injuries, and even deaths, resulted. See Law, pp. 126–7.

65 "Religious Doctrines and Dogmas: MAJOR THEMES AND MOTIFS: Covenant: NATURE AND SIGNIFICANCE." *Encyclopædia Britannica Online*. <http://members.eb.com/bol/topic?eu=119719&sctn=1>.

66 Fintan O'Toole, 'Over the top', *Sunday Tribune*, 17 February 1985.

67 Joe Jackson, 'The Bread Man Cometh . . .', *Hot Press*, 1 November 1990, pp. 44–45.

68 There are two texts of *Carthaginians*, the script text for rehearsal for the first production at the Peacock Theatre in 1988, published by Faber and Faber in 1988, and the version which is based on the

Druid production in 1992, included in *Frank McGuinness: Plays I*, published again by Faber and Faber in 1996. Unless otherwise stated, I use the 1992 Druid version in the discussion of the play.

69 Twenty-one years later, in 1993, the then British Prime Minister, John Major, acknowledged in a letter to the SDLP leader, John Hume, that the 13 civilians shot dead by the British army on Bloody Sunday were innocent. (See Kathleen Magee, 'Major acknowledges Bloody Sunday dead were innocent', *Irish Times*, 21 January 1993.) Patrick Mayhew, then the Home Secretary, however, 'denied any "criminal wrongdoing", therefore there was, is, and will be no need for an apology' in February, 1997. (See John O'Farrell, *Fortnight*, 14.) Mo Mowlam, the new Secretary of State for Northern Ireland of the Labour Government, said. 'We all should take responsibility . . . across the board . . . I have no difficulty with the concept. I just want to do it in a way that actually works.' (See *Irish Times*, 15 November 1997). Finally in 1998 on the eve of the 26th anniversary of the day, the Prime Minister, Tony Blair, announced that the government would re-investigate the whole incident.

70 It is said that Friel had already started writing this play before the event. At the time it first appeared in 1972, just 6 months after the event, Friel said that this was not a play about Bloody Sunday in Derry. He probably wanted to make it clear that this quick response was not a cheap and journalistic one. Still, it is obvious that Friel got much inspiration for his play from the event. See Elizabeth Hale Winkler, "Reflections of Derry's Bloody Sunday in Literature", in *Studies in Anglo-Irish Literature*, ed. H. Kosok, (Bonn: Bouvier, 1982).

71 'It is possible that there is no other memory than the memory of wounds.' (The epigraph to the 1988 text, taken from Polish poet, Czestaw Milosz)

72 Fintan O'Toole, 'You don't think I'm not as stupid as Yeats, do you', *Irish Times*, Saturday, 24 September 1988, Weekend: p. 3.

73 McGuinness said in an interview with Jaqueline Hurtley: 'We'd an unhappy time with *Carthaginians* but that's done now, forgotten; and then I did *Uncle Vanya*'. See *Ireland in Writing* (Amsterdam-Atlanta, GA: Rodopi, 1998), p. 65.

74 C. S. Lewis, *Allegory of Love: A Study of Medieval Tradition* (Oxford: Oxford University Press, 1958), p. 44.

75 Pine writes, in a survey of this area, that 'this hill outside the city was excluded from the world of the apprentices' protected guilds, for whom Derry was built, and it is almost as if in this social experiment, each element of an equation, town and country, which should have been reciprocally interactive and interdependent, became mutually polarised and exclusive. Perhaps there has always been an implicit failure in the Derry formula, an apprenticeship to the tensions of historical myth.' Richard Pine,

The Diviner: the Art of Brian Friel (Dublin: University College Dublin Press, 1999), p. 67.

76   Margaret Thatcher, then the Prime Minister, allowed Americans to use British airbases for an attack on Libya in March 1986.

77   Elizabeth Bulter Cullingford, "British Romans and Irish Carthaginians: Anticolonial Metaphor in Heaney, Friel, and McGuinness", *PMLA* (March 1996), pp. 222–239, p. 234.

78   Bobbie Sands had been on H-Block hunger strike in support of political status. On 5 May 1981, he died on the 66th day of his fast. He was the first of ten republican prisoners to die on hunger strike.

79   However, four years later, in 1992, the Druid version of the play simply describes the settings as 'a graveyard'. Once the symbolic machinery and allegorical impact of the play had matured, the obvious stage symbolism seemed no longer necessary.

80   Liz Penny, 'In the Forbidden City', *Theatre Ireland* 12, 1987, p. 62.

81   Fintan O'Toole, 'Over the Top', *Sunday Tribune*, 17 February 1985.

82   On the Troy-Rome-London sequence vs. Carthage-Derry sequence, see Cullingford.

83   Could this be seen as a parody of W.B.Yeats's opening scenes in *At the Hawk's Well* and *The Only Jealousy of Emer*, in which three musicians open the black cloth in the former, and a 'frail' bird is involved in the latter?

84   Penny, p. 62.

85   Pine, 'Frank McGuinness: A Profile', p. 29.

86   Fintan O'Toole, 'Seeing Is Believing', in *Seeing is Believing: Moving Statues in Ireland*, edited by Colm Tóibín, (The Lodge, Mountrath, Co. Laois: Pilgrim Press, 1985), p. 90.

87   Colm Tóibín, 'Introduction', in *Seeing is Believing: Moving Statues in Ireland*, p. 7.

88   Isabel Healy, 'A Miracle At Ballinspittle', in *Seeing is Believing: Moving Statues in Ireland*, p. 24.

89   James Liddy has briefly mentioned that 'the structure of the play . . . moves within the polarities of a liturgical week which must represent Holy Week.' See "Voices in the Irish Cities of the Dead: Melodrama and Dissent in Frank McGuinness's *Carthaginians*", *Irish University Review*, 25. 2. (1995), pp. 278–283, p. 279.

90   In the 1988 version, the play starts on Monday. The parallelism between the play's structure and Holy Week is still observed here. However, in the 1992 version, McGuinness makes it clear, starting his play on the Wednesday of Holy Week, which is generally known in Ireland as 'Spy Wednesday'.

91   The roll-call of the dead is one of the characteristics of Irish Theatre. Other examples can be seen in Synge's *Riders to the Sea*, Murphy's *Famine* and *Bailegangaire*. In *The Boxer*, a Neil Jordan film, this device of the roll-call is used most effectively.

92   The contemporary homosexual rights and civil rights movement had a roughly contemporary origin. Both started in the United

States in the late 1960s. Civil rights movements began in the southern states in 1963, the date of Martin Luther King's Alabama campaign. 'The beginning of militant homosexual activism can virtually be traced back to the hour. About 3:00 AM on June 28, 1969, the Stonewall Inn, a homosexual bar at 53 Christopher Street in Greenwich Village, was raided by New York City police. Instead of passively accepting the situation (as in the past), the some 200 homosexuals present began taunting the police and throwing debris; the riot lasted 45 minutes and resumed on succeeding nights. Protest rallies ensued, and homosexual rights organizations proliferated in the United States from the 1970s on.' (Encyclopaedia Britannica Online. "homosexual rights movement.")

93 This name shares the initals (F.McG) with Frank McGuinness.

94 It was Stephen Rea, the director and actor of the Field Day Theatre Company, who gave the idea of the play-within-a-play to McGuinness, when they were discussing a possible new play for Field Day. Rea said 'he was very, very tired of balaclava drama.' (BBC interview by Paul Allen, 'Kaleidoscope: Frank McGuinness Special', 1 May 1987.

95 "The History of Western Theatre: Medieval theatre: MORALITY PLAYS."Encyclopædia Britannica Online. <http://members.eb.com/bol/topic?eu=119719&sctn=1>.

96 J.L. Moreno, 'Reflections on my methods of group psychotherapy', Ciba Symposium II(1963), pp. 148–57.

97 Pine, 'Frank McGuinness: A Profile', p. 29.

98 Paul Holmes, 'Classical psychodrama: An overview', in *Psychodrama: Inspiration and Technique*, eds. Paul Holmes and Marcia Karp, (London: Routledge, 1991), pp. 7–13, p. 10.

99 Holmes, p. 11.

100 Holmes, p. 11.

101 Holmes, p. 11.

102 Holmes, p. 11.

103 In *The Crying Game* (1992), Neil Jordan's award-winning film, this point is emphasised as well. The British soldier, who is kidnapped by the IRA and eventually killed in a car accident when he is escaping, is played by a black actor, Forest Whitaker. This makes the stereotypical assessment of British soldiers as the oppressors and the Irish as the oppressed irrelevant, because this British soldier is also one of the oppressed, coming from a minority group.

104 Holmes, p. 12.

105 Holmes, p. 12.

106 A criticism against the actions of the British troops on Bloody Sunday is clear here.

107 William Shakespeare, *As You Like It*, Act 2 Scene 7.

108 See Lionel Abel, *Metatheatre*: A New View of Dramatic Form (New York: Hill and Wang, 1969).

109 Psychodrama as a form of therapy for the Ulster community was
     actually used by a member of Theatre Studies at the University of
     Ulster at Coleraine in the late 1980s. The director of the play used
     balaclavas for stage properties, as Dido does. On his way home
     after the rehearsal, he was stopped and searched at a police
     checkpoint in Derry and got into serious trouble when some
     twenty balaclavas were found in his car boot. (Interview with
     Professor Robert Welch)
110 It was Brian Friel's *Faith Healer* that inspired McGuinness to start
     writing a play.
111 Andrew E. Malone, *Irish Drama* (New York: Benjamin Blom, 1929,
     1965), p. 6.
112 Malone, p. 6.
113 Roche points out this aspect of storytelling in his discussion of
     Murphy's *Bailegangaire*. Anthony Roche, *Contemporary Irish Drama:
     from Beckett to McGuinness* (Dublin: Gill and Macmillan, 1994), pp.
     151–161.
114 Kristin Morrison, *Canters and Chronicles: The Use of Narrative in the
     Plays of Samuel Beckett and Harold Pinter* (Chicago: University of
     Chicago Press, 1983), p. 3.
115 Kenji Matsutani, *Karutago Kobo-shi* (The Rise and Fall of Carthage)
     in Japanese, (Tokyo: Hakusui-sha, 1991), p. 16.
116 McGuinness once said that: 'Beckett has affected us all; no one else
     can write the turning point of 20th-century drama, the end of
     Godot –"they do not move" – the gauntlet thrown down which
     we're all tempted to change in some way, if we're doing our job.
     We're not in the shadow of Beckett, but we've all been taken up in
     some way . . . Beckett's tramps go nowhere – quite rightly. Mine
     do.' See Pine.
117 Eamon McCann, *War and an Irish Town*: New Edition (London:
     Pluto Press, 1993), p. 3.

CHAPTER 2

Visualising his Verbal Theatre: McGuinness's Interpretation of the
Theatricality of Caravaggio's Paintings

1 The ending of *Innocence*, Caravaggio's laughter from backstage,
   might have been influenced by this scene.
2 Frank McGuinness, *Oisín i ndiaidh Na Feínne*[sic], in *Quarto: the
   Literary Magazine*, New University of Ulster, vol. 4, no. 2, April
   1978, p. 25. The correct title is: *Oisín i ndiaidh na Féinne.*
3 '*Oisín i ndiaidh Na Feínne*, p. 25.
4 This is what Friel did when he wrote *The Communication Cord*
   (1982), being a bit perplexed after the enthusiastic reception of
   Translations (1980). These plays are meant to be read and

considered 'in tandem' according to the playwright, but this
intention of Friel's is quite often neglected by critics and *The
Communication Cord* is not referred to as much as *Translations* is.

5 Fintan O'Toole, 'Innocence Uprooted', *Magill*, November, (1986),
pp. 48–54, p. 54.

6 There are two texts of *Innocence*, a separate edition published in
1986 by Faber and Faber and another included in *Frank
McGuinness: Plays 1* in 1996. Slight differences are to be found
between them. Further references are to the 1996 edition, unless
otherwise stated, and will be incorporated in the text.

7 Caravaggio was born in 1571? and died in 1610. The play is set in
Rome in 1607.

8 Frank McGuinness, *Plays 1* (London: Faber and Faber, 1996), p. xi.

9 Alfred Moir, *Caravaggio* (London: Thames and Hudson, 1989), p.
43.

10 Production Programme, p. 8.

11 Seamus Heaney, *Sweeney Astray* (Derry: Field Day, 1983, London:
Faber and Faber, 1984), p. ii.

12 Several critics have dealt with *Innocence* briefly as part of larger
discussions. See Riana O'Dwyer, 'Dancing in the Borderlands: The
Plays of Frank McGuinness', in *The Crows Behind the Plough*,
(Amsterdam: Rodopi, 1991), pp. 99–116, (pp. 109–111), and Jochen
Achilles, 'Religious Risk in the Drama of Contemporary Ireland',
Éire-Ireland, 28.3 (1993), 17–37, (pp. 32–35).

13 Eamonn Jordan, *The Feast of Famine* (Bern: Peter Lang, 1997).

14 Micheál Mac Gréil introduces striking statistics of Irish people's
attitudes to the 'Decriminalisation of Homosexuality' based on
research done in 1988–89. 'A plurality of the sample disagreed
with the view that: "Homosexual behaviour between consenting
adults should be a crime", i.e., 43.9% against and 35.1% for. This
result is very close to the responses of the Dublin sample in
1972–73, i.e., 45.2% *vs* 39.9%. Prior to the 1988–89 survey, the
European Court of Human Rights ruled against the criminalisation
of this behaviour in the Republic of Ireland as outlawed in the
Victorian criminal legislation of the second half of the 19th century
(which was in force at the time of the survey).' In 1993,
'Homosexual behaviour between consenting adults (over 17 years)
[was] legalised in the Republic.' See *Prejudice in Ireland Revisited,*
The Survey & Research Unit, Department of Social Studies,
(Maynooth: St. Patrick's College, 1996), pp. 399–400.

15 Jacqueline Hurtley's interview with McGuinness in *Ireland in
Writing: Interviews with Writers and Academics* (Amsterdam-Atlanta:
Rodopi, 1998), p. 62.

16 Lynda Henderson, 'Innocence and Experience', *Fortnight*,
November 1986, p. 26.

17 BBC Interview by Paul Allen, 'Kaleidoscope: Frank McGuinness
Special', 1 May 1987.

18   This is McGuinness's simple mistake. *Innocence* opened at Dublin's Gate Theatre on 7 October 1986.
19   Patrick Mason was the director of the production.
20   Frank McGuinness, *Plays 1*, p. xi.
21   Roger Hinks, *Michelangelo Merisi da Caravaggio: His Life, His Legend, His Works* (London: Faber and Faber, 1953), p. 87.
22   Henderson, p. 26.
23   BBC Interview, 1 May 1987.
24   Gerald McNamara, 'The Out Interview', *Out*, November/December, 1986, p. 20.
25   Barbara Walker, *Woman's Encyclopedia of Myths and Secrets* (San Francisco: Harper 1983), p. 213.
26   Frank Kermode, *The Sense of an Ending* (London: Oxford University Press, 1966), p. 27.
27   Willard Farnham, *The Medieval Heritage of Elizabethan Tragedy* (Berkeley: University of California Press, 1936), p. 39.
28   Jacobs Henry, 'Shakespeare, Revenge Tragedy, and the Ideology of Memento Mori', *Shakespeare Studies*, 1993, p. 96.
29   Moir writes that the population of Rome in 1600 was just 109,729. See *Caravaggio*, p. 11.
30   Frank McGuinness, *Plays 1*, p. xi.
31   "Bruno, Giordano." *Encyclopædia Britannica Online*. <http:// members.eb.com/bol/topic?eu=119719&sctn=1> [Accessed 5 April 2000].
32   Joe Vanek, 'Designing for the Gate', Production Programme, Dublin: the Gate Theatre, October, 1986, p. 24.
33   George Ferguson, *Signs & Symbols in Christian Art* (New York: Oxford University Press, 1954, 1977), p. 179.
34   Frank McGuinness, 'The Violent Kiss', *Irish Times*, 6 November, 1993.
35   Production Programme, p. 8.
36   According to Howard Hibbard, the man did not die of this wound. In the following year, 1606, in which the play is set, Caravaggio murdered a man, called Ranuccio Tomasoni, over a wager on a tennis match. See *Caravaggio* (London: Thames and Hudson, 1983), p. 206. Hibbard also recorded the document: "Lena che sta in piedi a piazza Navona . . . che è donna di Michelangelo" (Lena, who is to be found standing in Piazza Navona; who is Michelangelo's woman.) This woman actually posed for paintings such as *Madonna di Loreto* and *Madonna with St. Anne*. (See p. 191) In the play, Lena defines herself as 'a frequenter of the Piazza Navona'. p. 287.
37   Hibbard uses 'Magdalen' for 'Magdalena'.
38   Hibbard, p. 51.
39   Hibbard, p. 53.
40   Walker, p. 615.
41   Hibbard, p. 17.

42 Giorgio Bonsanti, *Caravaggio,* translated by Paul Blanchard (Milano: SCALA/Riverside, 1994), p. 8.

43 Moir, *Caravaggio* (London: Thames and Hudson, 1989), p. 66.

44 Eamon Jordan also points out the relation between the scene and the painting. See Jordan, p. 67.

45 Historically, Caravaggio was in Milan with his family until he was five. 'But by 1576 he had been sent back home to Caravaggio to escape the menace of the plague in the city.' See Moir, p. 8.

46 Moir, p. 64.

47 Joseph Campbell and Bill Moyers, *The Power of Myth* (New York: Doubleday, 1988), pp. 116–7.

48 Hibbard, p. 167.

49 This is Hibbard's misquotation. This line is from (John 20: 29).

50 Hibbard, p. 168.

51 BBC Interview, 1 May 1987.

52 Production Programme, p. 7.

53 Dante Alighieri, *The Divine Comedy,* translated by C. H. Sisson (Oxford: Oxford University Press, 1980), p. 47.

54 de Vries, p. 329.

55 de Vries, p. 329.

56 See McGuinness's version of *Peer Gynt* (London: Faber and Faber, 1990), p. 35.

57 McGuinness makes Paul in *Carthaginians* say this line. *Plays 1,* p. 311.

58 "Dante" *Encyclopaedia Britannica Online.* <http://members.eb.com/bol/topic?eu=119719&sctn=1>.

59 Programme note for *Dracula,* Galway, Druid Theatre, 1986.

60 Hibbard, p. 96.

61 Hibbard, p. 100.

62 BBC Interview, 1 May 1987.

63 This is another example of alterations McGuinness made in the 1996 edition, from which the following lines are taken. In addition to the change of the order, a slight alteration in phrasing can be seen as well.

> Whore: Who is the bird whose song is golden?
> Antonio: Lion, roar your lament of love.
> Lucio: Hound, play with the wounded lion.
> Antonio: Hare, lie with the sleeping hound.
> Whore: Steed, open your trusty mouth.
> Lucio: Dragon, breathe your web of fire.
> Antonio: Eagle, see with all-seeing eye.
> Whore: Bull, **weep for the cows and calves.**
> Lucio: Lizard, change colour for ever.
> Antonio: Unicorn, preserve the species.
> Chorus: Unicorn, protect the species. (*I,* 56)

64 Jordan, p. 65.

65 This painting is reproduced in the production programme.
66 Jordan quotes from McGuinness that 'Lena now has the same artistic powers as Caravaggio'. See Jordan, p. 67.

CHAPTER 3

'An Unhappy Marriage between England and Ireland': A Postcolonial Gaze at the Irish Past

1 Michael Parker and Roger Starkey (eds), *Postcolonial Literatures: Achebe, Ngugi, Desai, Walcott* (London: Macmillan, 1995), p. 5.
2 Declan Kiberd, who as Director invited Said to the Yeats Summer School, said: 'If you look at what was being written about Yeats in Ireland before that, the radical critics . . . were attacking Yeats as a kind of literary Unionist and saying that he was really an example of the problem rather than the solution . . . And that (Said's lecture) was a tremendous change.' See *Ireland in Writing: Interviews with Writers and Academics*, ed. by Jacqueline Hurley, (Amsterdam-Atlanta, GA, 1998), p. 172.
3 Seamus Deane, 'Introduction' in *Nationalism, Colonialism, and Literature*, by Terry Eagleton, Fredric Jameson and Edward E. Said, (Minneapolis, University of Minnesota Press, 1990), p. 3.
4 Deane, p. 6.
5 This open interview was held on 7 January 1998 prior to the performance of *Mutabilitie* at the Lyttleton in the Royal National Theatre, London.
6 Mic Moroney, 'Coming home', *Irish Times*, 29 November 1997: Saturday, 1.
7 Joseph Campbell and Bill Moyers, *The Power of Myth* (New York: Doubleday, 1988), p. 85.
8 Kevin Jackson, 'Speaking for the dead', *Independent*, 27 September 1989.
9 Frederick Engels, *The Condition of the Working-Class in England: From Personal Observation and Authentic Sources* (Moscow: Progress Publishers, 1973).
10 Frank McGuinness, *Mary and Lizzie* (London: Faber and Faber, 1989), p. 32. Further reference to the play will be incorporated into the text.
11 Edmund Wilson, *To the Finland Station: A Study in the Writing and Acting History* (W.H.Allen,1940, reprinted by Collins, the Fontana Library, 1960), p. 137.
12 Wilson, p. 262. Lizzie Burns died in 1878, and Engels married her to please her on her death bed. See Wilson, p. 338.
13 Douglas Kennedy, 'Poetic Politics', *New Statesman & Society*, 6 October 1989, pp. 50–51, p. 51.
14 Steven Marcus, *Engels, Manchester and the Working Class* (London:

Weidenfeld and Nicolson, 1974), p. 100, footnotes. He also introduces the very interesting psychological family background of Engels: 'one need only recall that Engels' favourite sister was named Marie and that his mother was named Elizabeth (and referred to as Elsie) to refresh one's sense of the depth of meaning that are determined in such matters.'

15 Kennedy, p. 50.
16 Jackson, 1989.
17 Jackson, 1989.
18 Henrik Ibsen, *Peer Gynt,* A Version by Frank McGuinness, (London: Faber and Faber, 1990), p. 35.
19 Michael Coveney, *Financial Times,* 28 September 1989. (Reprinted in the *London Theatre Record,* 24 September – 7 October 1989, p. 1318).
20 Richard Allan Cave, 'J'Accuse', *Theatre Ireland,* 21, 1989, p. 58.
21 Michael Billington, *Guardian,* 29 September 1989. (Reprinted in the *London Theatre Record,* 24 September – 7 October 1989, p. 1320).
22 Rhoda Koenig, *Punch,* 13 September 1989. (Reprinted in the *London Theatre Record,* 24 September – 7 October 1989, p. 1320).
23 Thomas Kilroy, *Double Cross* (London: Faber and Faber, 1986), p. 6.
24 de Vries, p. 475.
25 Milton Shulman mentioned these 'Irish harpies giggling on swings' in the *Evening Standard,* 29 September, (Reprinted in the *London Theatre Record,* 24 September – 7 October 1989, p. 1318.)
26 Nuala Ni Dhomnaill, 'Q & A', *Irish Literary Supplement,* Fall 1989, p. 42.
27 Humm, p. 75.
28 Humm, p. 169.
29 Kennedy, p. 51.
30 Wilson, pp. 132–3.
31 Kennedy, p. 51.
32 A key is one of the Great Mother's possessions. According to Neumann, 'she has for symbols the key, the phallic opening power of the male, the emblem of the Goddess, who is mistress of birth and conception'. Neumann, p. 170.
33 Neumann Erich, The Great Mother, trs. Ralph Manheims (Princeton, NJ: Princeton University Press, 1963), p. 170.
34 Camile Paglia, *Sexual Personae: Art and Decadence from Nefertiti to Emily Dickinson* (Harmondsworth: Penguin, 1992), p. 53.
35 Rees, Alwyn and Brinley, *Celtic Heritage* (London: Thames and Hudson, 1961), p. 47.
36 Ad de Vries, *Dictionary of Symbols and Imagery* (Amsterdam and London: North Holland Publishing Company, 1974), p. 379.
37 de Vries, p. 437.
38 The rhythm of this song reminds us of another cauldron, that of

the three witches in *Macbeth*. Its ingredients are strikingly similar.

> Scale of dragon, tooth of wolf,
> Witches' mummy, maw and gulf,
> Of the ravined salt-sea shark,
> Root of hemlock digged i'th' dark,
> Liver of blaspheming Jew,
> Gall of goat, and slips of yew
> Slivered in the moon's eclipse,
> Nose of Turk, and Tartar's lips,
> Finger of birth-strangled babe
> Ditch-delivered by a drab,
> Make the gruel thick and slab
> Add thereto a tiger's chaudron
> For th'ingredience of our cauldron. (*Macbeth*, Act 4, Scene 1)

39 Frank McGuinness, 'In the Forefront of Irish Writing: Michael Longley's Poems', *Irish Literary Supplement*, Spring 1986, p. 23.
40 This is not specified in the published text, but several critics recorded this in their reviews. See, for example, Coveney in the *Financial Times*, and Brown in the *Independent*.
41 de Vries, p. 67.
42 de Vries, p. 67.
43 This is reminiscent of a passage from Joyce Cary's *To be a Pilgrim*: 'England took me with her on a few stages of her journey. Because she could not help it. She, poor thing, was born upon the road, and lives in such a dust of travel that she never knows where she is. "Where away England, steersman answer me? We cannot tell. For we are at sea." She is the wandering Dutchman, the pilgrim and scapegoat of the world. Which flings its sins upon her as the old world heaped its sins upon the friars. Her lot is that of all courage, all enterprise; to be hated and abused by the parasite. But, and this has been one of the exasperating things in my life, she isn't even aware of this hatred and jealousy which surrounds her and, in the same moment, seeks and dreads her ruin. She doesn't notice it because she looks forward to the road. Because she is free. She stands always before all possibility, and that is the youth of the spirit. It is the life of the faithful who say, "I am ready. Anywhere at any time."' Joyce Cary, *To be a Pilgrim* (London: Michael Joseph, 1942), p. 342.
44 Jordan, p. 133.
45 Wilson, p. 134–5.
46 "Sleep and Dreams: Dreams and dreaming: DREAMLIKE ACTIVITIES." *Encyclopædia Britannica Online*. <http://members.eb.com/bol/topic?eu=119719&sctn=1>.
47 Coveney, *Financial Times*.
48 Jackson, 1989.
49 de Vries, p. 437.

50 Walker, p. 183.
51 Walker, p. 184.
52 *The Oxford Companion to the Bible*, eds. Bruce M. Metzger and Michael D. Coogan, (Oxford: Oxford University Press, 1993), p. 23.
53 Hélène Cixous, 'Sorties' (1986), in *A Critical and Cultural Theory Reader*, p. 153.
54 Jane Edwards, 'Frank's Spenser', *Time Out*, 19–26 November 1997, p. 158.
55 "mime and pantomime." *Encyclopædia Britannica Online.* <http://members.eb.com/bol/topic?eu=119719&sctn=1>.
56 Peter Holland, 'The Play of Eros: Paradoxes of Gender in English Pantomime', *New Theatre Quarterly*, 13. 51 (1997), 195–204, p. 200.
57 Holland, p. 203.
58 Jackson, 1989.
59 Frank McGuinness, *Someone Who'll Watch Over Me* (London: Faber and Faber, 1992). Further references to the play will be incorporated into the text.
60 The dedication was in Irish: 'Do Bhrian Fear Croga' means 'For Brian, Brave Man'.
61 The production programme for *Someone Who'll Watch Over Me* at the Gateway theatre in Chester explains the background of the play in detail. 'Since 1984, more than 30 Westerners, including four Britons were kidnapped by various Shia Fundamentalist Groups. Each group operated separately, but most were related to the pro-Iranian group Hezbollah. The Islamic Jihad, which held American journalist Terry Anderson and the Archbishop of Canterbury's special envoy Terry Waite, was the most prominent of these groups and demanded the release of 375 Shia and other prisoners held by Israel or the South Lebanon Army. The hostage 'crisis' ended in June 1992 when German hostages Heinrich and Struebig and Thomas Kemptner were released. Thus, one of the cruellest and most futile episodes in the history of the Middle East was brought to an end.'
62 Georgiana Brown, 'Three hostages to fortune', *Independent*, 10 July 1992.
63 Brian Keenan, *Irish Times*, 8 May 1993.
64 Brian Keenan, *An Evil Cradling*, London: Vintage Edition, 1993, p. 88.
65 Keenan, 1993, p. 93.
66 'Wounds' seems to be one of McGuinness's keywords or ideas. In the epigram to *Carthaginians*, he quotes Czeslaw Milosz: 'It is possible that there is no other memory than the memory of wounds.'
67 Brown, 1992.
68 E. Estyn Evans, 'Introduction' to *The Irish World*, ed. by Brian de Breffny, (London: Thames and Hudson, 1977), p. 8.
69 Edward, as a Dubliner, actually has less right to make a joke out of

it than a person from the North, or than the relatives of a dead English soldier.
70 Walker, p. 779.
71 Walker, p. 150.
72 Old Norse was the language chosen by McGuinness for his Master's degree in Medieval Studies at UCD.
73 Walker, p. 383.
74 Katharine Worth, 'Book Review on Frank McGuinness's *Someone Who'll Watch Over Me* ', *Irish University Review*, 23:2 (1993), pp. 324–326, p. 326.
75 In this chapter, the historical Edmund Spenser and the dramatic character, Edmund, are differentiated: the former is mentioned as 'Spenser' and the latter as 'Edmund', unless otherwise stated. The historical William Shakespeare and the dramatic character, William, are dealt with in the same way: the former is mentioned as 'Shakespeare' and the latter as 'William'.
76 The original title was *A Vewe of the Present State of Ireland*, but '*View*' has commonly been used by editors and critics.
77 David B. Quinn, "*A Vewe of the Present State of Ireland*", in *The Spenser Encyclopedia*, ed. A. C. Hamilton, (Toronto: University of Toronto Press, 1990, reprinted in 1997), p. 715.
78 Edward W. Said, *Culture & Imperialism* (London: Chatto & Windus, 1993), p. 5.
79 Frank McGuinness, *Mutabilitie* (London: Faber and Faber, 1997) Further reference to the play will be incorporated into the text.
80 Henry Morley, ed., *Ireland Under Elizabeth and James the First* (London: George Routledge and Sons, 1890), p. 13.
81 Seamus Deane, 'Introduction', in *Nationalism, Colonialism, and Literature*, by T. Eagleton, F. Jameson and E. W. Said, (Minneapolis: University of Minnesota Press, 1990), p. 7.
82 Edmund Spenser, *A View of the Present State of Ireland*, edited by W. L. Renwick, (originally published by Scholartis Press in 1934, Oxford: Clarendon Press, 1970), p. 171.
83 Edmund Spenser, *A View of the Present State of Ireland*, edited by Andrew Hadfield and Willy Maley, (Oxford: Blackwell, 1997), pp. xv–xvi.
84 Robert Welch, *The Kilcolman Notebook* (Dingle, Co.Kerry: Brandon Press, 1994).
85 John Whitley, 'The Arts: the Troubles with Shakespeare', *Daily Telegraph*, 20 November, 1997.
86 Sheldon P. Zitner, '*The Faerie Queene*, Book VII', in *The Spenser Encyclopedia*, ed. by A.C. Hamilton, Toronto: University of Toronto Press, 1990, reprinted in 1997, p. 288.
87 Jane Edwardes, 'Preview: Frank's Spenser', *Time Out*, November 19–26, 1997, p. 158.
88 Declan Kiberd, *Inventing Ireland* (London: Jonathan Cape, 1995), p. 11.

89 Andrew Hadfield has pointed out the fact that Spenser is included in the *Field Day Anthology of Irish Writing*. See *Spenser's Irish Experience: Wilde Fruit and Salvage Soyl* (Oxford: Clarendon Press, 1997), p. 6–7.

90 Peter Berresford Ellis, *A Dictionary of Irish Mythology*, (London: Constable, 1987), p. 122.

91 Kiberd, p. 15.

92 Jack Bradley wrote in the production note of *Mutabilitie* that 'the suggestion (that Shakespeare ever visited Ireland) is not as far-fetched as it might first appear. Indeed it has been the subject of academic debate since the turn of the century.' *Shakespeare and Ireland: History, Politics, Culture*, eds by Mark Thornton Burnett and Ramona Wray, to which McGuinness wrote 'Foreword', was published in 1997.

93 Kilcolman was attacked and burned in that year, and Spenser and his family fled to England.

94 Edmund Spenser, *A View of the Present State of Ireland*, edited by Andrew Hadfield and Willy Maley, (Oxford: Blackwell, 1997), pp. 101–2.

95 Mary Holland, 'Mini-Interview: So Shakespeare's the only one who can solve the Irish problem . . .', *Observer*, 16 November 1997.

96 'Platform', 9 January, 1998.

97 In an interview with Jacqueline Hurtley, McGuinness said that he had played Bolingbroke in the student production at UCD. See *Ireland in Writing*, Jacqueline Hurtley *et al* eds., (Amsterdam-Atlanta: Rodopi, 1998), p. 51.

98 Eleanor Knott & Gerald Murphy, *Early Irish Literature* (London: Routledge & Kegan Paul, 1966), p. 14.

99 Welch, pp. 387–8.

100 Kiberd, *Inventing Ireland*, p. 11.

101 John Whitley, 'The Arts: the Troubles with Shakespeare', *Daily Telegraph*, 20 November 1997.

102 Samuel Beckett, *The Complete Dramatic Works*, London: Faber and Faber, 1986, 1990, p. 101.

103 Oscar Wilde, *The Importance of Being Earnest and Other Plays* (Oxford: Oxford University Press, 1995), p. 253.

104 Wilde, p. 260.

105 Wilde was sent to school at Portora at Enniskillen, Co. Fermanagh, with his brother William, before he entered Trinity College, Dublin.

106 Edwardes, p. 158.

107 Which is also McGuinness's. He always keeps cats at home.

108 Mic Moroney, 'Coming home', *Irish Times*, Saturday, 29 November 1997.

109 Hadfield, p. 185.

110 Edmund Spenser, *The Mutabilitie Cantos*, ed. by S. P. Zitner,

(London: Nelson and Sons, 1968), p. 10.

111 Zitner, *'The Faerie Queene*, Book VII', in *The Spenser Encyclopedia*, p. 288.

112 Fosterage was a very important institution in Ireland. See Rees, pp. 240–1.

113 Mic Moroney, 'Coming home', *Irish Times*, Saturday, 29 November 1997, p. 1.

114 Mo Mowlam was replaced by Peter Mandelson in October 1999 and appointed Cabinet Office Minister. In September 2000, she announced her decision to retire from government, saying that she wants to do something different before she finally retires.

115 Mic Moroney, p. 1.

CHAPTER 4

'The Voice of the Voiceless': Representation of Women's Reality

1 Among McGuinness's works, *Mary and Lizzie* (1989), discussed in Chapter Three, could be added to this list.

2 Compared with Irish feminist films, which have been made especially in Northern Ireland in connection with the representations of the Troubles from a woman's point of view, it has become commonplace in Irish theatre to suggest a lack of women playwrights until Anne Devlin, Marie Jones, and Marina Carr made their appearance very recently.

3 Elain Showalter, 'Feminist Criticism in the Wilderness', in *The New Feminist Criticism: Essays on Women, Literature and Theory*, ed. by Elaine Showalter, First published by Pantheon Books, New York, 1985, reprinted by Virgo Press, London, 1989, p. 248.

4 Obviously, this name shares the initials (F. McG) with Frank McGuinness.

5 Ronan Farren, 'No category for Frank's new play', *Evening Herald*, 11 March 1982.

6 Sarah O'Hara, 'Productive lives', *Irish Press*, 17 March 1982.

7 'Towards Post-Feminisn?, *Theatre Ireland*, No 18, April-June 1989, p. 35.

8 It still is, in many aspects, but it is difficult to deny that Northern Ireland has, in the last ten years, striven for a more pluralist society.

9 A civil rights activist. In April 1969, when she was twenty-one, Devlin won a by-election to Westminster in the mid-Ulster constituency. She was the youngest MP in that assembly, the youngest woman MP ever to take a seat there, and the youngest MP elected under universal suffrage.

10 Derry Film and Video (Workshop), Channel 4 BBC, 1988. This film is highly acclaimed as one of the great feminist films of Northern

Ireland.
11 Women who go out to work are normal to McGuinness. He said, 'when I came to Dublin to study in 1971 I was a bit surprised about the fuss being made about women going out to work. ' See William Roche, 'The Tale of the Shirt Girls!', *Sunday Press*, 7 March 1982.
12 Farren, 'No category for Frank's new play'.
13 This version was rewritten for the Druid production in 1988.
14 Olive Schreiner, *Dreams and Dream Life and Real Life* (London: T. Fisher Unwin, 1912), pp. 99–100.
15 Frank McGuinness, *The Factory Girls* (Dublin: Monarch Line, 1982), p. 4.
16 Personal Interview.
17 However, only a reader can tell this, through the placement of quotation marks. See Chapter One on the use of 'word' and 'Word' in *Sons of Ulster*.
18 Nell McCafferty, 'The Death of Ann Lovett', in *The Abortion Papers: Ireland*, Ailbhe Smyth, ed., Attic Press, Dublin, 1992, 99–106, p. 99.
19 *Irish Times*, 1 October 1979.
20 After the referendum, the Eighth Amendment to the constitution was added: 'The State acknowledges the right to life of the unborn, and, with due regard to the equal right to life of the mother, guarantees in its laws to respect, and , as far as practicable, by its laws to defend and vindicate that right.' (Constitution, Article 40.3.3)
21 'Single parent' is now preferred to this rather pejorative phrase. But when this issue was raised in public debate for the first time in the Eighties, the term 'unmarried mother' was used.
22 Patsy McGarry, 'Pope's visit didn't stem ebbing tide', *Irish Times*, 2 October 1999.
23 Harkin's film, *Hush-a-Bye Baby* (Derry Film and Video, 1989) is a response to the Ann Lovett and 'Kerry-babies' cases.
24 Megan Sullivan, 'From Nationalism to "Baby X": An Interview with Northern Irish Filmmaker Margo Harkin', *Eire-Ireland*, 32: 2 & 3, 1997, pp. 40–51, p. 45.
25 Paula Meehan, *The Man Who was Marked by Winter*, Gallery Books, Oldcastle, County Meath, 1991, p. 42.
26 Nell McCafferty, *A Woman to Blame: the Kerry Babies Case*, Attic Press, Dublin, 1985, p. 8.
27 Nell McCafferty, 'Virgin on the Rocks', in *Seeing is Believing: Moving Statues in Ireland*, ed. by Colm Toibin, Pilgrim, Moutrath, 1985, pp. 53–58, p. 57.
28 Angela Bourke, unpublished paper: 'Silence in Two Languages: Nuala Ní Dhomhnaill and the Unspeakable', [Key note lecture at the Annual Graduate Irish Studies Conference "Breaking Silence", held at Harvard University and Boston College, March 1993, delivered 18 March 1993.

29 Colm Toibin (ed.), *Seeing is Believing: Moving Statues in Ireland,* Pilgrim, Mountrath, 1985, p. 7.
30 Personal interview.
31 Stanislaus Kennedy, *But Where Can I Go: Homeless Women in Dublin* (Dublin: Arlen House, 1985), p. 75. McGuinness wrote in a letter to Marie Heaney: I have so much time for Sr Stanislaus, I would do anything for her. See *Sources: Letters from Irish People on Sustenance for the Soul,* ed by Marie Heaney, (Dublin: Town House, 1999), p. 16.
32 Peter Thompson, 'Baglady the perfect package', *Irish Press,* 6 March 1985.
33 Fintan O'Toole, *The Irish Times: Book of the Century* (Dublin: Gill & Macmillan, 1999), p. 315.
34 *Mourne Observer,* 14 September 1956.
35 *Mourne Observer,* 28 October 1956.
36 Paul Allen, 'Kaleidoscope: Frank McGuinness Special', (BBC) 1 May 1987.
37 McGuinness wrote the screenplay of *Dancing at Lughnasa,* when it was made into a film in 1998.
38 Sarah O'Hara, 'Productive Lives', *Irish Press,* 17 March 1982.
39 Shane McGuinness, 'Breaking the barrier', *Sunday Tribune,* 10 May, 1987.
40 Sarah O'Hara, 'Productive lives'. (I regret to say that this is not always the case. Sometimes narrower feminism adopts these aspects which McGuinness attributed to men.)
41 For a discussion about windows and perspective, see Andrew Tomlinson, 'Windows and Souls: Contrary Imaginations in Film', unpublished DPhil thesis submitted to University of Ulster, 1997.
42 "Brunelleschi, Filippo" *Encyclopædia Britannica Online.* <http://members.eb.com/bol/topic?eu=119719&sctn=1>.
43 Stephen Heath, *Questions of Cinema,* (London: Macmillan Press, 1981), p. 28.
44 Heath, p. 28.
45 Jurgis Baltrusaitis, *Anamophic Art,* translated by W.J. Strachan (New York: Harry N. Abrams, 1976), p. 1.
46 According to Dr Anne McCartney, this song might have a Scottish origin.
47 Kristin Morrison, *Canters and Chronicles: The Use of Narrative in the Plays of Samuel Beckett and Harold Pinter* (University of Chicago Press, 1983), p. 3.
48 Kristin Morrison, p. 65.
49 An Interview with Jacqueline Hurtley in *Ireland in Writing: Interviews with Writers and Academics* (Amsterdam-Atlanta, GA: Rodopi 1998), p. 59.
50 Paul Allen, 'Kaleidoscope: Frank McGuinness Special', (BBC) 1 May 1987.
51 Frank McGuinness, *Dolly West's Kitchen* (London: Faber and Faber,

1999), p. 42.
52 *Sources: Letters from Irish People on Sustenance for the Soul*, ed. by Marie Heaney, (Dublin: Town House, 1999), p. 16.
53 See Martin McLoone, 'J'Accuse', Theatre Ireland, 21, 1989, p. 62.
54 This reminds one of Maela in *Carthaginians*, who spreads a dress over her daughter's grave.

CHAPTER 5

The Families at War: McGuinness's Irish 'Comedy of Bad Manners'

1 'Perhaps', Programme note for *The Caucasian Chalk Circle* (London: Loyal National Theatre, 1997).
2 Declan Kiberd, *Inventing Ireland* (London: Jonathan Cape, 1995), p. 35.
3 An Interview with Jacqueline Hurtley in *Ireland in Writing: Interviews with Writers and Academics*, (Amsterdam-Atlanta, GA: Rodopi, 1998), pp. 51–70, p. 55.
4 'Culture Ireland: The Bird Sanctuary', *Sunday Times*, 20 February 1994.
5 An interview with Jacqueline Hurtley in *Ireland in Writing: Interviews with Writers and Academics*, (Amsterdam-Atlanta, GA: Rodopi, 1998), pp. 143–176, p. 170.
6 Oscar Wilde, *The Importance of Being Earnest and Other Plays* (Oxford: Oxford University Press, 1995), p. 254.
7 Kiberd, p. 48.
8 Kiberd, p. 48.
9 Polly Devlin's attack on the play in the *Irish Times* (8 March 1994) provoked considerable debate. Heated exchanges were carried out in the readers' column for weeks. Sebastian Barry, Peter Denman, and Patrick Mason were among the ones who defended the play.
10 M. E. Collins, *History in the Making of Ireland: 1868 – 1966*, (Dublin: the Educational Company, 1993), p. 371.
11 Terence Brown, *Ireland: A Social and Cultural History 1922 – 1985*, (London: Fontana Press, 1981, 1985), p. 172.
12 See Patrick Lynch, 'The Irish Free State and the Republic of Ireland, 1921 – 1966', in *The Course of Irish History*, revised and enlarged edition, eds. by T. W. Moody and F. X. Martin, (Dublin: Mercier Press, 1967, 1984, 1994), pp. 324 – 341, and M. E. Collins, *History in the Making of Ireland: 1868 – 1966*, (Dublin: the Educational Company, 1993), pp. 370 – 384.
13 Mark Tierney, *Modern Ireland*, revised edition, (Dublin: Gill and Macmillan, 1972, 1978), p. 212.
14 Tierney, p. 211.
15 Robert Fisk, 'Turning our backs on the fire of life', Eye on the 20th Century 1940 – 1949, <http://www. Ireland. com/newspaper/

special/1999/eyeon20/1940e.htm>.

16 Michael Billington, You couldn't make it up', *Guardian*, 24 October 1999.
17 Oliver John, 'On a knife-edge', *What's On*, 17 May 2000, p. 59.
18 See, for example, Bruce Arnold, 'War drama had "no real theme"', *Irish Independent*, 8 October 1999.
19 Fintan O'Toole, *Tom Murphy: The Politics of Magic* (Dublin: Gill & Macmillan, 1994), p. 113.
20 Patrick Mason, 'Is the war over?', the programme note for the London production at the Old Vic.
21 Wilde, p. 267.
22 The very essence of this rather sentimental English hymn might well be explained by the fact that it was sung in both the wedding and the funeral of Diana, the Princess of Wales.

CONCLUSION

1 Joseph Campbell and Bill Moyers, *The Power of Myth* (New York: Doubleday, 1988), p. xix.
2 La Santa Sede (Vatican Home Page): <http://www.vatican.va/phome_en.htm>.
3 'Perhaps', Programme note for *The Caucasian Chalk Circle* (London: Loyal National Theatre, 1997).
4 An Interview with Jacqueline Hurtley in *Ireland in Writing: Interviews with Writers and Academics*, (Amsterdam-Atlanta, GA: Rodopi, 1998), pp. 51–70, p. 56.
5 Frank McGuinness, 'Don't Worry, be Abbey', *Fortnight*, Feb. 1995, p. 35.

INDEX

In entries other than his own the name of Frank McGuinness has been contracted to FM